SLOW COOKER

CENTRAL

SLOW COOKER

CENTRAL

Paulene Christie

ABC
Books

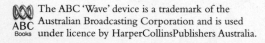 The ABC 'Wave' device is a trademark of the Australian Broadcasting Corporation and is used under licence by HarperCollinsPublishers Australia.

First published in Australia in 2015
by HarperCollins*Publishers* Australia Pty Limited
ABN 36 009 913 517
harpercollins.com.au

HarperCollins*Publishers*
Level 13, 201 Elizabeth Street, Sydney NSW 2000, Australia
Unit D1, 63 Apollo Drive, Rosedale Auckland 0632, New Zealand
A 53, Sector 57, Noida, UP, India
1 London Bridge Street, London, SE1 9GF, United Kingdom
2 Bloor Street East, 20th floor, Toronto, Ontario M4W 1A8, Canada
195 Broadway, New York NY 10007, USA

National Library of Australia Cataloguing-in-Publication entry:

Christie, Paulene, author.
  Slow cooker central / Paulene Christie.
  ISBN 978 0 7333 3431 3 (paperback)
  ISBN 978 1 4607 0501 8 (ebook)
  Electric cooking, Slow.
641.5884

Cover design by Hazel Lam, HarperCollins Design Studio
Internal design by HarperCollins Design Studio
Cover images by shutterstock.com
Author photograph by Tina Baills
Typeset in Adobe Jenson by Kirby Jones
Printed and bound in Australia by Griffin Press
The papers used by HarperCollins in the manufacture of this book are a natural, recyclable product made from wood grown in sustainable plantation forests. The fibre source and manufacturing processes meet recognized international environmental standards, and carry certification.

I dedicate this book to Simon and our three little miracles,
Caleb, Talyn and Ella.
You encourage me every day, in every way –
my hope is to always make you proud.

CONTENTS

INTRODUCTION

When I look back, I think my slow cooker journey began the same way it did for many of you, with the three 'S's – soups, stews and silverside. Throwing a heap of meat and veg into a machine, filling it up with water and letting it bubble away all day – that's what slow cooking is all about, right? Wrong!

I am a happily married and busy wife and mum of three young children, with a home to run, a high-pressure job involving shift work and never enough hours in the day. So the thought of having my family's evening meal all ready at the end of each long day was very enticing. But there are only so many soups and stew-type meals any family can want.

I turned to slow cooker recipe books next, buying every one I could find, but I very quickly wanted more. Being a total Facebook addict, I naturally looked there next for inspiration. And when a search for slow cooking pages or groups came up with nothing that fulfilled what I was looking for, I decided to create my own page and group. I had NO idea what I was beginning when I did so.

The Slow Cooker Recipes 4 Families Facebook group was born in late 2012. I hoped that maybe a few of my friends would join and maybe share a few recipes and ideas. I guessed that perhaps a few other people might find us and join the group.

Fast forward to April 2015 when we had more than 320,000 members, adding hundreds more each and every day.

The recipes members have shared in the group have been nothing short of amazing. Sure we get soups, stews and silverside amongst them – and some pretty good ones at that – but we also see so many amazingly innovative slow-cooker recipes, including food I'd never in a million years have thought to cook in a slow cooker. From lasagne, cakes and fudge, to scones, scrolls and muesli bars, and recipes for every type of meat you could imagine. There's also plenty for the vegetarians and those on healthy eating plans. And don't forget the desserts – cheesecakes, pavlova, crème brûlée, self-saucing puddings … we've got them all!

This was what I had been looking for when I started searching for recipes all those years before. This was amazing!

I managed the group myself until July 2014 when I appointed an incredible team of administrative people to assist me. These amazing, generous women give up their time each and every day to help run what has become a massive group. Without them I could never keep up!

What makes Slow Cooker Recipes 4 Families unique is that we are a 'group', not a page to 'like'. We are a group for sharing – be it recipes, knowledge, skills, support or conversation.

We have members from all over the globe, from every country you can imagine, and someone is always there thanks to the time differences. At any time of the day or night, 24/7, someone can ask a question on the group wall and usually have their answer within minutes. And sometimes hundreds of answers.

People ask questions while they are shopping, needing information about ingredients or sharing a find.

People ask questions as they put together a dish, needing a substitute for an ingredient or if they are unsure of a step.

People share what they are cooking that day, and lots come back to share photos of their finished creations.

It's such a supportive and encouraging family-type community where members can get instant advice and feedback when they need it most. And for those who are new to cooking, or new to slow cooking, they get a sense of pride in what they can achieve.

The design restrictions of Facebook for a group like ours soon meant we needed a new home. The members were begging for it and I wanted to see my 'baby' continue to grow and thrive. So we created a community fund drive and in no time the amazing members of our group helped me get www.slowcookercentral.com off the ground. The website, a sister site to the Facebook group, launched in August 2014.

The website was just as busy but a much quieter and more organised space than the Facebook group. All the recipes and information were easy to search, access and contribute to, without the constant Facebook chatter! And it also meant our great recipes and group knowledge were no longer restricted to only those in Facebook land.

Just like the Facebook group did before it, the website took off at an incredible rate and within 10 weeks we had our first 1 million hits!

We already have well over 1300 recipes in more than 40 categories to search or browse. All of our recipes are self-submitted by me or the members. Every single day I am inspired by the creativeness and inventiveness of our members and I want to thank you all – without you we wouldn't have this fabulous website.

Slow cooking has so many benefits. I'm often told by members who've never cooked previously, or who relied heavily on takeaway food, how they now make nutritious home-cooked meals every night for their family.

There's also the money you can save by cooking at home. One member of our Facebook group wrote to tell us that she had saved so much money, she actually had enough to buy a house by the beach. Slow cooking had transformed her life: '8 months ago, hubby and I would eat takeaway 3 nights, eat out 2 nights, and have either sausages or frozen pies the other 2 nights. I could NOT cook, and actually hated it. Detested it. I can now cook! And to top it off, I am about to move into a new house because I have an extra $180 in my wallet each week. Yes, EACH WEEK. That is a lot of money to go towards a new house!'

Slow cooking is also cheaper than running a conventional oven and stove. Experts estimate slow cookers to cost 4 cents per hour to run versus 60 cents per hour for conventional ovens. So even after 8 hours of slow cooking, you are still saving money. Another money-saving benefit comes from the fact you can buy much cheaper cuts of meat, because slow cooking makes even the most inexpensive meats fall-apart tender.

In most cases, slow cooking is a set-and-forget process, leaving us free to spend time with our families, time to ourselves or time to do what we need to get done.

Our recipes are created, cooked and submitted by regular home cooks, just like you and me. They definitely aren't so daunting that the average person is scared to try them. It is real food, cooked by real people, in real kitchens.

And thanks to the people at ABC Books and HarperCollins*Publishers*, we have been given this amazing opportunity to gather some of the best of our recipes right here in one place for you. When I was first approached about doing this book I was so excited about what an awesome opportunity was being given to us all. We ran a competition for our members to submit their favourite recipes to appear in this book, and so many shared tears of joy and overwhelming excitement to hear their recipe would feature here. The end result is a collection of some of the best slow cooker dishes I've seen, from people who range from beginner cooks to home chefs but who all share one thing in common – a passion for slow cooking!

This amazing collection of recipes was created, tested and submitted by the members of the Slow Cooker Recipes 4 Families Facebook page, slowcookercentral.com and also by me. These are some of our very best and most popular recipes, and I can't wait for you to try them.

So what are you waiting for – go get slow cooking :)

Paulene Christie

SLOW COOKER
HINTS & TIPS

Here's a great little collection of tips and tricks and frequently asked questions that we have gathered from the experience in our slow cooking community.

If you are cooking a cake or dessert in the slow cooker, be sure to read the section on cake tins first. The section on the tea-towel trick helps explain what that little strategy is all about – you will see it mentioned a lot in our recipes. It helps us make many of the unique and unusual dishes we create in our slow cookers! We've also covered some really important safety do's and don'ts to help you to get the very best out of your slow cooking experiments while minimising the risks that other cooks may unknowingly take.

So have a read through this section FIRST – and then your hardest decision will be deciding which great recipe from the book to cook!

Can I use frozen meat in the slow cooker?

In short, NO!

This is a very hotly debated topic that is discussed nearly every day in our Facebook group, Slow Cooker Recipes 4 Families. Some people choose to take this risk. In fact, you will often hear people saying that they have done so for years and it's never hurt them. However, according to the experts, this may be more due to pure luck than anything else.

It is up to you to make an educated and informed risk assessment for yourself. But I hope that the following information will help you make the smart choice.

Health concerns
Health and food technology experts say that for food safety reasons you should bring your food to temperatures of 60°C (140°F) as quickly as possible. It varies between machines, but in a slow cooker the LOW setting often cooks at around 94°C (200°F) and HIGH at 150°C (300°F). Check the manual that came with your machine and test the temperature using a thermometer. It's often preferred

to start the cooking process on HIGH (or AUTO – see more on the auto function below) to assist the food to reach this safe temperature as quickly as possible. This isn't mandatory though. I generally only do it with large roasts.

The bottom line is that cooking with frozen food significantly increases the amount of time it takes for that food to reach the safe temperature, and thus significantly increases the chances of you and your family getting food poisoning. Because of that, I for one WILL NOT take that risk with my loved ones. And don't just take my word for it! Here are qualified experts telling you exactly the same thing:

- 'Always thaw meat or poultry before putting it into a slow cooker' – United States Department of Agriculture – Food Safety and Inspection Service
- 'Do not put frozen ingredients in the slow cooker; defrost meat and poultry thoroughly in the refrigerator before slow cooking' – Web MD
- 'Do not cook frozen meat or poultry products in a slow cooker' – meatsafety.org
- 'Always thaw meat or poultry before putting it into a slow cooker. If frozen pieces are used, they will not reach 140°F quick enough and could possibly result in a food borne illness' – University of Minnesota

And that's just a sample. As I said previously, you are free to weigh up this risk for you and your family, but I hope this information helps you to never have to learn the hard way about taking risks with food safety.

Cooker care

Cooking meat when it is frozen also increases the risk of a ceramic slow-cooker bowl cracking due to the sudden temperature changes between frozen food and the heating bowl. If the bowl cracks, your slow cooker is unusable.

On a similar note, you should always remove the food from your slow cooker dish prior to refrigerating it. The nature of the thick ceramic bowl means it retains heat and thus takes a lot longer to cool down to safe refrigeration temperatures, once again leaving your food too long in the danger zone.

Safe defrosting

The safest way to defrost frozen meat is to put it in a bowl on a lower shelf of your fridge for 24 hours. Defrosting overnight may not be long enough, so ideally you should choose your meat for the following night the day before.

How can I thicken slow-cooker recipes with a high liquid content?

There are several methods you can use to thicken a sauce before serving a dish.

Cornflour (cornstarch)

Combine 2 tablespoons cornflour with 2 tablespoons cool tap water and mix until it becomes a thin, smooth paste. Put this paste straight into the slow cooker dish 20–30 minutes before serving, and stir briefly around whatever meat or vegetables are in the pot. Allow the dish to continue cooking, preferably on HIGH, or on LOW if the recipe requires.

This added cornflour will thicken the liquids in the recipe. If this amount of cornflour doesn't thicken the liquids sufficiently, you can repeat the process. But take care not to add too much cornflour to your recipe – once or twice is usually all that's needed. Some people ladle the liquid out of the slow cooker into a saucepan on the stove and add the cornflour there. How you do it is totally up to you.

Grated potato

Grate 1–2 raw potatoes and add them to the slow cooker about 30–45 minutes before serving. Stir through as much as you can around the solid ingredients. This will very quickly thicken the dish and continue to thicken it during the remaining cooking time.

Grated potato will only suit some recipes – those with vegetable or potato already in them, or that would work well with the addition of potato.

Instant potato flakes can also be used, as can gravy powder, again depending on the recipe.

Lift the lid

Another option is to remove the lid of the slow cooker, or at least place it ajar, for the last 30 minutes of cooking, to enable the sauce to thicken. This goes against the very nature of the slow cooker – having a sealed environment in which the cooking temperature is maintained constantly – but it is an available option if you're not a purist.

Use less liquid to begin with

Another natural consequence of slow cooking is the increased moisture content thanks to the condensation that drips from the lid down into the food during cooking. Many people think meat has to be covered in liquid to slow cook it, but in fact it needs very little liquid. If you find a dish is regularly ending up with far too much liquid, reduce the amount you add in the initial recipe next time you cook it.

The tea towel (dish towel) trick

Quite a few of the recipes in this book, and many in the Sweets chapter, will ask you to 'Cover the slow cooker, with a tea towel (dish towel) under the lid, and cook on HIGH.' The tea towel, which lies between the slow cooker bowl top and the lid of the slow cooker, acts to absorb condensation and stop it from dripping down into the food cooking inside. It's often used when you wouldn't want the cake or bread you're cooking to end up soggy.

This trick has been devised by home slow cooker enthusiasts and is not recommended officially or declared a safe practice by slow cooker manufacturers.

When using the tea towel trick, regular users suggest you fold up any excess fabric onto the lid of the slow cooker, securing it to the lid handle, so it doesn't hang down over the hotter outer casing of the slow cooker.

If you have concerns about the fire hazards related to this practice, you can research the safety issues involved and inform yourself about the pros and cons. I discovered through internet research that cotton fabric has an auto-ignition temperature of 407°C (765 °F), and your slow cooker will never come anywhere near these temperatures. Also, the tea towel absorbs liquid during this process, so it stays damp. However I would love to get feedback from anyone who has professional knowledge in this area.

Having said this, it is totally up to you to appraise the potential risks and decide whether it is safe to use the tea towel trick with your slow cooker.

It is not recommended to use the tea towel in general recipe cooking purely as a measure to reduce liquid in a dish. For risk minimisation with this technique, if you decide to use it, do so only for cakes and breads where water dripping onto them is a major issue.

Please make your own decision regarding the safety of this practice. If in any doubt, do not do this. I personally recommend you don't leave your home when you are using a tea towel in this way, so that you are able to keep an eye on your slow cooker and the tea towel.

How can I remove oil and fat from a slow cooker dish?

There are several methods you can use to remove oil from your dish. First and foremost, you can reduce the amount of fat going into the dish from the beginning.

Be choosy

Choose lean cuts of meat, trim visible fat from meat and add little to no oil to your slow-cooker recipes.

Prep it

Pre-browning or sealing meat in a frying pan is one way to remove some of the fat prior to cooking it in the slow cooker (read more about pre-browning and sealing meat on page 12).

Skim and discard

Perhaps the most obvious solution is to spoon that fat right out of there! Towards the end of the cooking process, the fat will often gather at the top of your dish so you can use a ladle or spoon to gently remove and discard it.

The ice-cube trick

Placing ice-cubes briefly on top of the dish will cause the fat to 'stick to' the ice-cube (because the lower temperature it brings about causes the fat to solidify). You can then discard the ice-cube and the oil right along with it.

The bread trick

Very briefly lay a piece of bread along the top of the dish. This will soak up the fat, which will be discarded with the bread or fed to a four-legged friend. But be very careful and always remove the bread with tongs, as it will be hot!

Some people use paper towel instead of bread to soak up the fats and oils, however if something was going to break down in my food, I would rather it were bread than paper.

Cool and skim

If you have the time or you are cooking a recipe in advance, you can cool the entire dish in the fridge overnight. The fat will solidify on top and you can remove it prior to reheating and serving the dish.

What does the AUTO function on my slow cooker do?

Many slow cookers have a LOW, HIGH, KEEP WARM and/or AUTO setting option. The AUTO function often means the dish will begin cooking at HIGH for approximately 2 hours, then the slow cooker will switch itself down to the LOW temperature setting. (The dial itself doesn't move and will remain pointing to AUTO.)

This feature can vary with different slow cooker models and brands, so always consult your user manual.

Is it safe to leave my slow cooker unattended all day while I am out of the house?

In short, yes ... with precautions.

Slow cookers are designed to run all day unattended without posing a fire hazard. There are, however, measures you can take to improve the safety of doing so.

I always place my slow cookers on top of my ceramic cooktop. This surface is designed to withstand high temperatures, after all. Just be sure never to accidentally have a hotplate turned on – I lost my first-ever slow cooker due to this because I melted its legs off! If you don't have this option, placing the cooker on a glass-top trivet or cutting board works in a similar way.

Ensure flammable objects are not touching or left too near the slow cooker. Move the slow cooker away from the wall and any curtains, etc.

Always have a working smoke alarm and electrical safety switch in your house so that if you are home and the worst were to somehow happen, you and your family can be alerted to the danger and/or the electricity supply will cease to the unit.

Is it okay to open the lid of my slow cooker to stir my dish or check on it?

Many of us have heard the tale that each time you open the lid of your slow cooker, it adds 30 minutes to the cooking time.

In practice, I have never personally found this to be true. If I am at home I am a habitual lid-lifter, often pausing to look at, stir, taste or even smell my dish throughout the day. And if anything, my dishes often cook much faster than the expected times.

However, slow cookers rely on the slow build-up of heat to cook food to perfection. Lifting the lid during cooking lets built-up heat escape and will lower the temperature in the slow cooker considerably. Stirring the contents allows even more heat to escape from the lower layers of the food. Once the lid is replaced, it will take a significant amount of time for the heat to build back up to its previous temperature, thus extending the cooking time of your dinner.

So the choice is up to you. Resist if you can, or don't. You will soon come to know your own slow cooker (or if you are like me and have several, you will get to know each of their little quirks and cooking times/temps).

Do I need to pre-brown, pre-cook or seal my meat prior to placing it in the slow cooker?

In short, no, you do not.

Some people like to do this step to add more depth of flavour (in their opinion) to the dish or to seal in juices.

It can also be helpful to liquefy fat from the meat, which can then be discarded prior to adding the meat to the slow cooker.

However it does add another step in the preparation of your dish, and more washing up to go with it.

So it's totally your choice but, for what it's worth, I rarely pre-brown, pre-seal, or pre-cook anything.

Can I prepare a meal in advance and store it in the slow cooker bowl in my fridge overnight, then put it on the next morning?

Yes, you can if you wish. But it comes with risks!

It is possible that heating a cold bowl can lead to it cracking.

Also, due to nature of the dish, it will retain that cold for a long time and thus take even longer to reach safe food cooking temperatures once you begin cooking, placing you at increased risk of food poisoning.

A great way around this is to prepare the dish in advance but store it in the fridge in another large bowl, for example a mixing bowl. The food can then be poured into the slow cooker bowl in the morning and turned on. You still have all the convenience but without any of the risk.

How do I cook a cake in my slow cooker?

Traditionalists might not be used to making cakes in a slow cooker – but with the right method it is possible!

First and foremost, the tea towel trick (see page 9) is very important as it prevents condensation dripping on your cake when it's cooking in the slow cooker. But what do you cook the actual cake in?

The slow cooker bowl

Line the inner bowl of your slow cooker with non-stick baking paper and pour your cake batter directly into it. You could also grease the inside of the bowl with butter, but I prefer to use baking paper as it gives you something to hold so you can easily lift the cake out once it is cooked.

A metal cake tin

When I use a metal cake tin, I like to elevate it off the bottom of the slow cooker to allow heat to circulate evenly around the cake. This can be achieved by resting the cake tin on a metal trivet, on metal egg rings or even on scrunched-up balls of aluminium foil. If you have any concerns about dry metal in your slow cooker, you can simply fill the bottom of your slow cooker insert with 2–3 cm of water, then sit the metal cake tin gently onto this water prior to cooking.

A silicone cake tin

As silicone cake tins are also intended for traditional ovens, they are perfectly safe for slow cooking and are in no danger of melting. You can use the methods listed above for elevating the cake tin from the base of your slow cooker bowl. When I use a silicone cake tin in a slow cooker with a non-ceramic bowl, I sit it directly onto the bottom of the slow cooker, without water, with no concerns.

As with all non-traditional slow cooking techniques, be sure to check the manual of your slow cooker first and only do what you feel comfortable doing.

What is the best way to clean my slow cooker bowl?

Most slow cooker bowls can simply be washed by hand and some are dishwasher safe (be sure to check your manual for what is safe for your model).

If there's a baked-on ring around your slow cooker insert dish that's hard to remove, the easiest way is to simply leave your slow cooker on and cooking after the food has been removed. Add water to a level above the baked-on ring and leave it on LOW for a couple of hours. It should clean away easily after that.

Some slow-cooker users suggest putting a dishwasher tablet in the slow cooker while the water is heating in it for up to 4 hours, but it is advisable to check the user manual before trying that one.

Do not wash your slow-cooker insert with cold water when it is hot. As with anything ceramic, the stoneware and lid will not withstand sudden temperature changes.

Neither the metal housing of the slow cooker nor the electrical lead should be placed in water.

Due to the porous nature of the base of the ceramic bowl, it should not be stood in water for extended periods as this water can be absorbed through the base. The bowl can be filled with water and left to sit, but not sit IN water.

Are there any 'diet' recipes?

Almost every dish can be adapted for weight loss or healthier options (with some obvious dessert-type exceptions).

Ways to adapt the original recipe to a more waist-friendly version include:

- using leaner cuts of meat
- adding extra vegetables to bulk out your meal
- choosing low-sodium versions of soups, stocks and sauces that may go into your dish
- choosing low-fat versions of cream and milk that may go into your dish
- serving with healthy side dishes like brown rice, salads and vegetables
- using wise portion control when serving
- even leftovers can be stored in measured portion-controlled healthy serves to prevent other bad impulse meals and snacks when you are time poor.

Does it cost less to run a slow cooker for 8 hours than an oven for 1 hour?

It certainly is cheaper!

Of course there are many variables to consider, including the size and model of your slow cooker, and the size and efficiency of your conventional oven, but overall the stats are well in favour of your slow cooker being the cheaper way to cook.

Even if it is over 8 hours instead of 1 hour!

Energy provider Ergon Energy advises that a slow cooker costs 4 cents per hour to run, while an oven costs 60 cents per hour. So running your slow cooker for 8 hours will cost 32 cents compared to 60 cents for just one hour of the oven (and that doesn't even account for oven pre-heating time).

Bargain!

Is it toxic to slow cook raw red kidney beans?

Yes, it is! Many online sources discuss the risks associated with ingesting raw kidney beans. One example that I think explains it best is found at www.choosingvoluntarysimplicity.com:

'Raw kidney beans contain especially large amounts of toxin and, amazingly, eating just four or five raw or improperly cooked kidney beans can make a person extremely ill. Ingesting larger amounts can actually cause death. Other beans, including white kidney beans, broad beans and lima beans, contain the same toxin in smaller but still dangerous amounts.'

If you'd like to read further on this issue, these websites would be good starting points:

+ www.choosingvoluntarysimplicity.com/crockpots-slow-cooking-dried-beans-phytohaemagglutinin/
+ www.medic8.com/healthguide/food-poisoning/red-kidney-bean-toxins.html

What staples should I keep in my pantry?

One of the best ways to ease into trying new recipes is to have a supply of staple items in your pantry – on hand and at the ready for your next kitchen session.

These may include:

Baking powder
Balsamic vinegar
Canned or dried fruits
Canned or dried vegetables

Canned soups: condensed cream of soups in various flavours (especially cream of mushroom and cream of chicken)

Coconut cream and milk
Cornflour
Couscous
Curry powder
Dry packet soup such as French
    onion and chicken noodle
Flour: plain and self-raising
Garlic: fresh or minced in jar
Ginger: fresh or minced in jar
Gravy powder/granules
Herbs & spices: fresh in your
    garden, frozen in tubes or dried
    in jars and packets – as many
    as you can gather!
Honey
Lentils
Mustard powder
Parmesan cheese: fresh or dried
Pasta

Powdered milk or UHT milk
Rice
Salt and freshly cracked black
    pepper
Sauces: sweet chilli, barbecue,
    tomato, Worcestershire, soy,
    mint, oyster, hoisin
Stock: powder, cubes or long life
    liquid (especially beef, chicken
    and vegetable)
Sugar: brown and white
Sweetened condensed milk
Tinned tomatoes
Tinned tuna
Tomato paste
Vinegar
Wine: red and white
Yeast

This is by no means an exhaustive list but it's a great start!

How do I convert oven/stove recipes for my slow cooker?

Now you're hooked on slow cooking, I bet you'll find there are heaps of your family's favourite recipes that are traditionally cooked in the oven or on the stovetop that you want to convert for a slow cooker. And, for almost all of them, there is no reason you can't!

Here are some simple pointers:

- Reduce the amount of liquid. Due to the condensation that forms in your slow cooker when in use, recipes cooked in slow cookers need much less liquid then their traditional stovetop or oven counterparts. As a general rule try reducing the total recipe liquid by approximately one-quarter.

- Use cheaper cuts of meat. Remember that almost any cut of meat – even the cheapest and toughest – is sure to be tender after slow cooking. So feel free to replace more expensive cuts of meat for a cheaper option.
- Adjust the amount of herbs and spices. Many people recommend reducing them by half when converting a regular recipe for a slow cooker.
- Adjust the time. See the chart below to convert your stove and oven times to slow-cooker times.
- Arrange the ingredients. When filling your slow cooker, put the root vegetables around the bottom and sides of your slow cooker, then place your meat on top.
- Take notes and experiment. It may take some trial and error to tweak your old favourites but it'll be worth it. Adjust liquids as you go (adding or removing) and keep an eye on cooking times. Take notes as you try new things so you'll always know just what worked the best for you. Soon you'll have a recipe you can use anywhere!

Stovetop & Oven Cooking Times	Slow Cooking on LOW Cooking Times	Slow Cooking on HIGH Cooking Times
15–30 mins	4–6 hours	1½–2½ hours
45 mins–1 hour	6½–8 hours	3–4 hours
1½–2½ hours	9–12 hours	4½–6 hours
3–5 hours	12½–18 hours	5–7 hours

SOUP

CHEESY CAULIFLOWER & BACON SOUP

I attempted a cauliflower soup when I first met my husband 12 years ago and he took one mouthful and put it down the sink! So I never made it again. Then a few months ago my 10-year-old son asked for cauliflower soup so I decided to attempt it again but added some new ingredients and topped it with bacon. The family loved it, even my husband who was at first hesitant to try it again. I serve it on a cold winter's night with a thick piece of sourdough bread. It warms your soul.

Serves 4–6 • Preparation 5 mins • Cook 5 hours

5 rashers bacon, diced and cooked, 2 tablespoons reserved for garnish
1 head cauliflower, broken into florets
1 carrot, cut into chunks
2 potatoes, peeled and cut into chunks
1 onion, coarsely chopped
2 garlic cloves, crushed
3 celery stalks, coarsely chopped
1 litre (35 fl oz/4 cups) salt-reduced vegetable stock
350 ml (12 fl oz) light evaporated milk
¼ cup plain (all-purpose) flour
125 ml (4 fl oz/½ cup) skim milk
1½ cups shredded reduced-fat cheddar cheese
Greek-style yoghurt, to serve

1. Put the bacon (reserving 2 tablespoons for the garnish), cauliflower, carrot, potato, onion, garlic, celery and stock in a slow cooker. Cover and cook on LOW for 4 hours, until the vegetables are soft.

2. In a jug, add 2 tablespoons of the evaporated milk to the flour and stir to make a paste. Add the remaining evaporated milk and the skim milk and stir until combined.

3. Add the flour and milk mixture to the slow cooker and stir through to thicken the soup. Increase the temperature to HIGH and cook for 1 hour.

4. Blend the soup in batches, leaving some chunks for texture, using a food processor, blender or stick blender. Add the cheese and stir until just melted. Season to taste with salt and freshly ground black pepper.

5. Serve in bowls with a dollop of yoghurt and scattered with the reserved bacon pieces.

Amanda Kirk

PEA & HAM SOUP WITH CHUNKY VEGETABLES

As a busy working single mum, I am always looking for ideas for easy and affordable meals. I had some leftover ham bones in the freezer and decided to make a soup with them, so I just threw them into the slow cooker with whatever vegies I had and hoped for the best. The end result was a bit bland so I added some relish, which turned out to be the key ingredient. I have since added more ingredients to perfect this soup. You could buy ham hocks from a butcher or supermarket, but I like to use ham bones from a baked ham, which we have for special dinners throughout the year – not just at Christmas. I keep some extra ham and chop up about 2 cups for extra meat also.

Serves 6 • **Preparation** 5 mins • **Cook** 5 hours

2 ham bones or hocks (not bacon bones, as they are too gritty)
2 cups chunky diced ham pieces
110 g (3¾ oz/½ cup) green split peas, rinsed thoroughly until the water runs clear, drained
220 g (7¾ oz/1 cup) yellow split peas, rinsed thoroughly until the water runs clear, drained
5 potatoes, peeled and diced
2 onions, diced
2 carrots, sliced
2 celery stalks, sliced
1 cup frozen corn kernels
¼ cup Lancashire relish or Worcestershire sauce
Crusty bread, to serve

1. Put the ham bones and diced ham in a slow cooker. Add the split peas, potato, onion, carrot, celery and corn. Pour over 1 litre (35 fl oz/4 cups) water, cover and cook on HIGH for 5 hours, stirring occasionally.

2. When 30 minutes from cooked, add the Lancashire relish or Worcestershire sauce and stir through.

3. Remove the ham bones or hocks and serve with crusty bread.

NOTE: Lancashire relish is a fruity version of Worcestershire.

Christine Webb

OUR FAVOURITE PEA & HAM SOUP

I've realised over time that you need to include the hock to get more meat in your soup, and the bacon bones for the lovely smoky aroma, so now I always use both. One day I was making soup and my sister told me the shopkeepers down the road were discussing the amazing smell. Apparently the whole neighbourhood loves it when I make this soup. It also freezes well.

Serves 6 • Preparation 5 mins • Cook 7–9 hours

Olive oil cooking spray
500 g (1 lb 2 oz/2¼ cups) green split peas, rinsed thoroughly until the water runs clear, drained
650 g (1 lb 7 oz) ham hock
375 g (13 oz) bacon bones
1 large potato, cut into 8 pieces
2 carrots, cut into large pieces
1.5 litres (52 fl oz/6 cups) hot water, to cover
Crusty bread, to serve

1. Spray the inside of a slow cooker with olive oil. Spread the split peas over the base and put the ham hock and bacon bones on top. Fill in the gaps with the potato and carrot pieces. Pour over enough hot water to just cover the hock and bacon bones. Cook on HIGH for 1 hour.

2. After 1 hour, reduce the temperature setting to LOW and cook for 6–8 hours.

3. Lift out the ham hock and bacon bones. Pull away and shred the meat, set aside and discard the bones.

4. Blend the split peas, potato and carrot with a stick blender or in a food processor or blender until smooth. Add boiling water a little at a time to thin the soup, if necessary.

5. Return the soup to the slow cooker and cook on HIGH for 5–10 minutes. Return the shredded meat to the soup and stir through.

6. Serve the soup in bowls with crusty bread on the side.

Vicky Kemp

EASY PEA & HAM SOUP

Pea and ham soup is a classic slow-cooker meal but I like to make things even easier by using meat that's already been taken off the bone so there's no need to do it at the end of cooking. If your butcher doesn't sell the ready cut chunks, use several ham hocks and, once cooked, discard the fat, cut the meat into chunks and return it to the soup.

Serves 8 • Preparation 5 mins • Cook 6–8 hours

500 g–1 kg (1 lb 2 oz–2 lb 4 oz) green split peas (depending on how thick you
    like your soup), rinsed thoroughly until the water runs clear, drained
2 onions, coarsely chopped
750g diced bacon chunks off the bone (not regular bacon)
1.5 L (51 fl oz/6 cups) water
Crusty bread rolls, to serve

1. Put the split peas, onion and bacon chunks in a 6 litre (24 cup) slow cooker. Add water to fill to 5 cm (2 inches) below the top of the slow cooker. Cover and cook for 6–8 hours on LOW, until thickened nicely and the solid split peas have all broken down.

2. Serve in big bowls with crusty bread rolls on the side.

Paulene Christie

CHICKEN & VEGIE SOUP

Nothing better for when it's cold or you are feeling sick or need comfort, this soup came about through experimentation. I added and took out ingredients until I found the mix I loved. It's nice in a bowl with a buttered crusty roll. Hope you enjoy it.

Serves 8–10 • Preparation 10 mins • Cook 6–8 hours

2 litres (70 fl oz/8 cups) chicken stock
2 skinless chicken breast fillets, chopped
3 stalks celery, coarsely chopped
1 onion, finely chopped
1 large leek, finely chopped
2 carrots, coarsely chopped
225 g (8 oz) broccoli florets and peeled stalks, chopped
2 teaspoons crushed garlic
2 teaspoons powdered vegetable stock
420 g (15 oz) tinned corn kernels, drained
410 g (14½ oz) tinned creamed corn
500 g (1lb 2 oz) Chinese cabbage, shredded
1 packet Singapore noodles
Salt and freshly ground black pepper, to taste

1. Put all the ingredients except the cabbage and noodles in a slow cooker and just cover with water. Cook on LOW for 6–8 hours.

2. Add the Chinese cabbage and Singapore noodles, season with salt and pepper. Cook for 30 minutes then serve.

Cheree Bone

☰— CHICKEN & CORN CHOWDER —●

Halfway between chicken soup and chicken casserole, this dish is my family's favourite on a cold winter's night.

Serves 6–8 • **Preparation** 15 mins • **Cook** 7¾ hours

1 onion, diced
4 potatoes, diced into small cubes
2 carrots, diced into small cubes
420 g (15 oz) tinned corn kernels, drained
410 g (14½ oz) tinned creamed corn
1 litre (35 fl oz/4 cups) chicken stock
3 rashers bacon, sliced
300 g (10½ oz) shredded cooked chicken (leftover barbecue chicken is fine)
200 ml (7 fl oz) thin (pouring) cream
Croutons or crunchy bread, to serve

1. Put the onion, potato, carrot, corn kernels and creamed corn, stock and bacon in a slow cooker. Cook on LOW for 7 hours.

2. Remove the lid and slightly mash the contents with a potato masher. Add the chicken and cream. Stir and cook, uncovered, on HIGH for another 30–45 minutes.

3. Serve in bowls with croutons on top or crunchy bread on the side.

Leisa Wallace

SUPER EASY CHICKEN SOUP

Sure there are many you can make from scratch, but you can throw this together in a flash and know a beautiful chicken soup will await you at day's end. Winner, winner chicken dinner! Very good for the soul!

Serves 6–8 • **Preparation** 5 mins • **Cook** 8 hours

1–2 kg (2 lb 4 oz–4 lb 8 oz) chicken wings and/or drumsticks
500 g (1 lb 2 oz) frozen diced vegetables
2 onions, diced
40 g (1½ oz) chicken noodle soup mix, dry
2–3 tablespoons chicken stock powder
Crusty bread rolls, to serve

1. Put all the ingredients in a slow cooker. Fill with water to about 5 cm (2 inches) below the top of the inner bowl. Cook for 8 hours on LOW.

2. When cooked, take the chicken out, remove the bones and return the chicken meat to the soup and stir.

3. Serve in bowls with crusty bread rolls.

Paulene Christie

THAI COCONUT CHICKEN SOUP (TOM KHA GAI)

Thai cuisine – and especially Thai soup – has always been a love of mine but I've never come across a good slow-cooker recipe for my favourite, tom kha gai or Thai coconut chicken soup. So I decided to try making my own using traditional Thai flavours. I tweaked it for flavour as I went along and was very happy with the result. It's a comforting, warming soup that I hope you'll enjoy.

Serves 6 • Preparation 15 mins • Cook 7 hours

800 ml (28 fl oz) tinned coconut milk
1 litre (35 fl oz/4 cups) chicken stock
2 tablespoons red curry paste
600 g (1 lb 5 oz) skinless chicken thigh or breast fillets, cut into bite-size pieces
1 lemongrass stalk, chopped into small pieces
3–4 large mushrooms, coarsely chopped
1 red capsicum (pepper), coarsely chopped
1–2 chillies, to taste, finely diced
1 tablespoon grated fresh ginger
2 tablespoons fish sauce
2 tablespoons light brown sugar
Lime juice, to serve
Fresh coriander (cilantro) leaves, to garnish

1. Put all the ingredients except the lime juice and coriander leaves in a slow cooker. Stir to combine and cook for 7 hours on LOW.

2. When 1 hour from cooked, taste and adjust seasoning with extra sugar or a splash of soy sauce.

3. Serve in bowls with a nice squeeze of lime and a scattering of coriander leaves.

Kate Treloggen

THAI CHICKEN & VERMICELLI NOODLE SOUP

Sometimes I add a tiny pinch of saffron – just ⅛ teaspoon – for a richer colour. And sometimes I use cooked prawns (shrimp) instead of the chicken. Add them with the noodles in the last 10 minutes of cooking.

Serves 6 • Preparation 15 mins • Cook 3½ hours

- 1.5 litres (52 fl oz/6 cups) chicken stock
- 400 ml (14 fl oz) tinned coconut milk (I use reduced-fat)
- 3 cm (1¼ inch) piece fresh ginger, finely sliced and cut into 1 cm (½ inch) length sticks
- 3 tablespoons fish sauce
- 1–2 red chillies, finely sliced (remove seeds if you prefer less heat)
- 1½ teaspoons ground turmeric
- 2 teaspoons light brown sugar
- 3 tablespoons fresh lime juice
- 500 g (1 lb 2 oz) frozen vegetables (a mixture of carrot, beans, broccoli, baby corn, bamboo shoots and bean sprouts)
- ½ cooked chicken, meat shredded coarsely
- 100 g (3½ oz) dry bean thread (also known as cellophane or glass) vermicelli noodles
- 3 tablespoons coarsely chopped coriander (cilantro), to serve

1. Turn a slow cooker on HIGH.

2. Combine the stock and coconut milk and add to the slow cooker. Add the ginger, fish sauce, chilli, turmeric, brown sugar and lime juice and stir to combine. Cover and cook on HIGH for 3 hours.

3. Add the frozen vegetables and shredded chicken and stir to combine. Cover and cook for 20 minutes, until the vegetables are al dente soft.

4. Add the noodles, broken into 20 cm (8 inch) lengths, to the slow cooker and stir to combine. Cover and cook for 10 minutes, until the noodles are soft.

5. Serve in bowls, scattered with the coriander, and lime wedges on the side.

Paulene Christie

CRAB & CORN SOUP

The crab meat truly shines in this dish that's so warming and mouth-wateringly delicious. I got the inspiration to cook this in the slow cooker when I saw the price at a local Chinese restaurant. Why pay extra when it's even better at home? I'm so proud of it.

Serves 4 • **Preparation** 15 mins • **Cook** 2 hours

1 cup crabmeat
1 teaspoon Chinese cooking wine
500 ml (17 fl oz/2 cups) boiling water
210 g (7½ oz) tinned corn kernels, drained
2 eggs, beaten
1 teaspoon salt
2 spring onions (scallions), finely chopped
½ teaspoon cornflour (cornstarch)
1 tablespoon water
Flat-leaf (Italian) parsley, to garnish

1. Squeeze the excess liquid from the crabmeat and put the crabmeat in a small bowl. Add the cooking wine and mix to combine.

2. Add the boiling water to a slow cooker and turn it on to HIGH heat.

3. Add the crabmeat, corn and eggs, stirring well with a quick motion.

4. Add the salt and spring onions and stir well. Mix the cornflour and water into a paste, and stir into the soup. Cook with lid off on HIGH for 2 hours until slightly thickened.

5. Serve in bowls. Garnish with finely chopped parsley.

Cheryl Barrett

CREAMY PUMPKIN SOUP

I came up with this recipe when I was experimenting with different soups. It's creamy with a hint of bacon and tastes yummy with fresh crusty bread. The best part is you can alter it to suit your own tastes.

Serves 4 • **Preparation** 20 mins • **Cook** 3 hours

1.5 kg (3 lb 5 oz) pumpkin (squash), peeled, seeded and chopped
1 onion, finely chopped
4 rashers bacon, chopped
1 litre (35 fl oz/4 cups) vegetable stock
½ cup thin (pouring) cream
¼ teaspoon freshly grated or ground nutmeg
Sour cream, to serve (optional)
Crusty bread, to serve

1. Put the pumpkin, onion, bacon and stock in a slow cooker. Cover and cook on HIGH for 2–2½ hours, or until the pumpkin is soft.

2. Transfer the mixture to a blender, in batches, and purée.

3. Return the puréed pumpkin to the slow cooker. Stir in the cream, nutmeg and freshly ground black pepper and cook for 30 minutes on HIGH, until heated through.

4. Serve the pumpkin soup with a dollop of sour cream and fresh crusty bread.

Sarah Rhodes

THAI PUMPKIN SOUP

I started using the coconut milk to try to reduce the heavy cream taste of my traditional soup. And now this soup is a favourite in our house and is a real winter night meal or an easy Sunday lunch.

Serves 4 • **Preparation** 15 mins • **Cook** 4–6 hours

½ pumpkin (squash), peeled and chopped
1 onion, chopped
3 rashers bacon, sliced
1 tablespoon chicken or vegetable stock
1 tablespoon finely grated fresh ginger
2 garlic cloves, crushed
420 ml (14½ fl oz) tinned coconut milk
500 ml (17 fl oz/2 cups) water
Coriander (cilantro) sprigs or fried shallots, to garnish

1. Put all the ingredients in a slow cooker, season with salt and freshly ground black pepper and stir. Cook on HIGH for 4 hours or LOW for 6 hours.

2. Blend the cooked mixture with a stick blender. Serve the soup in bowls sprinkled with the coriander or fried shallots.

Vicki Rossiter

PASTA E FAGIOLI SOUP

Warm, filling and great for chilly evenings, this soup makes the house smell divine while cooking, and works perfectly with fresh bread from a local bakery. It's hearty and healthy, and one of my family's favourite meals.

Serves 4–6 • Preparation 30 mins • Cook 4–8 hours

Cooking oil spray
900 g (2 lb) minced (ground) beef
1 onion, chopped
3 carrots, grated
1 cup chopped celery
840 g (1 lb 13 oz) tinned diced tomatoes
420 g (15 oz) tinned red kidney beans, drained
420 g (15 oz) tinned cannellini beans, drained
500 ml (17 fl oz/2 cups) beef stock
2 teaspoons ground oregano
2 teaspoons freshly ground black pepper
2 tablespoons chopped flat-leaf (Italian) parsley
1 teaspoon Tabasco sauce
250 g (9 oz) pasta sauce
225 g (8 oz) ditalini or other soup pasta
Crusty bread, to serve

1. Spray a large frying pan with cooking oil and heat over medium–high heat. Cook the mince until browned and drain.

2. Put the browned mince and the remaining ingredients, except the pasta, in a slow cooker. Cook on HIGH for 4–5 hours or LOW for 7–8 hours.

3. When the soup is cooked, cook the pasta according to the package directions. Drain and stir the pasta into the soup. Serve with crusty bread.

Melissa Hansen

QUINOA & TOMATO SOUP

My partner and I both work full-time jobs, have a healthy lifestyle and enjoy trying a wide variety of foods. I love to use my slow cooker as it is an easy way to get nutritious food whilst working full-time. I initially came up with this soup in the winter as a meal that was hearty, healthy and tasty. It is quick to make before I go to work as I can add all the ingredients whilst drinking my cup of coffee, and once I come home the house is filled with its welcoming aroma.

Serves 4–6 • **Preparation** 15 mins • **Cook** 4 hours

1 cup quinoa
800 g (1 lb 12 oz) tinned chopped tomatoes
400 g (14 oz) tinned red kidney beans, rinsed and drained
1 onion, chopped
1 garlic clove, chopped
2 tablespoons tomato paste (concentrated purée)
2 tablespoons olive oil
2 tablespoons Worcestershire sauce
1 tablespoon ground paprika
Crusty bread rolls, to serve

1. Put all the ingredients in a slow cooker and season with salt and freshly ground black pepper. Combine well. Cover and cook on HIGH for 3 hours.

2. Stir the soup and reduce the temperature to LOW. Cover and cook for 1 hour, adding water if the soup needs it.

3. Serve with crusty bread rolls.

Sara Grinter

MIDDLE EASTERN LENTIL SOUP

During our time living in Qatar in the Middle East we used to order this dish at restaurants in the winter months, and a Middle Eastern friend gave us this recipe. It is lovely served with warm puffy bread or any flat bread.

Serves 4–6 • Preparation 10 mins • Cook 4–6 hours

500 g (1 lb 2 oz) red lentils, washed and drained
1.5 litres (52 fl oz/6 cups) chicken stock
1 onion, diced
4 garlic cloves, crushed
1 tablespoon ground cumin
½ teaspoon cayenne pepper
½ cup lemon juice
1 large handful coriander (cilantro), chopped
Sour cream, to serve (optional)
Toasted flat bread, to serve

1. Put the lentils, stock, onion, garlic, cumin and cayenne pepper in a slow cooker and stir well. Cover and set the temperature to AUTO for 4–6 hours, or cook on HIGH for 1 hour and then LOW until the soup is cooked and smooth.

2. Just before serving, add the lemon juice and coriander. Serve in bowls with a spoonful of sour cream swirled through the soup, and a side of toasted flat bread.

Cheryl Costin

SNACKS & LIGHT MEALS

GRAPEFRUIT WITH HONEY & BROWN SUGAR

A simple, refreshing and delicious summer breakfast or snack.

Serves 1 • **Preparation** 5 mins • **Cook** 1 hour

1 grapefruit, cut in half
Honey, to drizzle
Brown sugar, to sprinkle
Plain yoghurt, to serve

1. Put 1 cup water in a slow cooker. Loosen up the grapefruit pulp with a spoon. Put the grapefruit halves cut-side up in the slow cooker. Drizzle the grapefruit with honey and sprinkle with brown sugar. Cover and cook on HIGH for 1 hour.

2. Allow the grapefruit to cool and serve with yoghurt.

sherrie sutcliffe

GREEK YOGHURT

Developing this recipe involved a bit of trial and error but it is extremely forgiving – if it's not working, just bring the temperature back up with hot milk. And if it doesn't thicken, use it as drinking yoghurt and whizz it up with frozen berries. It's easy to get it right, though, and you can use your yoghurt to make great dips or flavour with honey or fruit.

Makes approx 10 cups • **Preparation** 5 mins + 3½ hours cooling + 12 hours resting
Cook 3½ hours

3.5 litres (120 fl oz/14 cups) milk
1 cup yoghurt

1. Put the milk in a slow cooker and heat on HIGH for 3½ hours.

2. Turn the heat off and allow to cool in the slow cooker for 3½ hours.

3. Test the temperature, which should be between 44°C (112°F) and 47°C (117°F). (Reheat if temperature falls below this.)

4. When the milk is in the correct temperature range, remove 1 cup of the warm milk and mix it with the yoghurt. Return this milk and yoghurt mixture to the remaining milk.

5. Place the lid on the slow cooker and wrap in a blanket or towels and set aside for 12 hours.

6. Strain the yoghurt through muslin in a sieve over a bowl at room temperature.

Michelle Murray

BREAKFAST COB LOAF

My hubby LOVES nothing more than a cooked breakfast. So on Father's Day, when he was working all day and I had to go to work before he got home, I decided to surprise him with a breakfast for dinner! I added all his favourite ingredients and popped them in the slow cooker for 2 hours before he got home. The results were amazing. The cob bread was lovely and crispy, while the filling was cooked to perfection. Not only did he devour the lot, but I came home to a clean kitchen (only one dirty plate) and this is now one of his favourite breakfasts/dinners.

Serves 2–4 • **Preparation** 15 mins • **Cook** 2 hours

1 large cob loaf
220 g (7 oz) tinned baked beans
2 handfuls baby spinach leaves
3–4 rashers rindless shortcut bacon
50 g (2 oz) sliced mushrooms
10 cherry tomatoes, cut in half
3 eggs, plus 2 extra yolks
100 g (3½ oz) grated cheese
Flat-leaf (Italian) parsley (optional), coarsely chopped

1. Slice the top off cob loaf and scoop out the middle.
2. Layer the baked beans, spinach leaves, bacon, mushroom, cherry tomatoes, eggs and extra egg yolks. Season with salt and freshly ground black pepper. Sprinkle over the cheese and top with the parsley.
3. Line a slow cooker with baking paper. Put the cob in the slow cooker on top of the baking paper and cook for 2 hours on HIGH, with a tea towel (dish towel) under the lid to stop condensation.
4. Carve and serve the cob bread warm.

Amanda Markham

EGG-STYLE TOAD IN THE HOLE

I like to serve this with grilled streaky bacon and fresh tomato. It's also great wrapped in foil for an easy-to-grab breakfast for hubby or the kids heading off to work or school.

Serves 4 • **Preparation** 5 mins • **Cook** 30 mins

Cooking oil spray
4 thick slices sourdough bread
2 teaspoons butter (optional)
4 eggs
Fresh chives, to garnish
Grilled bacon and tomato, to serve

1. Line the insert of a slow cooker with baking paper. Spray the paper lightly with cooking oil. Preheat the slow cooker to HIGH.

2. Use a scone cutter or glass to cut out a circle from the centre of each slice of bread. Butter the bread if you like. Lay each piece of bread, buttered-side down, on the baking paper in the slow cooker. Gently crack an egg into the hole in each slice of bread. Sprinkle with freshly ground black pepper.

3. Cover, putting a tea towel (dish towel) under the lid, and cook on HIGH for 30 minutes.

4. Serve the egg-style toad in the holes sprinkled with chives and with grilled bacon and tomato on the side.

Paulene Christie

═══ STUFFED BREKKIE CAPSICUMS ═══

I use the same ingredients to make scrambled eggs or an omelette, and I'd made Italian stuffed capsicums before, so I thought I'd turn it around, and stuff the other brekkie ingredients inside the capsicum instead. It was so yummy and I can start it cooking before going to bed and wake up to a great cooked breakfast.

Makes 4 • Preparation 20 mins **• Cook** 3–6 hours

1 tablespoon butter
1 brown onion, diced
200 g (7 oz) bacon rashers, diced
1 cup sliced mushrooms
1 large tomato, diced
1 handful baby spinach leaves
1 cup grated cheddar cheese, plus extra to sprinkle
4 red capsicums (peppers)
6 eggs, whisked with ¼ cup milk

1. Heat the butter in a frying pan over medium heat. Add the onion and bacon and cook briefly to brown slightly. Set aside.

2. Put the mushroom, tomato, baby spinach leaves and cheese in a bowl with the bacon and onion. Mix well and season with salt and freshly ground black pepper.

3. Slice the tops off the capsicums and scoop out the insides. Lightly stuff the capsicums with the mushroom mixture and stand them up against each other in a slow cooker. If you need, scrunch up foil into balls and stuff between the capsicums to help keep them upright.

4. Pour the egg mixture into the capsicums. Sprinkle the extra cheese on top. Cover the slow cooker and cook on HIGH for 3 hours or LOW for 6 hours.

5. Serve the stuffed capsicums for breakfast on their own or with a slice of toast.

Leisa Wallace

STUFFED BREAKFAST TOMATOES

For people who have busy weekends with children's sports, or for holidays away in the caravan, this is for you – a one-pot cheap, easy and no-fuss breakfast with variety.

Serves 6 • Preparation 15 mins • Cook 2–3 hours

6 tomatoes
6 rashers bacon
6 eggs
1 small handful chives, chopped
420 g (15 oz) tinned spaghetti
420 g (15 oz) tinned baked beans
½ teaspoon minced garlic (optional)
2 teaspoons Worcestershire sauce (optional)

1. Slice the tops off the tomatoes and set aside. Scoop out the tomato flesh with a teaspoon, reserving it for later use.

2. Use the bacon, cut to size, to line the inside of the tomato shells. Put 1–2 teaspoons tomato pulp in the bottom of each tomato shell and crack an egg into each one. Season with salt and freshly ground black pepper, sprinkle with chives and replace the tomato lids.

3. Combine the spaghetti, baked beans, garlic and Worcestershire sauce and ¼ cup water in a medium bowl. Transfer the mixture to the base of a slow cooker.

4. Sit the tomatoes upright in the spaghetti mixture. Cover and cook on LOW for 2–3 hours, until the tomatoes and eggs are cooked.

Cheryl Barrett

⇛— MINI QUICHES —●

Can you do mini quiches like you would in the oven? You sure can! Just use silicone cupcake cases placed directly in your slow cooker, and a tea towel (dish towel) under the lid to absorb any moisture – which makes it easy to lift them straight out when you're done and turn them out of the cases.

Makes 12 • Preparation 5 mins • Cook 1–1½ hours

100 g (3½ oz) bacon rashers, diced
2 mushrooms, finely diced
½ red capsicum (pepper), finely diced
½ cup finely diced spring onions (scallions)
6 eggs, whisked
Dash of milk
½ cup grated tasty cheese

1. Distribute the bacon, mushroom, capsicum and spring onion evenly between the 12 cups of a silicone muffin/cupcake tray. Combine the egg and milk in a small bowl, pour an even amount into each cup and sprinkle the tops with cheese.

2. Place the filled silicone cases gently into a slow cooker, directly onto the base. Spread a tea towel (dish towel) under the slow cooker lid to absorb the moisture. Cook on LOW for 1–1½ hours, or until the mini quiches are set.

Paulene Christie

QUICK & EASY QUICHE SQUARES

A great healthy addition to school lunches or to have in the fridge as a snack, these quiche squares can be made with whatever ingredients you have on hand. You can also increase the quantities to make bigger squares. I rarely do two quiches exactly the same.

Makes 24 squares • **Preparation** 10 mins • **Cook** 1 hour

8 eggs
⅓ cup low-fat milk
200 g (7 oz) lean, fat-trimmed bacon (or ham or cooked chicken), diced
2 spring onions (scallions), thinly sliced
½ red capsicum (pepper), finely diced
4 small mushrooms, finely diced
⅛ red onion, finely diced
⅓ cup corn kernels

1. Put the eggs and milk in a large bowl and whisk to combine. Add the remaining ingredients, season with salt and freshly ground black pepper, and stir to combine.

2. Line a slow cooker with baking paper. Pour the mixture into the slow cooker. Place a tea towel (dish towel) under the lid and cook on LOW for 1 hour, or until the quiche is set.

3. When cooked, remove the quiche from the slow cooker using the paper to lift it out. Slice into small squares.

Paulene Christie

 ZUCCHINI SLICE

Good in lunchboxes or for dinner with a salad.

Serves 6 • **Preparation** 10 mins • **Cook** 2½ hours

Cooking oil spray
400 g (14 oz) zucchinis (courgettes), grated and excess liquid squeezed out
2 carrots, grated
1 brown onion, thinly sliced
4 rashers bacon, thinly sliced
1½ cups grated tasty cheese
1 cup self-raising flour
6 eggs, beaten
Salad, to serve

1. Spray a slow cooker insert well with cooking oil spray.

2. Combine all the ingredients in a large bowl and season with salt and freshly ground black pepper. Pour the mixture into the slow cooker. Cover, putting a tea towel (dish towel) under the lid, and cook on HIGH for 2½ hours.

3. Serve the zucchini slice with salad.

Leisa Wallace

BACON & VEGETABLE FRITTATA

I came up with this recipe because I wanted something full of vegetables for my two little boys that is easy and convenient to make. I have done quiches in the past but never frittata, so I experimented and came up with bacon and vegetable frittata. And to my surprise, it came out the perfect shape and texture, and tasted awesome. My boys both loved it and the recipe is versatile – you can swap around and add whatever vegetables you choose.

Serves 4–6 • **Preparation** 20 mins • **Cook** 4 hours

6 eggs, beaten
2 teaspoons garlic powder
2 teaspoons onion powder
1 cup self-raising flour
1 cup grated cheddar cheese
1 onion, diced
2 carrots, grated
150 g (5½ oz) bacon pieces
1 cup frozen peas
1 cup small cauliflower and broccoli florets
2 tomatoes, diced
Salad and garlic bread, to serve

1. Line a slow cooker with baking paper.

2. Put all the ingredients in a large bowl, season with salt and lots of freshly ground black pepper and mix well. Transfer to the slow cooker and smooth the top.

3. Cover with a tea towel (dish towel) under the lid and cook on HIGH for 4 hours.

4. Serve the frittata on its own or with a simple salad and garlic bread.

Lisa Beaton

BACON, SPRING ONION & CHEESE POTATO BAKE

I wanted to do something different to roast potatoes with our family roast so I decided to take a gamble and try something new. I had used French onion soup mix in potato bakes in the oven, so I thought I'd do the same in my slow cooker but with a bit more of a twist. I didn't want extra liquid in it, so I tucked it up nicely in foil and precooked the bacon to try to prevent it being too oily.

Serves 4–6 • Preparation 30 mins • Cook 6–8 hours

Cooking oil spray
8 potatoes, peeled and cubed
200 g (7 oz) bacon pieces, cooked on baking paper in the oven
3 spring onions (scallions), chopped
1 cup shredded cheddar cheese
300 ml (10 fl oz) thin (pouring) cream
40 g (1½ oz) French onion soup mix
Salad, to serve

1. Line a slow cooker with foil. Lightly spray with cooking oil spray.

2. Layer the potato, bacon, spring onions and cheese until all used. Combine the cream and French onion soup, and pour over the layered potato and bacon. Cover the top with foil.

3. Cook on LOW for 6–8 hours.

4. Serve the potato bake as a side dish with a roast or with salad.

Lisa Beaton

CREAMY POTATO BAKE

A great side dish to any main meal or barbecue, this dish is adaptable –
increase the bacon, leave out the garlic, whatever you like. It's a lovely creamy
and cheesy taste sensation. Every slow cooker is different, so if you worry your
potato bake is getting too dry you can add more milk and cream or just milk.
This is perfectly sized for the 1.5 litre (52 fl oz/6 cup) baby slow cookers.

Serves 4–6 as a side • Preparation 10 mins • Cook 4–5 hours

Cooking oil spray
3 large potatoes, thinly sliced
1 small onion, diced
3 bacon rashers, trimmed of fat if you like
½ cup milk
½ cup cooking cream
1 teaspoon cornflour (cornstarch)
1 tablespoon minced garlic
½–¾ cup grated cheese

1. Spray the insert of a slow cooker with cooking oil. Spread a third of the potato
   slices over the bottom of the slow cooker. Scatter over half the onion and bacon.
   Spread another third of the potato slices on top, and the remaining onion and
   bacon. Top with the remaining potato.

2. Combine the milk, cream, cornflour and garlic in a medium bowl. Season with
   salt and freshly ground pepper, stir and pour over the potato layers in the slow
   cooker.

3. Cover and cook on HIGH for 2 hours.

4. Reduce the temperature setting to LOW and cook for 2–3 hours or until potatoes
   are tender. (Auto function for 5 hours will achieve the same result.)

5. When 30 minutes before cooked, scatter over the grated cheese and cook until
   melted.

Paulene Christie

SWEET POTATO & POTATO LAYER BAKE

My partner introduced me to this recipe, which belongs to his mother. It is originally an oven-cooked dish and minus the spring onion. I've never been a massive fan of sweet potato but I love this recipe. I always serve it as a side with meat and vegetables, but it could also be served on its own. Full credit to Bec Widdison.

Serves 4–6 as a side • **Preparation** 10 mins • **Cook** 4 hours

1 sweet potato, thinly sliced
3–4 potatoes, thinly sliced
600 ml (20 fl oz) thin (pouring) cream
40 g (1½ oz) French onion soup mix, dry
2 rashers bacon, finely chopped
6 spring onions (scallions)
½ cup shredded tasty cheese

1. Start with a layer of sweet potato over the base of a slow cooker. Follow with a layer of potato and pour over enough of the cream to cover the potato. Scatter over the soup mix, and some bacon and spring onion pieces. Repeat layering like this, finishing with the remaining cream. Sprinkle the shredded cheese over the cream.

2. Cook on HIGH for 4 hours.

Kareena Whennen

POTATO & SWEET POTATO BAKE

I love sweet potato and so I tend to find an excuse to add it to anything I can, like this twist on the classic potato bake.

Serves 6 as a side • **Preparation** 10 mins • **Cook** 4–6 hours

Cooking oil spray
4 potatoes, thinly sliced
1 large sweet potato, thinly sliced
2 rashers bacon, rind removed and diced
1 onion, thinly sliced
420 g (15 oz) tinned condensed cream of mushroom,
    asparagus or celery soup
1 tablespoon minced garlic
1 tablespoon mustard
½–¾ cup grated cheese

1. Spray the bowl or insert of a slow cooker with cooking oil.

2. Spread a layer of potato slices over the base of the slow cooker. Top with a layer of sweet potato slices, and repeat layering until half the potato and sweet potato slices have been used. Top with the bacon and onion, then continue the potato and sweet potato layers until all are used.

3. Put the soup in a medium bowl with the garlic and mustard and mix to combine. Pour the mixture over the potato and sweet potato layers.

4. Cover and cook on LOW for 4–6 hours, or until the potato is tender and not crunchy.

5. When 30 minutes from cooked, sprinkle the cheese over the top and continue to cook until the cheese has melted.

Paulene Christie

HASSELBACK POTATOES

We love potatoes in our family. And this recipe for Hasselback potatoes made in the slow cooker is perfect for us as a married couple, both of us working, with three children coming and going from one sporting commitment to another every night of the week. Quick, easy and yummy – that's my kind of cooking.

Serves 6 as a side • **Preparation** 10 mins • **Cook** 2–3 hours

6 potatoes, skin on
3 rashers bacon, finely chopped
1 cup shredded tasty cheese
Sour cream or guacamole, to serve

1. Make thin, evenly spaced cuts about 5 mm (¼ inch) apart in the base of the potatoes. Do not cut right through to the base. Push the bacon into the cuts.

2. Line a slow cooker with baking paper. Put the bacon-filled potatoes on top of the baking paper in the slow cooker. Sprinkle cheese over the potatoes.

3. Cover, putting a tea towel (dish towel) under the lid and cook on HIGH for 2–3 hours.

4. The potatoes are ready to serve when they are tender and the cheese is melted and crisp. Serve with sour cream or guacamole.

NOTE: Use feta cheese, sundried tomatoes, black or green olives, spring onions (scallions), garlic or anything your heart desires as the filling.

Natasha Dacey

SCHWARTZIES POTATOES

A great filling potato dish for the family.

Serves 6–8 as a side • **Preparation** 10 mins • **Cook** 3–8 hours

4 tablespoons butter
2 onions, finely chopped
5 rashers bacon, finely chopped
1 tablespoon crushed garlic
2 x 1 kg (2 lb) packets frozen potato gems (tater tots)
500 ml (17 fl oz/2 cups) sour cream
420 g (15 oz) tinned cream of mushroom soup
40 g (1½ oz) French onion soup mix, dry
1 cup grated cheese, plus extra to scatter

1. Melt the butter in a medium frying pan over medium–high heat. Add the onion, bacon and garlic and cook for 4–5 minutes, or until the bacon is browned and the onion is clear. Set aside.

2. In a large bowl, combine sour cream, soup mixes and cheese and whisk together. Add in potato gems along with the bacon mixture. Stir gently to combine, then pour into a slow cooker.

3. Cover, with a tea towel (dish towel) under the lid, and cook for 3–4 hours on HIGH or 6–8 hours on LOW.

4. When 30 minutes from cooked, scatter over the extra shredded cheese.

Duane Rasmussen

EGG & BACON PIE

We have chickens and get plenty of fresh eggs, so I have cooked egg and bacon pie in the oven a number of times and my husband is a real fan. On this occasion I had a load of eggs to use up and decided to try making a pie in the slow cooker. The result was fantastic and my husband was extremely happy because he had it cold for his lunch break too.

Serves 4 • **Preparation** 15 mins • **Cook** 3 hours

Cooking oil spray
2 sheets puff pastry
2 tomatoes, sliced
4 rashers bacon
8 eggs
1 handful grated tasty cheese
Grated parmesan cheese, to sprinkle

1. Spray a slow cooker with cooking oil and line with baking paper. Put one of the pastry sheets on the base of the slow cooker. Spread the tomato slices over the pastry and season with salt and freshly ground black pepper. Lay the bacon over the tomato.

2. Crack 6 of the eggs carefully over the bacon and allow them to spread.

3. Whisk the remaining 2 eggs and pour over the egg and bacon to fill in the gaps. Scatter over cheese. Cover with the remaining sheet of pastry.

4. Cover the slow cooker with a tea towel (dish towel) under the lid. Cook on HIGH for 3 hours.

5. Serve with a sprinkling of freshly grated parmesan cheese.

Chris McInnes

STUFFED MUSHY

A nice breakfast and a great snack, this dish came to be from my love of experimenting with ingredients and it worked really well. These ingredients will make one big one and you can easily multiply the ingredients to make more.

Makes 1 • Preparation 5 mins • Cook 1 hour 10 mins

1 large mushroom (a jumbo one, as big as possible)
1 tablespoon cream cheese
1 teaspoon bacon bits
1 teaspoon finely diced capsicum (pepper)
1 teaspoon chopped spring onion (scallion)
1 tablespoon finely grated cheddar cheese

1. Remove its stalk and sit the mushroom on a work surface. Spread the cream cheese on its underside (which will be facing upward), and sprinkle over the bacon, capsicum, spring onion and cheese. Repeat for however many mushrooms you are cooking.

2. Pour ½ cup water in the base of a slow cooker and carefully sit the mushroom on the base. Cover and cook on HIGH for 1 hour.

3. Heat the grill (broiler) to high. Carefully transfer the mushroom from the slow cooker to a baking tray and grill (broil) to brown the cheese. Serve the stuffed mushy on its own or with toast.

sherrie sutcliffe

BAKED BEANS

I love baked beans. My partner is a personal trainer and once fought for Queensland and Australian boxing titles, so along with the fit lifestyle comes the need for healthy and nutritious food. We have eggs, egg whites, ham and tomato every morning for breakfast but I like to mix it up a bit by adding baked beans. My partner pointed out the high sugar content of tinned baked beans, so I decided to make my own healthy version. We now have baked beans every morning and everyone is happy.

Serves 4–6 • **Preparation** 6 mins • **Cook** 6–8 hours

Cooking oil spray
1 onion, finely chopped
8 rashers bacon, finely chopped
700 g (1 lb 9 oz) passata (puréed tomato)
4 x 420 g (15 oz) tinned cannellini beans, thoroughly rinsed and drained
1 tablespoon golden syrup (light treacle)
1 teaspoon smoked paprika

1. Spray the base of a slow cooker with cooking oil. Put the onion and bacon in the slow cooker on HIGH, cover and cook until the onion is translucent and the bacon is almost cooked.

2. Add the passata, beans, golden syrup and paprika to the slow cooker, adding more paprika if you like. Cover and cook on HIGH for 6 hours or on LOW for 8 hours.

Zara Charles

MEDITERRANEAN BAKED BEANS

A breakfast, lunch or dinner that is canola, dairy, egg, gluten, lactose and soy free.

Serves 4 • Preparation 5–10 mins • **Cook** 6–7 hours

800 g (1 lb 12 oz) tinned butter beans, rinsed and drained
1 red onion, quartered then sliced
2 garlic cloves, crushed
500 g (1 lb 2 oz) passata (tomato purée)
100 g (3½ oz) sundried tomatoes in oil
1 teaspoon dried oregano
1 teaspoon sweet paprika
Pinch of sea salt
2 tablespoons honey
100 g (3½ oz) speck, diced
1 large handful baby spinach leaves
1 cup feta cheese, coarsely crumbled (optional)

1. Put all the ingredients except the spinach and feta in the slow cooker. Stir to combine, cover and cook for 6–7 hours on LOW.

2. When almost cooked, add the spinach and stir through, allowing it to soften a little.

3. Serve the baked beans in bowls with the feta cheese sprinkled on top, if you like.

Felicity Barnett

COOKED TOMATO WITH A WHOLE EGG COOKED IN THE MIDDLE

A different way to enjoy tomatoes and egg – for breakfast, lunch or dinner. Multiply the ingredients to serve more people.

Makes 1 • **Preparation** 5 mins • **Cook** 1 hour

1 large tomato
1 egg

1. Slice the top off the tomato and discard. Scoop out the middle.
2. Put 1 cup water into the base of a slow cooker. Carefully place the tomato in the base and crack an egg into the middle. Cover and cook on HIGH for 1 hour.
3. Serve the tomato with its egg centre with a slice of toast.

sherrie sutcliffe

SLOW-COOKER RISOTTO

Absolutely perfect and pretty much foolproof, this recipe enables anybody who's really busy to enjoy a wholesome meal that still tastes like you slaved over a stove to make it. Also, the fact you don't have to slowly add stock and keep stirring is a bonus! You can add one or any combination of the following ingredients as well: chicken, mushroom, roasted pumpkin and baby spinach.

Serves 4–6 • Preparation 15 mins • Cook 3¼ hours

2 tablespoons butter
1 onion, finely chopped
1 tablespoon crushed garlic
2 cups arborio rice
1.25 litres (44 fl oz/5 cups) chicken or vegetable stock
60 ml (2 fl oz/¼ cup) white wine (or the same amount of extra stock)
½ cup grated parmesan cheese, or cheese of your choice

1. Preheat a slow cooker to LOW and allow to heat for 15 minutes or so.

2. Meanwhile, heat the butter in a frying pan over medium heat. Add the onion and garlic and cook until the onion becomes translucent. Transfer the onion and garlic to the slow cooker. Add the rice to the slow cooker and mix to coat in the butter mixture. Pour in the stock and white wine. Stir, cover and cook on LOW for 2 hours.

3. Stir well and add the pre-browned meat and/or vegetables of choice (unless using spinach, which should be added in the last 5 minutes). Cook for another hour, or until all the stock is absorbed.

4. When the risotto is cooked, add and stir through the cheese, then serve immediately.

Amie Barrett

HIDDEN VEGETABLE MAC & CHEESE

I wanted a version of the supermarket instant mac and cheese that would be healthy and nutritious for my family. So I created my own healthy hidden vegetables mac and cheese.

Serves 4 • **Preparation** 15 mins • **Cook** 2 hours

½ small cauliflower (about 350 g/12 oz), broken into small florets
500 g (1 lb 2 oz) butternut pumpkin (squash), chopped into ½ cm (¼ inch) cubes
1 cup shredded strong-tasting (mature or vintage cheddar) cheese
125 g (4½ oz) cream cheese
1 tablespoon onion flakes
½ tablespoon dried oregano
1½ cups full cream (whole) milk
Wholemeal macaroni elbows, cooked, to serve

1. Put the chopped cauliflower and pumpkin in the base of a slow cooker. Scatter the shredded cheese over the cauliflower and pumpkin, crumble over the cream cheese, and scatter over the onion flakes and oregano. Pour the milk over the top.

2. Cover and cook for 2 hours on HIGH.

3. Blend the cauliflower and pumpkin mixture with a stick blender. Add the cooked wholemeal macaroni elbows, stir through and serve. You can also transfer the mixture to a heatproof dish, sprinkle with some extra grated cheese and place under the preheated grill (broiler) until the top is crisp and golden.

Justine Kamprad

◼━ CURRIED LENTIL LASAGNE ━●

Once, years ago, I made curried lentil lasagne as I didn't have any mince but I had spices, lentils and lasagne sheets. When I saw people cooking lasagne in their slow cookers and loving the results, I made a gluten- and lactose-free version for my daughter. There is a little hard cheese in there, which luckily she can eat. The resulting flavours after slow cooking were stunning.

Serves 6 • **Preparation** 25 mins • **Cook** 2 hours

1 tablespoon vegetable oil
1 onion, chopped
1 teaspoon curry powder
½ teaspoon smoky paprika
1 carrot, grated
425 g (15 oz) tinned brown lentils, rinsed
425 g (15 oz) tinned tomatoes
140 g (5 oz) tomato paste (concentrated purée)
Cooking oil spray
½ packet lasagne sheets
CHEESE SAUCE
40 g (1½ oz) butter
3 tablespoons plain (all-purpose) flour
3 cups milk (lactose-free if needed)
1 cup grated cheese

1. Heat the oil in a large saucepan over medium–high heat. Add the onion and cook for 2–3 minutes, until browned. Add the curry powder and cook for 1 minute. Add the paprika, carrot, lentils, tomatoes and tomato paste and bring to the boil, stirring. Reduce the heat to medium–low and simmer until thick. Set aside.

2. To make the cheese sauce, melt the butter in a large saucepan over medium heat. Slowly stir in the flour. Keep stirring, slowly adding the milk. Add half the cheese, and stir until thick.

3. Spray the bowl of a slow cooker with cooking oil. Spoon half the lentil mixture into the slow cooker, then add a layer of lasagne sheets, breaking a sheet into pieces to fit the edge. Spoon over half the white sauce. Add the remaining lentil mixture, a layer of lasagne sheets and the remaining white sauce. Top with the remaining grated cheese.

4. Cover, putting a tea towel (dish towel) under the lid, and cook on HIGH for 2 hours.

Sandra Rielly

HAM, EGG & CHEESE BUNS

I was wondering whether a recipe like this would work so I tried it – for dinner that night my hubby ate two and I had one. Delicious. I zapped the one left over in the microwave the next day and it tasted like a fresh bun. And now I'm thinking we might just have these tonight.

Serves 4 • **Preparation** 30 mins • **Cook** 1½–2 hours

4 bread rolls
4 slices ham
½ small onion, chopped
½ capsicum (pepper), diced
1 spring onion (scallion), diced
4 eggs
½ cup shredded cheese

1. Cut the top off each bun and scoop out some of the bread. Lay a slice of ham in each bun. Add the onion, capsicum and spring onion.
2. Crack an egg into a cup and slide it gently into a bread roll. Sprinkle with cheese and gently replace the top of the roll. Repeat with the remaining eggs and rolls.
3. Cover the buns with a tea towel (dish towel) and cook on HIGH for 1½–2 hours.
4. Serve as a snack or add a side salad to make a meal.

Carol McJannett

SAVOURY BREAKFAST TIGER BUNS

My daughter Kayla and granddaughter Aaliyah are usually not great breakfast eaters, but I got inspiration from Kayla's love of crusty tiger buns and made them with a savoury filling and hot melted cheese. They were an instant hit, and make an easy tasty breakfast treat that the whole family can enjoy.

Serves 4 • **Preparation** 15 mins • **Cook** 1 hour

Cooking oil spray
6–8 rashers middle bacon, diced
¾ onion, diced
½ red capsicum (pepper), diced
4 bread rolls (I use 'tiger' rolls, baked with stripes)
3 eggs, beaten
1 tablespoon milk
Tasty cheese, thinly sliced or grated, to top

1. Line a slow cooker with baking paper and preheat to HIGH.

2. Heat a medium frying pan sprayed with cooking oil over medium–high heat. Cook the bacon, onion and capsicum for 2–3 minutes, stirring to combine, until just cooked.

3. Cut the tops off the bread rolls and hollow the rolls out, setting aside the bread lids for later. Spoon the bacon, onion and capsicum mixture evenly inside the rolls.

4. Combine the eggs and milk in a small bowl, season with salt and pepper, and pour over the bacon mixture in the rolls.

5. Put the sliced or grated tasty cheese on top of the egg mixture. Replace the bread lids on the rolls and put the rolls in the slow cooker. Cover and cook for 1 hour, or until the egg mixture has cooked.

Deb McCoy

THREE-LAYER BREAD

I love bread of all kinds but have always picked the toppings off to eat first, so I came up with the idea of having layers of ingredients so the bread is packed full of flavour. I make it at least once a week and the whole family loves it.

Serves 4–6 • **Preparation** 30 mins • **Cook** 2 hours 10 mins

2 cups self-raising flour
1 cup plain yoghurt
1 teaspoon dried yeast
1 small egg (optional, if the dough is dry)
250 g (8 oz) spreadable cream cheese
3 tablespoons sweet chilli sauce
12 salami slices
150 g (5 oz) shredded bacon or ham
150 g (5 oz) grated tasty cheese, plus extra to sprinkle
1 spring onion (scallion), finely sliced
Dried shallots, to sprinkle

1. To make the dough, put the flour, yoghurt and dried yeast in the bowl of an electric mixer and beat slowly using the dough hook attachment for 5 minutes. If the mixture is too dry, add the egg.

2. Gather together the dough and put on a sheet of baking paper on a floured work surface. Divide the dough into three portions and flatten out to make three rounds, using your hands rather than a rolling pin.

3. Preheat the slow cooker to HIGH. Combine the cream cheese and sweet chilli sauce in a bowl. Spread ⅓ of the cream cheese mixture over one round of dough, and top with ⅓ of the salami slices, bacon, cheese and spring onion. Add the next round of dough and repeat layering. Finish with a generous sprinkling of cheese and dried shallots on top.

4. Transfer the dough stack to the slow cooker. Cover, putting a tea towel (dish towel) under the lid, and cook on HIGH for 1 hour.

5. Lift out the bread stack, put a wire rack in the base, and replace the bread stack, to prevent the bottom from being overcooked.

6. Cook for 1 hour. Preheat the regular oven to high when 30 minutes away from the bread being cooked.

7. Put the bread in the hot oven for 5–10 minutes to brown off the top.

Sharon Paull

CHEESE & GARLIC BEER BREAD

After seeing other bread recipes, I came up with my own kind. When I added this recipe and picture to the Slow Cooker Facebook page, it had nearly 500 likes with everyone wanting the recipe. Even my kids love this bread and, no, it doesn't taste like beer!

Makes 1 loaf • **Preparation** 15 mins • **Cook** 2 hours

Cooking oil spray
450 g (1 lb/3½ cups) self-raising flour, sifted
½ teaspoon salt
3 tablespoons sugar
125 g (4½ oz) grated cheddar cheese
355 ml (12½ fl oz) beer (use one that's not bitter if possible)
2 level tablespoons minced garlic
Sesame seeds, to sprinkle

1. Trace around the bottom of the slow cooker onto baking paper, cut out the shape and use it to line the bottom of the slow cooker. Spray a generous amount of cooking spray all over the slow cooker insert.

2. Sift the flour, salt and sugar together in a medium bowl. Add the cheese, beer and half the garlic. Mix the ingredients together to form a thick dough.

3. Put the dough on a floured board and shape it to fit the slow cooker.

4. Put the dough in the slow cooker and smear the remaining garlic over the top. Sprinkle the top with sesame seeds.

5. Cover, with a tea towel (dish towel) under the lid, and cook on HIGH for 2 hours.

6. After 1 hour of cooking, turn the slow cooker insert halfway around in case of any hot spots.

7. The bread is cooked when a skewer inserted comes out clean. Turn off the slow cooker and let the bread rest there for 10 minutes. It should then just fall out of the slow cooker insert when tipped over. Set the bread aside for 10 minutes before slicing it, otherwise it will fall apart. Spread the bread with butter and enjoy.

Leisa Wallace

SCROLLS

The thing with these scrolls is, no two batches have to be the same. You can vary what toppings you use and whether you go sweet or savoury. My kids' favourites are the cheese and Vegemite version and the diced ham, green tomato relish and cheese combination.

Makes approx 15 • **Preparation** 15 mins • **Cook** 1½ hours

2 cups self-raising flour
½ teaspoon salt
75 g (2½ oz) butter, cut into small cubes
125–250 ml (4–9 fl oz/½–1 cup) milk

1. Put the flour, salt, butter and milk in a medium bowl. Mix until the dough just comes together.

2. Turn out onto a lightly floured work surface and knead until smooth. Roll the dough into a 20 x 30 cm (8 x 12 inch) rectangle. Add the topping of your choice (see below for options) then carefully roll the dough into one big roll and cut into slices.

3. Line a slow cooker with baking paper and put the slices on the bottom, close together. Cover and cook on HIGH for 1½ hours.

4. To ice sweet scrolls, combine ½ cup icing sugar and 1 tablespoon milk and pour over while the scrolls are warm or pipe on when they are cooled.

TOPPINGS

Cinnamon Brush dough with 1 tablespoon melted butter and sprinkle over a mixture of 2 tablespoons light brown sugar and 2 teaspoons cinnamon sugar.

Apple & Cinnamon Brush dough with 1 tablespoon melted butter, spoon over 1 tablespoon stewed apple and sprinkle over a mixture of 2 tablespoons light brown sugar and 2 teaspoons cinnamon sugar.

Cheesy-mite Spread the dough with Vegemite and top with grated cheese.

Pizza-style Spread the dough with pizza sauce and top with pizza toppings of your choice.

Ham & Relish Spread dough with red or green tomato relish and top with shredded ham and cheese.

ALTERNATIVE DOUGH OPTIONS

Cream scrolls Combine 2 cups self-raising flour, 2 teaspoons sugar and 1¼ cups thin (pouring) cream.

Yoghurt scrolls Combine 2 cups self-raising flour and 1 cup Greek-style yoghurt.

Paulene Christie

FOCACCIA BREAD

One of the early crazes to sweep our Facebook group was the focaccia bread base recipe that could be adapted in so many ways – simple cheese and garlic, cheese and Vegemite, pizza style, Greek style, whatever! The recipe produces a heavy damper-like bread so the more toppings you add, the better the resulting flavour.

Makes 1 focaccia • **Preparation** 10 mins • **Cook** 1½ hours

3 cups self-raising flour
2 cups warm water
½ teaspoon salt
Toppings of your choice (see below)

1. Line the inner bowl of a slow cooker with baking paper and spray with cooking oil spray. Preheat the slow cooker to HIGH while you prepare the ingredients.

2. Mix the flour, water and salt in a bowl with a handful or so of your chosen topping ingredients (no kneading required).

3. Put the bread mixture in the slow cooker on the baking paper. Top with the remaining topping ingredients.

4. Cover, with a tea towel (dish towel) under the lid to catch condensation and prevent your bread going soggy, and cook on HIGH for 1½ hours.

TOPPING SUGGESTIONS

Pizza Anything you'd put on a pizza you can put on this focaccia – ham and pineapple, vegetarian, whatever you like.

Herb & Garlic Brush the focaccia with oil and scatter over chopped fresh herbs or dried herbs and lots of finely chopped garlic.

Sun-dried Tomato & Olive Brush the focaccia with oil and scatter over chopped sun-dried tomato and halved pitted olives.

Ham & Cheese Scatter over shredded ham and coarsely grated cheese of your choice.

Parmesan & Chive Brush the focaccia with olive oil and scatter over a mixture of grated parmesan cheese and chopped fresh chives.

Paulene Christie

PIZZA FOCACCIA

I know this is one recipe I can cook knowing the whole family will enjoy it – even my fussy husband and two kids who all like cheese and bacon. Variations to the toppings/mix-ins include garlic, cheese and herb; mushroom, cheese and bacon; or any combination you desire!

Makes 1 focaccia • **Preparation** 10 mins • **Cook** 1½–2 hours

3 cups self-raising flour
500 ml (17 fl oz/2 cups) warm water
1 large pinch of salt
FILLING
1½ cups grated cheddar cheese
1½ cups bacon bits
½ cup chopped spring onions (scallions)
140 g (4½ oz) pizza sauce
227 g (8 oz) tinned crushed pineapple in syrup, drained

1. Line the bowl of a slow cooker with baking paper.

2. Combine the flour, water and salt in a medium bowl and mix well (no kneading required).

3. Add 1 cup of the cheese, 1 cup of the bacon bits and the spring onions to the dough and combine. Put the dough in the slow cooker insert and spread it evenly over the baking paper in the base. Spread the pizza sauce over the top of the dough, followed by the crushed pineapple and the leftover bacon bits.

4. Cover with a tea towel (dish towel) under the lid, and cook on HIGH for 1½–2 hours.

5. The focaccia is done when the cheese on top has browned.

Courtney Murray

SPAGHETTI GARLIC BREAD BAKE

This recipe is one of my family's favourites. Cheap and easy to make and you can add any extra ingredients that you enjoy. We always have garlic bread with our spaghetti bolognese so I thought, Why not slow cook the two together? I carefully lifted it out to check for any burning of the garlic bread and mine was crunchy in some places which was lovely. Serve with a delicious salad and you can't go wrong. Enjoy!

Serves 4 • **Preparation** 30 mins • **Cook** 1–1½ hours

Cooking oil spray
500 g minced (ground) beef
1 x 500 g (1 lb) jar spaghetti sauce (I use red wine and garlic)
3 garlic cloves, chopped
2 loaves store-bought, buttered and sliced garlic bread
50 g (1¾ oz) grated parmesan cheese
50 g (1¾ oz) spaghetti (or pasta of choice)
Cheddar cheese, sliced or grated, to top
Green salad, to serve

1. Heat a large frying pan sprayed with cooking oil over medium–high heat. Add the garlic and the mince in batches, breaking it up with a wooden spoon and cooking until the mince is browned.

2. Transfer the browned mince and garlic to a slow cooker. Add the pasta sauce to the slow cooker and mix well. Cover and cook on HIGH for 1 hour.

3. Transfer the mince sauce from the slow cooker to a large bowl. Cover and set aside.

4. Wash and dry the slow cooker. Line the base and side with baking paper. Arrange the slices of garlic bread over the base and sides of the slow cooker, buttered side against the baking paper, to form a bowl shape. Cut the slices in half again if you don't have enough garlic bread to cover the base and side. Sprinkle half the parmesan cheese over the garlic bread on the base of the slow cooker. Add half the pasta and spread it over the garlic bread. Add half the meat sauce and spread it over the pasta. Add the remaining parmesan cheese, the rest of the spaghetti and the last of the meat sauce. And top with the cheddar cheese.

5. Cook for 1 hour on HIGH or 1½ hours on LOW.

6. Serve with green salad.

Sharon Burke

CAJUN BOILED PEANUTS

A fantastic snack food that adults and kids will love, these peanuts are delicious. On a family vacation in the US, my husband stumbled across a 'Boiled Peanut' stand alongside the road and that's when we discovered the Cajun Boiled Peanut. My family loves them and I hope whoever makes these enjoys them just as much. I make a batch on Friday and the kids eat them all weekend until they are gone.

Some batches of peanuts may cook faster than others, and slow cookers vary, so as long as the peanuts are cooking and covered in water, just cook until you reach the desired tenderness of the peanut you want. Feel free to build on the flavours by adding more heat as wanted, salt as desired or even some onion, a dash of oregano, or whatever you fancy.

Makes 6–8 cups • Preparation 10 mins • Cook 16–48 hours

4–6 tablespoons salt
4 tablespoons Cajun seasoning
2 tablespoons flaked red pepper
1 tablespoon cayenne pepper
1 tablespoon garlic powder or 2 teaspoons minced garlic
1 chopped jalapeno, including seeds (optional)
1 chicken stock cube (optional)
1 tablespoon sugar (optional)
900 g (2 lb) raw peanuts in the shell

1. Put all the seasonings in a slow cooker then cover with the peanuts. Add cold water to cover the peanuts, which will rise as the water is added.

2. Cover and cook on HIGH for 16–24 hours or on LOW for 24–48 hours, adding hot water as needed to keep the peanuts immersed as they cook.

3. The peanuts are ready when they are tender and have absorbed all the flavours.

ReBecca Byrd

RED MEAT

HOMEMADE BEEF STOCK

With so many folk liking to cook their recipes 'from scratch', it's important to start off with the very base of the recipe being homemade too. This rich, goodness-packed beef stock is so much more flavoursome than the store-bought variety, and with just a few ingredients thrown in and left to bubble away your work here is mostly done.

Makes 1.6 litres (55½ fl oz) • **Preparation** 10 mins • **Cook** 20 hours

1.5 kg (3 lb 5 oz) meaty beef bones
2 onions, cut in half
2 carrots, coarsely chopped
2 celery stalks, coarsely chopped
1 teaspoon whole black peppercorns
½ bulb garlic, peeled
1 leek, white part rinsed and coarsely chopped
3 thyme stalks
3 rosemary stalks
4 fresh or dried bay leaves
2 tablespoons apple cider vinegar

1. Put all ingredients in a 6 litre (24 cup) slow cooker. Fill with about 3 litres (12 cups) water, or until the water level is 5 cm (2 inches) from the top of the inner bowl. Cover and cook on LOW for up to 20 hours for full depth of flavour and concentration.

2. Use a slotted spoon to remove and discard all the solid pieces from the stock.

3. Pour the remaining liquid contents through a fine sieve over a large bowl to remove any remaining solid pieces of food or herbs. If you don't have a sieve, you can take a new clean pair of pantyhose, cut off one leg, secure the toe end with a knot and stretch it over a bowl to form a fine sieve.

4. Refrigerate overnight or long enough for any fat in the dish to solidify on top of the stock.

5. Use a slotted spoon to carefully remove and discard the solidified fat.

6. Refrigerate and use within 3–4 days, or freeze and use within 3 months.

Paulene Christie

BEEF GOULASH

This recipe is great for a winter's night. It goes really well with mashed potato or served on a bed of pasta shells. A really good hearty meal.

Serves 4–6 • **Preparation** 10 mins • **Cook** 8 hours

1 kg (2 lb 4 oz) chuck steak (stewing beef), cut into 3 cm (1¼ inch) cubes
3 carrots, sliced
4 potatoes, cut into 4 cm (1½ inch) cubes
4 teaspoons mild sweet paprika
4 teaspoons tomato paste (concentrated purée)
1 large onion, coarsely chopped
3 garlic cloves, minced
500 ml (17 fl oz/2 cups) beef stock
Mashed potato or pasta shells, to serve
Sour cream and coarsely chopped parsley, to garnish

1. Put all the ingredients in a slow cooker and mix well. Cover and cook on LOW for 8 hours.
2. Serve over mashed potato or pasta shells and top with a dollop of sour cream and parsley.

Chrystal Briggs

SWEET STEAK SUPREME

An awesomely flavoured steak dish that will literally melt in your mouth and leave you wanting more! Serve with a salad and chips or with vegetables. It would also go perfectly in a burger.

Serves 4–6 • **Preparation** 15 mins • **Cook** 5 hours

Cooking oil spray
1 kg (2 lb 4 oz) stewing or rump steak
⅓ cup soy sauce
1 onion, halved and sliced
1½ teaspoons minced garlic
½ teaspoon grated fresh ginger
1½ teaspoons sugar
420 g (15 oz) tinned diced tomatoes
2 green capsicums (peppers), quartered and sliced
1 teaspoon beef stock powder
Chips and salad or vegetables, to serve

1. Spray the searing insert of a slow cooker or a medium frying pan over medium–high heat with cooking oil. Add the steak and cook for 1–2 minutes, or until sealed and just browned. Transfer the steak to a slow cooker.

2. Combine the soy sauce, onion, garlic, ginger and sugar in a bowl and pour over the steak in the slow cooker. Cover and cook on LOW for 4 hours.

3. Add the tomatoes, capsicum and beef stock powder. Mix, cover and cook on LOW for 1 hour.

4. Serve the steak with chips and salad or vegetables.

Simon Christie

CREAMY STEAK

A delicious recipe that's similar to stroganoff but so much simpler – it's perfect for when you are in a hurry. I usually serve it with rice or mashed potato.

Serves 4–6 • Preparation 15 mins + 1 hour marinating **• Cook** 5–6 hours

2 tablespoons minced garlic
Pinch of sweet mild paprika
500 g–1 kg (1 lb 2 oz–2 lb 4 oz) diced skirt steak, rump steak or similar cut
Cooking oil spray
1 onion, sliced
3 tablespoons Worcestershire sauce
420 g (15 oz) tinned condensed cream of mushroom soup
125 ml (4 fl oz/½ cup) milk or thin (pouring) cream
40 g (1½ oz) French onion soup mix, dry
3 tablespoons tomato paste (concentrated purée)
Rice or mashed potato, to serve

1. Combine the garlic and paprika in a medium bowl and season with salt and freshly ground black pepper. Add the steak and toss to coat with the seasoning. Cover and refrigerate for up to 1 hour to marinate.

2. Spray a large frying pan with cooking oil spray. Heat over medium–high heat, add the onion and cook for 2–3 minutes, until golden brown. Add the steak and Worcestershire sauce and cook for 1–2 minutes, to brown the steak. Transfer the steak and onion to a slow cooker.

3. Put the cream of mushroom soup, milk or cream, French onion soup mix and tomato paste in a medium bowl and stir until combined. Pour the mixture over the steak in the slow cooker and cook on LOW for 5–6 hours.

4. Serve the creamy beef with rice or mashed potato.

Duane Rasmussen

MARY'S SAZZY WINTER STEW

I created this recipe because my husband loves stews but the recipes I used always lacked flavour. With a Maltese background, we grew up with all sorts of stews from rabbit to fish, and Mum knew how to pack a punch with flavour. This recipe is economical and you can use almost all the vegies you have on hand in the fridge. And everyone in the family loves it.

Serves 4 • Preparation 15 mins • Cook 8½ hours

Dash of olive oil
1 onion, chopped
1 teaspoon minced garlic
600 g (1 lb 5 oz) chuck (stewing) steak, or any budget beef cut, cubed
2 carrots, cubed
3–4 potatoes, cubed
¼–½ cup frozen corn kernels
¼–½ cup frozen peas
2 beef stock cubes
Pinch of sugar
2–3 tablespoons tomato paste (concentrated purée)
½ teaspoon dried oregano
½ teaspoon ground cumin
1–2 tablespoons cornflour (cornstarch), for thickening
Bread rolls, to serve

1. Heat a dash of olive oil in a frying pan over medium-high heat. Add the onion and garlic and cook until the onion is browning. Add the beef and cook until sealed and coated with browned onion. Transfer to a slow cooker.

2. Add the carrot, potato, corn, peas, stock cubes, sugar, tomato paste, oregano and cumin to the slow cooker. Season with salt and freshly ground black pepper and stir to combine. Add ¼ cup water, or enough to make a nice stewy consistency for the gravy.

3. Cover and cook on HIGH for 1 hour 30 minutes.

4. Reduce the temperature to LOW and cook for 7 hours.

5. When 30 minutes from cooked, check thickness of the stew. If it is too watery, mix the cornflour with a little water and stir through the stew to thicken.

6. Enjoy with warm bread rolls.

Mary Campbell

STEAK & MUSHROOM PIE

My stepfather made this for a Sunday family dinner and I hassled him until he gave me the recipe. I changed a couple of things and now it's a favourite in my house! I have used the same recipe and made mini steak pies for parties. I usually serve it with mashed potatoes, honey carrots and green beans – the sweetness of the carrots, creaminess of the mash and crunch of the beans works so well together with the richness of the pie.

Serves 4 • **Preparation** 20 mins • **Cook** 6 hours 20 mins

500 g (1 lb 2 oz) stewing beef, cut into 2 cm (¾ inch) cubes
1 onion, finely chopped
200 g (7 oz) Swiss brown mushrooms, chopped
375 ml (13 fl oz/1½ cups) beef stock
Splash of Worcestershire sauce
1–2 teaspoons cornflour (cornstarch) or gravy powder, for thickening
1 tablespoon butter, melted
2 sheets frozen puff pastry
1 egg, lightly beaten
Green beans, carrots and mashed potato, to serve

1. Put the beef, onion, mushrooms, stock and Worcestershire sauce in a slow cooker and season with salt and freshly ground black pepper. Stir to combine, cover and cook on LOW for 5 hours, until the meat is tender.

2. Mix the cornflour or gravy powder with a little water and add to the slow cooker. Stir through, leave the lid off and increase the temperature setting to HIGH. Cook until the sauce thickens, scooping out any excess if necessary. Turn off the slow cooker, transfer meat mixture to a clean bowl or dish and cool, covered, in the fridge.

3. Preheat the oven to 180°C (350°F). Grease a 22 cm (9 inch) pie dish with the melted butter. Line the base with 1 sheet of pastry and trim the edge. Add the meat mixture to the pie base and smooth the top. Lay the remaining pastry sheet over the top and crimp the edge to seal it. Brush the top of the pastry with the beaten egg. Bake until the pastry is golden.

4. Serve the pie with beans, carrots and mashed potato.

Imogen Bizilis

MASSAMAN CURRY

My husband and I love flavour-packed meals, and my toddler is no different, so I played around with my favourite meal and came up with my massaman curry recipe.

Serves 4–6 • Preparation 10 mins • Cook 4–8 hours

2 tablespoons vegetable or peanut oil
1 kg (2 lb 4 oz) stewing beef, cut into large chunks
800 ml (28 fl oz) tinned coconut cream
400 ml (14 fl oz) tinned coconut milk
140 g massaman curry paste, or yellow curry powder of your choice
2 brown or red onions, coarsely chopped
2 cinnamon sticks
2 star anise
2 dried or fresh bay leaves
4 potatoes, peeled and cut into large chunks
1½ tablespoons light brown sugar
1 tablespoon soy sauce
2 tablespoons lime juice
Coriander (cilantro) sprigs, to garnish
Coconut rice and steamed green beans and carrot, to serve

1. Heat the oil in a frying pan over medium–high heat. Add the beef and sear quickly to seal.

2. Remove the beef from the frying pan and put in a slow cooker, along with all the ingredients except the coriander. Cook on LOW for 6–8 hours or on HIGH for 4–6 hours.

3. Serve over coconut rice with steamed green beans and carrots, and a garnish of coriander sprigs.

Lizzie Mewburn

FRENCH ONION STEAK

It's a great family recipe and everyone who has tried it, loves it. I adapted a recipe I had to suit the slow cooker, and I make a version with lamb chops as well. Tasty and tender, it leaves a smile on everyone's dial.

Serves 4 • Preparation 15 mins • Cook 3–4 hours

2–3 onions, cut into 1–2 cm (½–¾ inch) thick slices
125 ml (4 fl oz/½ cup) beef stock
Olive oil spray
1–1.5 kg (2 lb 4 oz–3 lb 5 oz) rump steak, or steak of choice
40 g (1½ oz) French onion soup mix, dry
2 tablespoons butter
1 tomato, sliced
1–2 tablespoons cornflour (cornstarch), to thicken
3 drops Worcestershire sauce (optional)
Mashed potato, corn on cob and carrots or chips and salad, to serve

1. Cover the base of a slow cooker with the onion slices. Splash over the stock. Season with salt and freshly ground black pepper.

2. Spray a large frying pan with oil and heat over medium–high heat. Season the steak with freshly ground back pepper and sear quickly in the frying pan.

3. Put the soup mix in a shallow bowl. Remove the steak from the frying pan, put it in the bowl and coat it well with the soup mix.

4. Put the steak in the slow cooker and put knobs of butter between the pieces of steak. Put the tomato slices on top of each steak. Cover and cook for 1 hour on HIGH.

5. Reduce the heat to LOW and cook for 2–3 hours.

6. Remove the steak from the slow cooker and keep warm. Mix the cornflour with a little water, add to the slow cooker and stir through. Turn the temperature up to HIGH and add the Worcestershire sauce, if you like.

7. Serve the steak with the thickened sauce, mashed potato, carrots and corn on the cob or chips and salad.

Cheryl Barrett

SEMI-SALSA SLOW-COOK BEEF

This is a winter-warmer recipe that fills the mouth with flavour and the belly with goodness. Created from found ingredients, it's designed to be flexible depending on what's in your pantry.

Serves 6 • Preparation 15 mins • Cook 4–7 hours

1 leek, thinly sliced
3 stalks celery, thinly sliced
4 spring onions (scallions), thinly sliced
3 garlic cloves, thinly sliced
6 mushrooms, coarsely chopped
1 large onion, coarsely chopped
600 g (1 lb 5 oz) stewing beef, coarsely chopped
1 teaspoon ground oregano
1 teaspoon ground basil
2 teaspoons minced garlic
1 teaspoon ground chilli
Hoisin sauce, to taste
40 g (1½ oz) French onion soup mix, dry
40 g (1½ oz) tomato soup mix, dry
100 g (3½ oz) soup mix (dried barley, lentils and split green peas)
400 g (14 oz) tinned crushed tomatoes
Mashed potato or boiled rice, to serve

1. Put all the ingredients in a slow cooker and combine. Add enough water to cover the ingredients, cover and cook for 4 hours on HIGH or 6–7 hours on LOW.

2. Serve with mashed potato or boiled rice.

Jess van Netten

BLADE ROAST IN BRANDY CREAM SAUCE

My grandma used to make this on Sundays and I love it because it's a little different from normal roast.

Serves 6 • **Preparation** 5 mins • **Cook** 6–8 hours

2 kg (4 lb 8 oz) blade roast
2 teaspoons butter, melted
1 garlic clove, crushed
2 teaspoons dijon mustard
250 ml (9 fl oz/1 cup) beef stock or water
2 tablespoons brandy
300 ml (10½ fl oz) thin (pouring) cream
1 tablespoon cornflour (cornstarch)
Mashed potato and steamed vegetables or roast vegetables and green beans, to serve

1. Put the blade steak in a slow cooker. Combine the butter, garlic, mustard and stock in a small bowl and pour over the meat. Cook on LOW for 6–8 hours.

2. When the roast is cooked, take out the meat, cover with foil and set aside. To make the sauce, increase the slow cooker temperature to HIGH. Add the brandy and cream to the slow cooker and stir. Combine the cornflour with ¼ cup of the cooking liquid and return to the slow cooker, stirring until the sauce thickens.

3. Serve with the gravy and mashed potato and steamed vegetables or over roast vegetables and steamed green beans.

sherrie sutcliffe

SLOW-COOKED LASAGNE

Eat some now and freeze the rest for lunches and easy nights, because this recipe will make plenty of delicious lasagne.

Serves 8 • **Preparation** 20 mins • **Cook** 4 hours

Olive oil cooking spray
1 large onion, diced
5 garlic cloves, crushed
1 kg (2 lb 4 oz) minced (ground) beef
250 g (9 oz) tomato paste (concentrated purée)
400 g (14 oz) tinned whole tomatoes, crushed with a fork
1 handful basil leaves, coarsely chopped
1 small handful flat-leaf (Italian) parsley leaves, coarsely chopped
1 handful oregano leaves, coarsely chopped
250–375 g (9–13 oz) fresh or dried lasagne sheets
Garden salad, to serve

WHITE SAUCE
3 tablespoons butter
3 tablespoons plain (all-purpose) flour
1 litre (35 fl oz/4 cups) milk
White pepper, to taste
500 g (1 lb 2 oz) tasty cheese, grated

1. Spray a large frying pan with olive oil and heat over medium–high heat. Cook the onion and garlic until soft. Add the mince and break down with a wooden spoon until just brown. Add the tomato paste, crushed tomato, basil, parsley and oregano and stir to combine.

2. To make the white sauce, melt the butter in a medium saucepan over medium heat. Add the flour and cook, stirring, for 1 minute, until the colour changes. Gradually add the milk, stirring continually, adding more as the mixture thickens. Add white pepper to taste and stir in three-quarters of the cheese. Remove the saucepan from the heat.

3. Spoon a layer of the meat sauce over the base of a slow cooker. Top with a lasagne sheet and follow with a layer of white sauce. Repeat until all the meat sauce and lasagne sheets are used and finish with a layer of white sauce. Sprinkle over the remaining grated cheese. Cook on LOW for 4 hours.

4. When 1 hour before cooked, spread a tea towel (dish towel) over the slow cooker and under the lid to help the cheese brown (see Hints & Tips, page 9).

5. Serve the lasagne with a garden salad.

Melodie Tapp

— MY FIRST BEEF STEW —

It was my first attempt at a stew – and actually my first ever slow-cooked meal – and I still cook this recipe because it's hearty and delicious. You can put the leftovers into a pie maker with puff pastry for great pies.

Serves 6 • Preparation 30 mins • Cook 6 hours

1 kg (2 lb 4 oz) stewing steak, diced
5 potatoes, peeled and cut into chunky pieces
1 red capsicum (pepper), coarsely chopped
1 onion, coarsely chopped
1 swede (rutabaga), peeled and coarsely chopped
1 parsnip, peeled and coarsely chopped
1 turnip, peeled and coarsely chopped
2 celery stalks, coarsely chopped
1 cup frozen peas
3 carrots, coarsely chopped
1 zucchini (courgette), coarsely chopped
440 g (15½ oz) tinned chopped or crushed tomatoes
½ cup barbecue sauce
6 beef stock cubes, crumbled
2 teaspoons plain (all-purpose) flour
2 teaspoons gravy powder
Bread rolls or boiled rice, to serve

1. Put the beef and vegetables in a slow cooker.

2. Combine the barbecue sauce, stock cubes and 500 ml (17 fl oz/2 cups) water in a bowl. Pour over the beef and vegetables in the slow cooker. Cook on LOW for 6 hours, until the carrot is soft.

3. When 5 minutes before cooked, combine the flour and gravy powder with ¼ cup of the cooking liquid. Add the mixture to the slow cooker. Stir until the sauce is the right consistency. Keep cooking on LOW for another 5 minutes.

4. Serve with crusty bread rolls or boiled rice.

Karen Schreck

CLASSIC STEW

It's our all-time favourite slow-cooker dish that we have at least once a week – when the weather's not roasting, that is. The recipe came about with my wife and I adding whatever ingredients we wanted, and even now we sometimes swap ingredients about, using different meat – other beef cuts, lamb, pork or chicken – and different veg, whether it is fresh, frozen or tinned. And it really does taste as good as it smells.

Serves 2–4 • Preparation 5 mins • Cook 8–9 hours

Baby potatoes (as many as you like), cut in half
500 g (1 lb 2 oz) minced (ground) beef or meat of your choice
1 onion, coarsely chopped
2 garlic cloves, crushed
Pinch of dried mixed herbs
500 g (1 lb 2 oz) frozen mixed vegetables
570 ml (20 fl oz) meaty stock
Suet dumplings (prepared as per packet instructions) (optional)
1–2 tablespoons cornflour (cornstarch) or gravy powder, to thicken
Crusty bread, to serve

1. Put the potatoes in the slow cooker and sprinkle with salt and freshly ground black pepper. Add the mince, onion, garlic, herbs and mixed vegetables. Pour the stock over all the ingredients. Cook on HIGH for 1 hour.

2. Reduce the temperature to LOW and cook for 7–8 hours.

3. When 1 hour from cooked, add the dumpling mixture, if using.

4. Remove the dumpling, if using, and divide into portions.

5. Mix the cornflour or gravy powder with some of the cooking liquid and return to the slow cooker. Stir until thickened.

6. Serve with crusty bread.

Jamie Harrower

⊨— BEEF & SHERRY CASSEROLE —⬤

Super quick and easy, this casserole has sherry as well as red wine, which adds a lovely sweetness.

Serves 6 • **Preparation** 10 mins • **Cook** 8 hours

1 kg (2 lb 4 oz) stewing beef, diced
3 carrots (or other vegetables of choice), coarsely chopped
1 garlic clove, crushed
1 brown onion, coarsely chopped
400 g (14 oz) tinned diced tomatoes
125 ml (4 fl oz/½ cup) sherry
125 ml (4 fl oz/½ cup) red wine
3 fresh or dried bay leaves
2 teaspoons dried thyme
Rice or mashed potato, to serve

1. Put all the ingredients in a slow cooker and mix well. Cook on LOW for 8 hours.

2. Serve with rice or mashed potato.

Heidi Cook

⇒— 'ROAST' BEEF —●

Slow-cooked 'roast' beef spends all day cooking in the amazing herbs and flavours of this sauce. Serve it as it is with traditional gravy if you prefer but I like to drizzle a few spoons of the sauce over the finished roast for a flavour-packed sauce. Great accompanied by roast vegetables or even served on bread rolls for an easy roast beef and gravy roll recipe.

Serves 6 • Preparation 10 mins • Cook 6 hours

Cooking oil spray (optional)
1 kg (2 lb 4 oz) beef roast
½ cup salt-reduced liquid beef stock
1 tablespoon wholegrain mustard
1 tablespoon tomato paste (concentrated purée)
1 tablespoon Worcestershire sauce
2 garlic cloves, crushed
1 teaspoon fresh thyme leaves
1 teaspoon fresh rosemary leaves
1 teaspoon cracked black pepper
Roast vegetables, to serve

1. You can brown the meat first or put it straight into the slow cooker. I prefer to brown mine. Spray a large frying pan with cooking oil spray. Heat the oil over medium–high heat, add the roast and cook for 5–10 minutes, until browned, then move roast to a slow cooker bowl.

2. Combine all the other ingredients and pour over the meat in the slow cooker. Cover and cook on LOW for 6 hours, basting every now and then, and turning the meat once during cooking.

3. Slice the roast and drizzle with a little of the juices. Serve with your favourite roast vegetables.

Paulene Christie

═══ COLA BEEF ═══

A well-known if controversial dish, as some people don't like using soft drinks in cooking. You may prefer to use a low-sugar cola – it's totally up to you as both work – or to use steak or diced beef, or even other red meats. Keep in mind the volume of cola in each actual serve will be minimal.

Serves 6–8 • **Preparation** 5 mins • **Cook** 8 hours

1.5–2 kg (3 lb 5 oz–4 lb 8 oz) roasting beef
1 onion, diced
375 ml (13 fl oz/1½ cups) cola soft drink, or diet cola
40 g (1½ oz) French onion soup mix, dry
420 g (15 oz) tinned condensed cream of mushroom soup
1 tablespoon cornflour (cornstarch), to thicken
Vegetables, to serve

1. Put the beef in a slow cooker. Scatter over the onion.

2. Put the cola, soup mix and mushroom soup in a medium bowl and combine. Pour the mixture over the beef in the slow cooker.

3. Cover and cook on LOW for 8 hours.

4. Remove the beef and set aside. If the sauce needs thickening, combine the cornflour with a little water and add to the sauce in the slow cooker. Stir until the sauce thickens.

5. Carve the beef and serve with the sauce and vegetables of your choice.

Paulene Christie

CORNED BEEF

There are many versions of slow-cooked corned beef or silverside, but this seems to be the one people most commonly like to use.

Serves 4 • **Preparation** 5 mins • **Cook** 6–8 hours

1 large onion, cut into quarters
1.5 kg (3 lb 5 oz) piece corned beef/silverside, rinsed
2 garlic cloves, crushed
4 whole cloves
4 black peppercorns
2 fresh or dried bay leaves
500 ml (17 fl oz/2 cups) hot water
Vegetables, to serve

1. Put the onion and garlic on the base of the slow cooker. Put the meat on top of the onion.

2. Combine the cloves, peppercorns, bay leaves and hot water in a bowl and pour over the meat. Cover and cook on LOW for 6–8 hours.

3. Serve the corned beef with vegetables of your choice.

Paulene Christie

MARINATED CORNED BEEF
IN RICH GRAVY

I am disabled and bed-bound for 23 hours per day, with carers who come for only a short time daily, so I get a carer to prepare the meat and marinade and put them in the fridge, and later that night I transfer them to the slow cooker. Next day the carer finishes off the dish and freezes it as single serve meals. So that's how this recipe came to be. The marinade came about because I wanted more flavour in the corned beef, and now I end up with a super-rich shredded meat and gravy, as well as a strong beef stock. Nothing wasted.

Serves 6–8 • Preparation 10 mins + 8 hours marinating **• Cook** 9–11 hours

1.2 kg (2 lb 10 oz) corned beef/silverside, trimmed of fat
4 tablespoons Worcestershire sauce
4 tablespoons sweet chilli sauce
1 tablespoon light brown sugar
1 teaspoon minced garlic
1 teaspoon minced fresh ginger
1 large onion, sliced
2 carrots, cut into rounds
Warm water, to cover
2 tablespoons white vinegar
2 tablespoons cornflour (cornstarch)
1 tablespoon gravy powder
Mashed potato and steamed vegies, or soft bread rolls, to serve

1. Wash the meat under cold water and pat dry with paper towel.

2. To make the marinade, put the Worcestershire sauce, sweet chilli sauce, brown sugar, garlic and ginger in a large bowl. Mix well and add the corned beef, coating it well with the marinade. Add the onion and carrot slices and coat well with the marinade. Cover the bowl with plastic wrap and put it in the fridge, leaving it there for 8 hours or overnight.

3. Put half of the marinated carrot and onion slices over the base of a slow cooker. Put the meat on top and pour over the remaining marinade, carrot and onion. Add enough warm water to cover the meat. Add the vinegar. Cover and cook on HIGH for 1 hour.

4. Reduce heat to LOW and cook for 8–10 hours.

5. Lift the meat out of the slow cooker and shred it coarsely, leaving some pieces slightly thicker.

6. To make the gravy, put the cooked onion and carrot in a blender or food processor with a few tablespoons of the cooking juices. Purée and add more of the juices to make at least 1 litre (35 fl oz/4 cups) and mix well.

7. Transfer the stock mixture to a large frying pan and cook over medium heat, allowing the liquid to reduce. Mix the cornflour and gravy powder in 2 tablespoons of water and add to the pan, stirring until the gravy thickens.

8. Add the shredded meat to the gravy and serve with mashed potatoes and vegetables or on rolls. Keep the remaining super-rich beef stock in the fridge or freezer to use for another recipe.

Vicky Kemp

SLOW-COOKED BEEF CHEEKS

I was inspired to make this dish after trying beef cheeks at a restaurant. No local supermarkets or butchers had beef cheeks – they all looked at me funny when I asked if they sold them, and one butcher even asked if I wanted them for dog food. But I eventually found a butcher further afield that sold them and came up with my own recipe after three or four times. It tastes so good and the meat just melts in your mouth!

Serves 4 • **Preparation** 10 mins • **Cook** 10–12 hours

4 beef cheeks
1 cup bacon pieces
1 large brown onion, diced
1 stalk celery, sliced
2 carrots, sliced
3 dried bay leaves
1 small handful thyme sprigs
1 small handful flat-leaf (Italian) parsley, coarsely chopped
3 garlic cloves, sliced
250 ml (9 fl oz/1 cup) red wine
250 ml (9 fl oz/1 cup) beef stock
250 ml (9 fl oz/1 cup) chicken stock
2 tablespoons tomato paste (concentrated purée)
Mashed potato, to serve

1. Put the beef cheeks in a slow cooker. Add the bacon, onion, celery, carrot, bay leaves, thyme, parsley and garlic. Combine the wine, stocks and tomato paste in a large bowl and season with salt and freshly ground black pepper. Stir to combine and pour the liquid over the beef cheeks. Cover and cook on LOW for 10–12 hours, until the beef cheeks are very tender and falling apart.

2. Remove and discard the bay leaves and thyme sprigs. Carefully transfer the beef cheeks to a plate. Break up the stewed contents of the slow cooker with a potato masher to make a thick sauce.

3. Serve the beef cheeks with mashed potato and the sauce over the top.

Leisa Wallace

McGINNES BEEF STEW

I have customised this using the multitude of Beef & Guinness recipes around. It has the perfect balance of flavour and freshness, I think. You can serve it as a stew or use it as a filling for delicious pot pies. And you can omit the potato and serve the stew with mashed potato.

Serves 4–6 • Preparation 5–10 mins • Cook 8 hours

1 kg (2 lb 4 oz) beef topside, diced, or other stewing beef cut
3 potatoes, peeled and cut into chunks
2 carrots, coarsely chopped
2 red onions, coarsely chopped
3 celery stalks, coarsely chopped
4 garlic cloves
8 button mushrooms, cut into quarters
3 tablespoons Worcestershire sauce
350 ml (12 fl oz) beef stock
1½ cans Guinness
40 g (1½ oz) tomato paste (concentrated purée)
1 large handful mint, leaves torn
1 small handful thyme sprigs
1 cup frozen peas
1 tablespoon gravy powder, optional
Vegetables, to serve

1. Put all the ingredients except the peas and gravy powder in a slow cooker. Mix, cover and cook on LOW for 8 hours.

2. When 1 hour away from cooked, add the peas.

3. When cooked, if you want the sauce thicker, combine the gravy powder with a little water and add to the slow cooker. Stir and cook until thickened. Serve with your favourite vegetables or as a filling for pot pies.

Wendy McGinnes

BEEF POT ROAST

My family loves this recipe – it turns out perfect every time and the beef is tender enough that even toddlers like it.

Serves 4–6 • **Preparation** 10 mins • **Cook** 4–6 hours

Cooking oil spray
1 kg (2 lb 4 oz) roasting beef
40 g (1½ oz) French onion soup mix, dry
250 ml (9 fl oz/1 cup) beef stock
2 fresh or dried bay leaves
1 tablespoon cornflour (cornstarch)
1 tablespoon wholegrain mustard
Sweet potato mash and leafy greens, to serve

1. Spray a large frying pan with cooking oil and heat over medium–high heat. Add the beef and brown on all sides. Transfer to a slow cooker.

2. Combine the soup mix, stock and bay leaves in a bowl and pour the mixture over the meat in the slow cooker. Cook on LOW for 4–6 hours, until the meat is tender.

3. Remove the beef and set aside on a plate.

4. Mix the cornflour with enough water to make a smooth paste. Add the cornflour mixture to the slow cooker, stirring until it thickens. Add the mustard, return the meat to the pan and cover in the sauce.

5. Slice the beef, spoon over the sauce and serve with sweet potato mash and leafy greens.

Vicki Rossiter

PACKET-FREE CHILLI CON CARNE

I started making this to save time and money on takeaway food. I make a batch and keep it in my freezer for nights when cooking is too hard or we are very busy. It can be served as chilli con carne with rice, as a filling for tacos, quesadillas or tortilla stacks, and as a topping for potatoes.

Serves 10–12 • **Preparation** 20 mins • **Cook** 6–8 hours

Olive oil spray
6 onions, coarsely chopped
3 red capsicums (peppers), coarsely chopped
1 teaspoon sweet mild paprika
¼ teaspoon cayenne pepper
1 teaspoon chilli powder
1 tablespoon ground cumin
1 tablespoon ground coriander
1.5 kg (3 lb 5 oz) lean minced (ground) beef
2 fresh or dried bay leaves
3 teaspoons dried oregano, or 1 handful fresh oregano, leaves picked
1.2 kg (2 lb 10 oz) tinned red kidney beans, drained and rinsed
400 g (14 oz) tinned chopped tomatoes
10 garlic cloves, finely chopped
Basmati rice, plain yoghurt, avocado and shredded lettuce, to serve

1. Spray a large frying pan with olive oil and heat over medium heat. Add the onion and capsicum and cook until soft. Add the paprika, cayenne pepper, chilli, cumin and coriander and cook for 1 minute, until the spices are fragrant. Transfer to a slow cooker.

2. Add the mince to the frying pan and cook until browned. Transfer to the slow cooker. Add the bay leaves, oregano and two-thirds (2 tins) of the red kidney beans to the slow cooker.

3. Put the remaining red kidney beans, tomatoes and garlic in a food processor or blender and blend until smooth. Add half a tin of water, mix through and transfer to the slow cooker. Cook on LOW for 6–8 hours.

4. Remove the bay leaves when the chilli con carne is cooked. Divide into 4 portions and eat, or freeze, thaw and reheat as needed. Serve with basmati rice, yoghurt, avocado and shredded lettuce.

Justine Kamprad

STROGANOFF MEATBALLS

No need for the heavy creams in standard stroganoff recipes in this one, so good for those watching their waistline, and the use of mustard and sweet paprika gives it an original taste. Serve it with mashed sweet potato or pumpkin, or with pasta.

Serves 4 • **Preparation** 15 mins • **Cook** 4 hours

500 g (1 lb 2 oz) minced (ground) beef
1 egg, lightly beaten
1 brown onion, sliced
2 teaspoons minced garlic
3 teaspoons sweet paprika
2 tablespoons tomato paste (concentrated purée) or tomato pasta sauce
    (passata)
2 tablespoons dijon mustard
2 tablespoons gravy powder
¼ cup white wine
½ cup beef or chicken stock
1 cup sliced mushrooms
Mashed sweet potato or pumpkin, or pasta, to serve

1. Combine the mince and egg and roll into small meatballs, about 1 level tablespoonful each. Set aside.

2. Put the onion, garlic, paprika, tomato paste, mustard, gravy powder, wine and stock in a slow cooker and stir to combine. Gently place the meatballs on top of the liquid.

3. Cook on LOW for 4 hours, waiting for the meatballs to seal before stirring.

4. When 15 minutes from cooked, add mushroom.

5. Serve with mashed sweet potato or pumpkin, or pasta.

Jenny Ford

PORCUPINES

A simple favourite in our family, and the variations include adding herbs to the meatballs or substituting the tomato soup with any pasta sauce of your choice.

Serves 4–6 • Preparation 15 mins **• Cook** 2½ hours

500 g (1 lb 2 oz) minced (ground) beef
1 egg
1 cup white rice
1 brown onion, coarsely grated
840 g (1 lb 14 oz/2 tins) tinned condensed tomato soup
Garlic-and-onion mashed potato and steamed green vegetables, to serve

1. To make the meatballs, combine the mince, egg, rice and onion well in a large bowl. Season with salt and freshly ground black pepper. Roll into small meatballs.

2. Pour the tomato soup and one tin of water into a slow cooker and mix. Drop the meatballs gently into the liquid. Cook on HIGH for 2½ hours without stirring meatballs or lifting the lid.

3. Serve with garlic-and-onion mashed potato with a side of green vegies.

Jenny Ford

EASY CHEESY MEATBALLS

Sure you can make your own meatballs, but when you just have enough time spare to throw together a few simple ingredients and race out the door, this is the dish for you!

Serves 4 • **Preparation** 5 mins • **Cook** 4½ hours

500 g (1 lb 2 oz) pre-made spaghetti sauce
500 g (1 lb 2 oz) packet pre-made beef meatballs
⅔ cup mozzarella cheese
Thin spaghetti, to serve
Finely grated parmesan cheese, to serve
Garlic bread, to serve

1. Pour the spaghetti sauce into a slow cooker. Add the meatballs and stir gently to combine with the sauce. Cover and cook on LOW for 4 hours.

2. When 30 minutes from cooked, scatter the mozzarella cheese over the meatballs and sauce. Cover and cook on LOW for 30 minutes, or until the cheese has melted.

3. Cook the spaghetti and serve in bowls with the meatballs and sauce, with parmesan sprinkled on top and garlic bread on the side.

Paulene Christie

SPAGHETTI BOLOGNESE

Traditional Italian flavours come together to make this classic bolognese sauce. Leave it simmering away all day and all you have to do at dinner is to cook some fresh pasta and top with cheese to serve. No need to pre-brown the meat – though some prefer to do so – I prefer to use lean mince and skim any additional fat that rises to the top prior to stirring and serving.

Serves 6–8 • Preparation 5 mins • Cook 8 hours

1 kg (2 lb 4 oz) lean beef mince
820 g (1 lb 13 oz/2 tins) tinned crushed tomatoes with basil and garlic
2 small onions, diced
1 cup sliced mushrooms
1 tablespoon minced garlic
1 teaspoon beef stock powder
¼ teaspoon dried oregano
½ teaspoon dried Italian mixed herbs
⅓ cup barbecue sauce
2 tablespoons Worcestershire sauce
Spaghetti and grated parmesan cheese, to serve

1. Combine all the ingredients in a slow cooker. Cover and cook on LOW for 8 hours.

2. Serve with spaghetti and grated parmesan cheese.

Paulene Christie

SPAGHETTI BOLOGNESE NO. 2

Just like what my mum served us from the stove as children, this bolognese sauce is, well, very saucy, and has the great tomato taste you want. No need to pre-brown the mince, and this sauce copes well with the KEEP WARM setting.

Serves 6–8 • **Preparation** 10 mins • **Cook** 6 hours

500 g (1 lb 2 oz) premium minced (ground) beef
500 g (1 lb 2 oz) tomato-based spaghetti sauce
200 g (7 oz) tinned condensed tomato soup
2–3 garlic cloves, finely chopped
1 onion, finely diced
8 mushroom cups, coarsely chopped
1 large carrot, grated
1 teaspoon dried Italian mixed herbs
3 tablespoons barbecue sauce
2 tablespoons Worcestershire sauce
Spaghetti and grated parmesan cheese, to serve

1. Combine all the ingredients in a slow cooker. Cook on LOW for 6 hours.

2. Serve with spaghetti and top with grated parmesan cheese.

Paulene Christie

POTATO GEM CASSEROLE

A slow-cooker adaptation of a well-known oven recipe, it's easy to assemble and great for a casual weekend dinner for the whole family.

Serves 4 • Preparation 5 mins • Cook 2–3 hours

Cooking oil spray
0.5–1 kg (1 lb 2 oz–2 lb 4 oz) minced (ground) beef
1 small onion, chopped
420 g (15 oz) tinned diced tomatoes
420 g (15 oz) tinned condensed cream of mushroom or chicken soup
½–1 x 1 kg (2 lb) packet frozen potato gems (tater tots)
2 cups grated cheddar cheese
Side salad or vegetables, to serve

1. Spray a large frying pan with oil and heat over medium–high heat. Add the mince and cook for 4–5 minutes, stirring, until browned. Add the onion and tomatoes, stir to combine, and pour the mixture into a slow cooker.

2. Add the soup, stir to combine and gently place the potato gems on top of the mixture. Cover and cook on LOW for 2–3 hours.

3. When 30 minutes before cooked, scatter the cheese over the top and allow to melt. Great served with salad or vegetables.

Paulene Christie

MEXICAN POTATO GEM CASSEROLE

Serve this casserole with a dollop of sour cream and some mashed avocado for a Mexican taste sensation. Pre-browning of the minced meat isn't needed, but if you choose to do so, reduce the first cooking time down to 1 hour.

Serves 4 • **Preparation** 5 mins • **Cook** 6 hours

1 kg (2 lb 4 oz) lean minced (ground) beef
2 tomatoes, diced
1 red onion, diced
1 green capsicum (pepper), diced
1–2 packets taco seasoning mix
420 g (15 oz) tinned diced tomatoes
1 x 1 kg (2 lb) packet frozen potato gems (tater tots)
¾ cup grated cheese (I use low-fat)
Sour cream and mashed avocado, to serve

1. Put the mince in a slow cooker (no need to pre-brown). Add the tomato, onion, capsicum, taco seasoning and tinned tomatoes and stir to combine. Cook on LOW for 4 hours.

2. Then add the potato gems on top of the mince. Cook on LOW for 2 hours.

3. When 30 minutes from cooked, scatter the grated cheese over the mince and potato gems, and continue cooking.

4. Serve with a dollop of sour cream and a spoonful of mashed avocado.

Paulene Christie

⫸ SAVOURY MINCE ⫷

This is the epitome of the throw-in-what-you-have style of slow cooking. Start with the mince and add whatever vegetables you have on hand – frozen or finely diced fresh. No two batches of my savoury mince are ever the same.

Serves 4–6 • Preparation 5 mins • Cook 6 hours

500 g (1 lb 2 oz) lean minced (ground) beef
2 garlic cloves, minced
1–2 cups diced mixed vegies (fresh or frozen)
1 beef stock cube
210 g (7½ oz/½ tin) tinned condensed tomato soup
1 onion, diced
2 tablespoons Worcestershire sauce
2 tablespoons barbecue sauce
2 tablespoons tomato sauce
1 tablespoon instant gravy mix (roast meat or brown onion flavour)
½ cup water
Mashed potato and fresh corn on the cob, to serve

1. Put all the ingredients in a slow cooker and stir to combine. Season with salt and freshly ground black pepper. Cover and cook on LOW for 6 hours.

2. Serve with mashed potato and fresh corn on the cob.

Paulene Christie

⇒— TERIYAKI BEEF NOODLES —●

I created this one evening when the cupboards were bare and I felt like something different. With a dash of this and a little of that, I had an amazing dish that had us coming back for more. I used fresh pasta instead of noodles and fresh Italian herbs because that was what was in the cupboard that night. It surprised us all by tasting so ridiculously good. I served it with vegetable wontons for a little extra kapow.

Serves 4 • **Preparation** 5 mins • **Cook** 6 hours

500g (1 lb 2 oz) beef schnitzel, sliced
1 large onion, chopped
Vegetables of choice, diced
½ cup teriyaki sauce
2 vegetable stock cubes dissolved in 1 cup boiling water
250g (9 oz) dried rice noodles (or cooked pasta!)
450 g (1 lb) frozen wontons (optional)
Handful fresh coriander, chopped

1. Put the schnitzel, onion, vegetables, teriyaki sauce and stock in a slow cooker and mix to combine. Cover and cook on LOW for 5 hours 40 minutes.

2. Make up the noodles, and wontons if using, as per packet instructions. Add to the slow cooker and mix through. Cook for 20 minutes and serve in bowls.

4. Scatter over chopped fresh coriander or herbs of choice.

Megan Morris

DEB'S WINTER STEW

My stew is so easy and tasty, it's great for beginners and large families. It's a regular stew with added flavours like soy sauce and paprika, and I don't add green vegies as they go soggy and you can always add them as a side dish. I usually make this once a week in winter – I prepare it the night before, leave it in the fridge and put it in the slow cooker before I go to work. It's wonderful coming home to such a nice smell after a long day at work and it's easy for teenagers to serve themselves if they are hungry before I get home.

Serves 4–6 • Preparation 15 mins • Cook 4–10 hours

1 kg (2 lb 4 oz) stewing steak, cut into bite-size pieces
1–2 tablespoons sweet paprika, or paprika of your choice
¼ cup plain (all-purpose) flour
Cooking oil spray (optional)
3–4 potatoes, chopped
2–3 carrots, chopped
1 parsnip, chopped
1 turnip, chopped
1 swede (rutabargo), chopped
440 g (15½ oz) tinned chopped tomatoes
1–2 tablespoons tomato paste (concentrated purée)
2 tablespoons soy sauce
1 litre (35 fl oz/4 cups) beef stock
1 cup frozen peas
Crusty bread or mashed potato, to serve

1. Put the meat, paprika and flour, and salt and freshly ground black pepper to taste, in a ziplock bag and shake to coat the meat all over.

2. If you have the time and would like to, brown the meat before putting in the slow cooker. Spray a large frying pan with oil and heat over medium–high heat. Add the meat in several batches, turning until just browned.

3. Put the coated meat in the slow cooker with the remaining ingredients except the peas. Cover and cook on HIGH for 4–6 hours or on LOW for 8–10 hours.

4. When 20 minutes from cooked, add the peas to the slow cooker and stir.

5. Serve with crusty bread or mashed potato.

Deb Youle

EASY CHEESY NACHO LASAGNE

I love nachos and lasagne, so it only seemed fitting that I combine them. It was a huge hit with my family and it's easy to make.

Serves 4–6 • **Preparation** 10 mins • **Cook** 1–1½ hours

Cooking oil spray
500 g (1 lb 2 oz) minced (ground) beef
200 g (7 oz) tomato-based pasta sauce
230 g (8 oz) packet corn chips
1 cup homemade or pre-made cheese sauce
½ cup grated cheddar cheese
Sour cream, to serve

1. Spray a large frying pan with oil and heat over medium–high heat. Add the mince and cook for 4–5 minutes, stirring, until browned.

2. Add the pasta sauce, mix to combine and reduce the heat to medium. Cook for 2 minutes and set aside.

3. Spray a slow cooker bowl with oil. Put a layer of corn chips on the bottom, add a layer of meat sauce and a layer of cheese sauce. Continue layering until the meat sauce, cheese sauce and corn chips are all used. Sprinkle over the grated cheese. Spread a tea towel (dish towel) over the slow cooker to prevent soggy corn chips (see Hints & Tips, page 9). Cover with lid and cook on HIGH for 1–1½ hours.

4. Serve the nacho lasagne with sour cream.

Shayna Manoah

━ BEEF SINGAPORE NOODLES ━

You could make this one with pork as well. It tastes like it has come straight from a takeaway noodle shop.

Serves 4–6 • **Preparation** 15 mins • **Cook** 4 hours

500 g (1 lb 2 oz) eye fillet steak, sliced
4 spring onions (scallions), thinly sliced
2 brown onions, sliced
2 celery stalks, diced
2 carrots, cut into matchsticks
425 g (15 oz) tinned baby corn
2 teaspoons curry powder of your choice
1 teaspoon minced garlic
½ teaspoon finely grated fresh ginger
¼ cup soy sauce
2 tablespoons oyster sauce
1 tablespoon chicken stock powder
1 teaspoon sesame oil
250 g (9 oz) dried rice noodles

1. Put all the ingredients except the noodles in a slow cooker and mix to combine. Cover and cook on LOW for 3 hours 45 minutes.

2. Make up the noodles as per packet instructions or cover with boiling water for 2 minutes then drain. Add the noodles to the slow cooker and mix through. Cook for 15 minutes and serve in bowls.

Angela Beswick

SINGAPORE NOODLES WITH BEEF AND CHICKEN

I'm a mum of one, and another on the way, so I love quick simple meals that are easy to prepare. My family loves noodles and this recipe is easy to jam pack full of vegies for the kiddies. I hope you enjoy my recipe as much as we do!

Serves 4 • **Preparation** 10 mins • **Cook** 4 hours

250 g (9 oz) beef steak (cut of choice), sliced
200 g (7 oz) skinless chicken breast fillet, sliced
4 spring onions (scallions), thinly sliced
1 capsicum (pepper), sliced
2 celery stalks, diced
2 carrots, diced
200 g (7 oz) tinned baby corn
½ cup frozen peas
1 teaspoon curry powder
1 teaspoon minced garlic
½ teaspoon grated fresh ginger
¼ cup soy sauce
2 tablespoons oyster sauce
1 tablespoon chicken stock powder
1 teaspoon sesame oil
250 g (9 oz) dried rice noodles

1. Put all the ingredients except for noodles in a slow cooker and cook on LOW for 3 hours.
2. Add 1 cup of water and the noodles, and cook for 1 more hour.

Brooke Clack

LAYERED MEXICAN MINCE & CORN CHIPS

This Mexican mince dish is really popular in our house as we all love Mexican food and corn chips. So combining all our favourites together, I came up with this yummy, filling meal.

Serves 6 as a snack • **Preparation** 15 mins • **Cook** 3–4 hours

Cooking oil spray
1 kg (2 lb 4 oz) minced (ground) beef
1 packet taco seasoning mix
200 ml (7 fl oz) mild tomato salsa
175 g (6 oz) packet corn chips, crushed
1 cup grated cheddar cheese
250 g (9 oz) sour cream, to serve
2 spring onions (scallions), chopped, to garnish

1. Spray a large frying pan with cooking oil and heat over medium-high heat. Add the mince and cook, breaking up with a wooden spoon, until browned. Add the taco seasoning and sauce, mix and set aside.

2. Scatter half the crushed corn chips over the base of a slow cooker. Spoon over the meat mixture, cover with grated cheese, and scatter over the remaining crushed corn chips. Spread a tea towel (dish towel) over the slow cooker to prevent soggy corn chips (see Hints & Tips, page 9). Cover with lid and cook for 3–4 hours on low.

3. Serve with a dollop of sour cream and a sprinkling of spring onion.

sherrie sutcliffe

RIGATONI PIE WITH AMERICAN CHEESE

The Wisconsin cheddar cheese makes this rigatoni pasta dish, as it is an aged cheddar that has a bite to it. Every kid loves spaghetti bolognese but this is a fun take on the age-old dish. The cheese oozes down with every bite, the sauce infuses the pasta and kids love the flavour – but they have no idea that I hid so many vegetables in the sauce when I made it. Eating healthy does not have to be boring.

Serves 4 • **Preparation** 10 mins • **Cook** 2 hours

500 g (1 lb 2 oz) rigatoni pasta, slightly undercooked, drained and rinsed
½ cup grated parmesan cheese
Cooking oil spray
320 g (11 oz) prepared bolognese sauce
1 cup grated Wisconsin cheddar cheese, or any aged cheddar
Small handful basil leaves, to garnish
Green salad, to serve

1. Put the rigatoni in a medium bowl and shake over the parmesan cheese. Toss to combine.

2. Lightly spray a 23 cm (9 inch) spring-form pan with oil. Pack the rigatoni, standing on their ends, into the pan tightly. Pour the bolognese sauce over the pasta, pushing the sauce down into the holes. Transfer the pan to a slow cooker and cook on HIGH for 2 hours with a tea towel (dish towel) under the lid.

3. Carefully remove the pan and put on a heatproof surface. Preheat the grill (broiler) to medium–high. Scatter the American cheese over the pasta and grill until the cheese has melted.

4. Scatter over fresh basil leaves and serve with a green salad on the side.

Wayne Gatt

⚡— KOREAN BEEF TACOS —●

We love tacos but find it works out to be expensive to buy packet taco mixes. Living on a tight budget I wanted to work out a cheaper and nicer recipe that I could do at home. The sauce is more of a basic Korean marinade, which I found on the internet, but cooking it with the meat makes a nice sauce once the meat juices are released. This is also nice to have on rice if you don't want to make tacos. It has a nice fresh flavour which is loved by our whole family. You can also use beef topside, but that is more expensive, or pork or chicken.

Makes 8 • Preparation under 5 mins **• Cook** 8 hours

1 kg (2 lb 4 oz) piece beef bolar blade
5 garlic cloves, crushed
¼ onion, diced
⅓ cup light brown sugar
¼ cup soy sauce
1 tablespoon rice wine or white vinegar
1 teaspoon sesame oil
6 mm (¼ inch) piece fresh ginger, peeled and grated
1 jalapeno chilli, diced (optional)
8 flour tortillas
Shredded lettuce and grated carrot salad, to serve

1. Put the beef in a slow cooker.

2. Combine the garlic, onion, brown sugar, soy sauce, vinegar, sesame oil, ginger and chilli, if using, in a small bowl. Pour over the meat in the slow cooker. Cover and cook on LOW for 8 hours.

3. Remove the beef and shred. Combine the shredded meat with the sauce and serve on the tortillas with the salad.

Karen Stuckings

PIZZA LASAGNE

I can eat pizza anytime of the day but it is generally so high in fat. I decided to take my recipe and convert it into a low-fat, higher-fibre and higher-protein recipe to enable me to eat it without guilt – and I have a longer-lasting feeling of satisfaction and fullness due to the whole wheat pasta and non-fat yoghurt. It's also Weight Watchers friendly, which enables my family and me, here in San Diego, California, USA, to enjoy this wonderful meal often. I hope y'all enjoy it as much as our family does.

Serves 6–8 • Preparation 20 mins • Cook 2½–5 hours

Cooking oil spray (optional)
450 g (1 lb) lean minced (ground) beef
70 g (2½ oz) thinly sliced salami (pepperoni, or turkey pepperoni if you can get it)
900 g (2 lb) Italian pasta sauce
4 cups shredded light mozzarella cheese
½ cup grated parmesan cheese
115 g (4 oz) reconstituted powdered egg or 2 eggs, lightly beaten
225 g (8 oz) non-fat Greek-style yoghurt
185 g (6½ oz) wholemeal (whole wheat) lasagne sheets
Green salad, to serve

1. Brown the mince, if desired. Spray a large frying pan with cooking oil and heat over medium–high heat. Add the mince and cook, breaking up with a wooden spoon, until browned.

2. Put the raw or browned mince in a medium bowl with the pepperoni and pasta sauce and stir to combine.

3. In a separate bowl, combine 2 cups of the mozzarella, the parmesan, the egg product or eggs and the yoghurt.

4. Pour 1 cup of the meat mixture over the base of a slow cooker. Cover with a layer of lasagne sheets. Spread a quarter of the cheese mixture over the lasagne sheets and top with a quarter of the meat sauce.

5. Repeat the layering with lasagne sheets, half of the remaining cheese mixture, the remaining lasagne sheets, and the remaining cheese mixture. Top with the remaining meat mixture and the remaining mozzarella. Cook for 2½ hours on HIGH or 5 hours on LOW.

6. Serve the lasagne with a green salad.

Larell Adney Strickland

ENCHILADA TORTILLA LASAGNE

A delicious meal for the weight-conscious! Mexican restaurants are found in abundance where I live in San Diego, California, USA. I decided to try and make a lasagne involving Mexican ingredients, especially with cheese and tortillas, along with low-fat, high-fibre and high-protein ingredients. This means the recipe can easily be cooked by Weight Watchers members and yet it tastes delicious for ALL your family to eat! Trust me, you'll all enjoy it.

Serves 6–8 • **Preparation** 15 mins • **Cook** 3–6 hours

Cooking oil spray
450 g (1 lb) lean minced (ground) beef
840 g (1 lb 14 oz/2 tins) tinned condensed cream of chicken soup
770 g (1 lb 11 oz/2 tins) vegetarian refried beans
1 cup mild tomato salsa
2 cups shredded reduced-fat cheddar cheese
12 corn tortillas (standard size)

1. Spray a large frying pan with cooking oil and heat over medium–high heat. Add the mince and cook, breaking up with a wooden spoon, until browned.

2. Transfer the mince to a large bowl with the soup, refried beans, salsa and 1 cup of the cheese. Mix to combine.

3. Put 4 tortillas on the bottom of a slow cooker. Spread over a third of the meat mixture. Repeat two more times, ending with the meat mixture. Top with the remaining cheese.

4. Cover and cook on HIGH for 3–4 hours or LOW for 6 hours.

Larell Adney Strickland

OSSO BUCO WITH A MEXICAN TWIST

Serve this delicious slow-cooker meal with a glass of red wine.

Serves 2 • Preparation 30 mins • Cook 6–8 hours

Plain (all-purpose) flour, for dusting
Garlic and herb salt, for dusting
Freshly ground black pepper, for dusting
2 pieces osso buco
Cooking oil spray
420 g (15 oz) tinned diced tomatoes
½ jar taco sauce
1 packet taco seasoning mix
250 ml (9 fl oz/1 cup) red wine
250 ml (9 fl oz/1 cup) beef stock
2 teaspoons dried oregano
2 stalks celery, coarsely chopped
2 zucchini (courgettes), coarsely chopped
2 mushrooms, coarsely chopped
1 onion, coarsely chopped
Mashed potato and crusty bread, to serve

1. Put flour in a large bowl and season with the garlic and herb salt and black pepper. Coat the osso buco with the seasoned flour, shaking off any excess.

2. Spray a medium frying pan with cooking oil. Heat over medium–high heat and cook the osso buco for 3 minutes each side until sealed. Set aside.

3. Put the tomatoes, taco sauce, taco seasoning mix, red wine, beef stock and oregano in a large bowl and stir to combine.

4. Combine the celery, zucchini, mushroom and onion in a large bowl.

5. Spread the vegetable mixture over the base of a slow cooker. Top with the osso buco and the tomato mixture. Cover and cook on LOW for 6–8 hours.

6. Serve the ossu buco with mashed potato and crusty bread.

Lynn Hastie

MONGOLIAN BEEF

This Mongolian beef recipe was created thanks to my OCD husband. One day, he complained to me that my fridge was full of jars of sauce – hoisin sauce was the one I pulled out that day. With help from Google, I found a recipe from a website and tweaked it to how I like it. I'm glad that the recipe is now liked by other families.

Serves 4 • Preparation 10 mins • Cook 3½–4 hours

650 g (1 lb 7 oz) chuck steak, sliced
30 g (1 oz/¼ cup) cornflour (cornstarch)
1 tablespoon olive oil
1 onion, thinly sliced
1 tbsp minced garlic
3 spring onions (scallions), sliced diagonally into 1 cm (½ inch) pieces
60 ml (2 fl oz/¼ cup) soy sauce
¼ cup light brown sugar
½ teaspoon minced fresh ginger
60 ml (2 fl oz/¼ cup) hoisin sauce
Dash of sesame oil
Rice and stir-fried vegetables, to serve

1. Put the steak and cornflour in a ziplock bag. Shake the bag to evenly coat the steak and set aside for 10 minutes.

2. Heat the olive oil in frying pan over medium–high heat. Shake off any excess cornflour and cook the steak for 2–4 minutes, until evenly browned. Transfer the steak to a slow cooker.

3. Put the onion, garlic and spring onion in the slow cooker.

4. Combine the soy sauce, brown sugar, ginger, hoisin sauce, sesame oil and 60 ml (2 fl oz/¼ cup) water in a small bowl. Pour over the meat in the slow cooker and cook on LOW for 3½–4 hours.

5. Serve the Mongolian beef with steamed rice and stir-fried vegetables.

Cheng Ibberson

⚏— SWISS STEAK —●

Who says you can't do steak in a slow cooker? My husband loves this dish, and I can't go past a creamy mushroom sauce on a steak. If you want to make a lower-fat version, leave out the cream and you will still have a lovely mushroom sauce.

Serves 4–6 • **Preparation** 10 mins • **Cook** 3–6 hours

4 tablespoons vegetable oil
250 g (9 oz) mushrooms, sliced
1 kg (2 lb 4 oz) beef blade steak, seasoned with salt and black pepper
1 onion, sliced
1 tablespoon thyme leaves
1 teaspoon sweet paprika
¼ cup plain (all-purpose) flour
¾ cup chicken stock
¼ cup apple cider vinegar
½ cup thickened (whipping) cream
Green salad and chunky cut potato chips or wedges, to serve

1. Heat 1 tablespoon of the vegetable oil in the searing insert of a slow cooker, or in a frying pan on the stove. Add the mushroom and cook for 5 minutes, or until brown. Transfer the mushroom to a plate, or if using a frying pan for the browning, straight to the slow cooker at this point.

2. Heat 1 tablespoon of the oil in the searing insert or same pan. Add the seasoned steak and cook for 1–2 minutes, or until sealed and just browned. Transfer the steak to the plate with the mushroom, or if using a frying pan for the browning, add steak to the mushroom in the slow cooker.

3. Heat the remaining oil in the searing insert or same pan. Add the onion, thyme and paprika. Cook, stirring, for 1 minute. Add the flour and cook, stirring continuously, for 1 minute. Add the stock and vinegar, stirring and scraping together all the browned bits from the bottom of the pan.

4. Transfer the onion mixture and mushroom to the slow cooker if not already in there. Put the steak on top, cover and cook on HIGH for 3–4 hours or LOW for 4–6 hours.

5. Remove the steak from the slow cooker and keep warm. Add the cream to the liquid in the slow cooker and stir to combine. Allow to cook for 10 minutes.

6. Serve the steak with the sauce spooned over and a green salad and chunky cut potato chips or wedges on the side.

Paulene Christie

BEEF & RED WINE CASSEROLE

A traditional slow cooker recipe that many have tried. Adjust the vegetables to suit yourself. Leave it chunky or blend some of the dish first then add it back in for a thicker soup type finish. A great way to use up all of your leftover vegetables before shopping day. Lovely served as a complete meal with crusty bread rolls on the side.

Serves 4–6 • Preparation 10 mins • Cook 3–8 hours

¼ cup plain (all-purpose) flour
Salt and cracked black pepper, to season
1.5 kg (3 lb 5 oz) blade steak, cubed
2 tablespoons vegetable oil
1 brown onion, sliced
4 garlic cloves, crushed
½ cup tomato paste (concentrated purée)
2 tablespoons beef stock powder
125 ml (4 fl oz/½ cup) red wine
1 tablespoon oregano leaves
400 g (14 oz) tinned diced tomatoes
2 cups sliced mushrooms
Baby potatoes and green beans, to serve
Crusty bread rolls, to serve

1. Put the flour, salt and pepper in a bowl, add the steak and toss to coat.

2. Heat the oil in a frying pan, browning the meat quickly in batches, stirring often. Remove the browned meat and add to a slow cooker.

3. Using the same frying pan, cook the onion and garlic for 2 minutes or until beginning to brown. Add the tomato paste, stock powder and wine, and cook for 2 minutes, stirring constantly. Add this mixture to the beef in the slow cooker and stir in the oregano, tomatoes and mushrooms until combined.

4. Cover and cook for 3–4 hours on HIGH or 6–8 hours on LOW.

5. Serve the casserole with the cooking juices, baby potatoes, steamed green beans and crusty bread rolls on the side.

Paulene Christie

SAUSAGES IN BARBECUE & MUSTARD SAUCE

Slice these sausages into bite-size pieces and serve them on toothpicks at your next party. Or just leave them whole and enjoy them with salad or steamed vegies.

Serves 6 • **Preparation** 5 mins • **Cook** 4 hours

1 kg (2 lb 4 oz) thin beef sausages
½ cup barbecue sauce
1 tablespoon white vinegar
2 tablespoons mild American mustard
½ cup light brown sugar
1 tablespoon soy sauce
1 garlic clove, minced
Salad or steamed vegies, to serve

1. Put the raw sausages in a slow cooker (pre-browning is optional but not required).

2. Combine the barbecue sauce, vinegar, mustard, brown sugar, soy sauce and garlic in a bowl and stir to combine. Pour over the sausages in the slow cooker. Cover and cook on LOW for 4 hours.

3. Allow to remain in the slow cooker on the WARM setting for another couple of hours if you need.

4. Slice or serve whole with salad or steamed vegetables.

Paulene Christie

SAUCY SLOW-COOKER SAUSAGES

Some like to brown their sausages first, to remove the extra fat before slow cooking. That's fine if you wish to, but I choose low-fat sausages instead and add them from raw. This approach maintains the combine-and-walk-away style of slow cooking at its best. You can also halve this recipe easily.

Serves 6–8 • Preparation 5 mins • Cook 6–8 hours

16 thin beef sausages
2 onions, diced
½ cup barbecue sauce
½ cup tomato sauce
3 tablespoons Worcestershire sauce
40 g (1½ oz) French onion soup mix, dry
1–2 tablespoons cornflour (cornstarch), for thickening

1. Put the sausages (no need to pre-brown or pre-boil them) and onion in a slow cooker. Combine the barbecue, tomato and Worcestershire sauces and the soup mix in a jug. Add 375 ml (13 fl oz/1½ cups) water, mix well and pour over the sausages in the slow cooker. Cook on LOW for 6–8 hours.

2. If you need to thicken the sauce, mix in 1–2 tablespoons of cornflour towards the end of cooking.

Paulene Christie

CURRIED SAUSAGES

Who doesn't love a good curry made in the slow cooker? This version doesn't have the cream base of some and can be cooked with low-fat sausages so that it's more friendly on the waistline. Load it up with vegetables for maximum goodness.

Serves 6 • **Preparation** 5 mins • **Cook** 6–8 hours

500 g (1 lb 2 oz) thick or thin sausages
1 large onion, diced
4 potatoes, cubed
3 carrots, coarsely chopped
1 cup frozen peas
1–2 tablespoons curry powder, according to taste
750 ml (26 fl oz/3 cups) beef stock
2 tablespoons cornflour (cornstarch), to thicken
Rice, to serve

1. Put the sausages in a slow cooker. (I put mine in raw but you can pre-boil them and remove the skins.) Add the onion, potato, carrot, peas, curry powder and stock. Cook on LOW for 6–8 hours.

2. When cooked, check whether the sauce needs thickening. Remove the sausages and, if required, add the cornflour combined with a little water and stir through. I like to slice the sausages then return them to the sauce in the slow cooker for serving.

3. Serve the curried sausages with rice.

Paulene Christie

SAUSAGES IN BROWN ONION GRAVY

A classic dish made easy, with a rich, thick and glossy gravy that develops during the hours of slow cooking. Serve it straight from the slow cooker, pouring the gravy over your sausages and mash.

Serves 6 • **Preparation** 10 mins • **Cook** 5 hours

Cooking oil spray
1 kg (2 lb 4 oz) thin beef sausages
2 onions, sliced
½ cup rich meat gravy powder
Mashed potato and vegetables, to serve

1. You can put the raw sausages directly in the slow cooker or pre-cook them. To pre-cook them, spray a large frying pan with cooking oil and heat over medium–high heat. Cook the sausages for 2–3 minutes in batches to seal and brown them. Transfer the sausages to a slow cooker. Spray the pan with oil again and cook the onion for 3 minutes, until translucent.

2. Transfer the sausages and onion to the slow cooker. Combine the gravy powder with a little water, then add more to make up to 1 litre (35 fl oz/4 cups). Pour the gravy mixture over the sausages in the slow cooker. Cook on HIGH for 1 hour, then reduce to LOW and cook for 4 hours.

3. Serve with mashed potato and vegetables.

Paulene Christie

COUNTRY TOMATO SAUSAGE CASSEROLE WITH BACON

Quick, easy and budget friendly, this full-flavoured sausage dish will be a hit with the whole family. Be sure to spoon some of the sauce over the sausages on the plate! I don't do it, but some people like to brown the sausages quickly with the onion and garlic before putting them in the slow cooker.

Serves 4 • **Preparation** 10 mins • **Cook** 5 hours

8 thin beef sausages
1 onion, diced
1 large garlic clove, crushed
200 g (7 oz) diced bacon
410 g (14½ oz) tinned chopped tomatoes with basil and garlic
¼ teaspoon dried thyme
¼ teaspoon ground sage leaves
Mashed potato and steamed vegetables, to serve

1. Put the sausages (raw or browned quickly with the onion and garlic) in a slow cooker. Add the remaining ingredients and stir well to combine. Cook on LOW for 5 hours.

2. Serve the sausages with mashed potato and steamed vegies, with plenty of the sauce spooned over the top.

Simon Christie

SAUSAGE PAPRIKASH

Use a teaspoon of mashed roasted garlic instead of the crushed raw garlic for a more intense flavour.

Serves 6–8 • Preparation 5 mins • Cook 2 hours

12 sausages of choice
420 g (15 oz) tinned condensed tomato soup
40 g (1½ oz) French onion soup mix, dry
1 tablespoon Worcestershire sauce
1½ teaspoons smoked paprika
½ teaspoon crushed sea salt flakes
1½–2 teaspoons crushed garlic
Mashed potato, steamed broccolini and carrots, to serve

1. Put all the ingredients in a slow cooker and mix thoroughly. Cover and cook on HIGH for 1½ hours.

2. Remove the sausages and slice into bite-size pieces then return them to the slow cooker. Cook for 30 minutes on HIGH.

3. Serve with creamy mashed potato, steamed broccolini and julienne carrots.

Christy Roth

CURRIED SAUSAGES

A lovely creamy version of curried sausages, the leftovers can be frozen for lunch or easy dinners.

Serves 6 • **Preparation** 10 mins • **Cook** 6 hours

12 sausages
1 large onion, diced
270 ml (9½ fl oz) tinned coconut cream
1 tablespoon curry powder
2 tablespoons beef stock powder
1 cup frozen baby peas
Rice and pappadums, to serve

1. Cut the sausages into bite-size pieces and put them in a slow cooker. Scatter the onion over the sausages.

2. Put the coconut cream and curry powder in a bowl or jug. Stir to combine and pour the mixture over the sausages. Mix the beef stock powder with 150 ml (5 fl oz) water and pour the mixture over the sausages.

3. Cover and cook for 5½ hours on LOW.

4. Add the peas to the slow cooker and stir through the curry. Replace the lid and cook for 30 minutes.

5. Serve the sausages with plenty of the curry sauce over rice and with pappadums on the side.

Geoff Tapp

SAUSAGE LASAGNE

I created this recipe after looking for a way to use up leftover sausages after an Australia Day barbecue, as well as wanting to make lasagne – my hubby's favourite – in the slow cooker. Now I make it with different flavoured sausages and it's a winning dish every time.

Serves 4 • Preparation 20 mins • Cook 4–6 hours

Cooking oil spray
6–8 beef sausages, browned and chopped
1 large onion, diced
1 capsicum (pepper), coarsely chopped
425 g (15 oz) tinned diced tomatoes
1 tablespoon crushed garlic
1 teaspoon dried oregano
250 g (9 oz) lasagne sheets
Grated cheese, for sprinkling
Salad, to serve

CHEESE SAUCE
500 ml (17 fl oz/2 cups) milk
1 cup grated cheddar cheese
1 tablespoon butter
1 tablespoon plain flour

1. To make the cheese sauce, melt the butter in a saucepan on stovetop. Stir in the flour and cook for 1–2 minutes. Remove from the heat and gradually add the milk, whisking continuously to ensure a smooth consistency. Return pan to the heat and cook over a low heat for 10 minutes, stirring continuously. Remove from heat, add the cheese and stir to combine. Season with salt and freshly cracked pepper.

2. Spray the bowl of a slow cooker well with cooking oil. Set temperature to LOW.

3. Put the sausages, onion, capsicum, tomatoes, garlic and oregano, plus salt and freshly ground black pepper in a bowl and mix to combine.

4. Cover the base of the slow cooker with some sausage mixture, then put lasagne sheets to cover over the top. Spoon enough cheese sauce over the lasagne sheets to cover. Repeat layers until all the mixtures are used. Sprinkle the extra cheese on top. Cover and cook on HIGH for 4 hours or LOW for 6 hours.

5. Serve the sausage lasagne with a simple salad.

Jesseca Huber

STICKY BARBECUE & MUSTARD MEATBALLS

The reason I made the meatballs was because I was craving something barbecue-flavoured and sweet. I gathered up what I had in the fridge and cupboard and chucked it together and this is what I came up with. I served it for dinner and the children (aged 16, 11 and 1) and my partner loved it.

Serves 4 • Preparation 20–30 mins • Cook 2–3 hours

½ cup tomato sauce (ketchup)
2 tablespoons soy sauce
2 tablespoons light brown sugar
2 tablespoons apricot or plum jam (jelly), or honey if you like
2 teaspoons dijon mustard, or to taste
10 pork or beef sausages or 800 g (28 oz) sausage mince

1. Put the tomato sauce, soy sauce, sugar, jam, mustard and ½ cup water in a slow cooker. Mix well, until the brown sugar and jam are dissolved. Set the slow cooker to HIGH while you prepare the meatballs.

2. Squeeze the filling from the sausages. You should get 5 small meatballs from each sausage. Roll small amounts of the sausage meat (or mince, if using) into balls. Add to the slow cooker and cook on HIGH for 2–3 hours with a tea towel (dish towel) under the lid so the sauce goes thick and sticky.

Maxine Streets

STICKY BARBECUE-FLAVOURED SAUSAGES

We live rurally so getting to the supermarket is something we only do every three or four weeks. We decided we wanted sausage casserole with barbecue sauce for dinner one night but discovered we had no mix, so I googled a recipe – and discovered it was horrible! Over the next couple of years I changed all the ingredients, one by one, until I had the sauce exactly the way my family loves it. There is only one ingredient from the original recipe but we now have a recipe my family are happy to eat any time!

Serves 2–6 • **Preparation** 10 mins • **Cook** 3 hours

Whole or sliced pre-cooked sausages, as many as desired
1 onion, finely sliced
2–3 garlic cloves, minced
2 tablespoons soy sauce
1 cup tomato sauce (ketchup), or use 1 cup tinned crushed tomatoes and 2 tablespoons tomato paste (concentrated purée)
¼ cup light brown sugar
2 tablespoons malt vinegar
1 teaspoon mustard powder
Mashed potato or rice, to serve

1. Put the sausages in the base of a slow cooker. Combine the onion, garlic, soy sauce, tomato sauce, sugar, vinegar and mustard powder in a bowl. Mix to combine and pour over the sausages in the slow cooker. Cook on LOW for 3 hours.

2. Serve the sausages in their sauce with mashed potato or rice.

Carla ZenThings Rako

LAMB OBSESSION

I stumbled upon this dish by accident just by combining a few things I thought would go nicely together. Little did I know it would become my signature dish. I almost never ate lamb before I created this recipe but we have it pretty much every week in our house now.

You can make it using various cuts of lamb – chops, steaks, leg, shanks, diced and even minced – because all lamb loves obsession! I even use this recipe on beef and chicken, just omitting the mint. Even the most hardened mushroom-haters swear they can't taste the mushrooms in this, let alone the mushroom-haters who happily eat it without their knowledge. And even if you don't like mint – I admit I don't – try it here because it creates a perfect little zing with the lamb.

Serves 4–6 • **Preparation** 5 mins • **Cook** 6 hours

6–8 lamb chops, or cut of your choice up to 2 kg (4 lb 8 oz)
1 onion, diced
420 g (15 oz) tinned condensed cream of mushroom soup (no water added)
40 g (1½ oz) French onion soup mix, dry
1–2 tablespoons Worcestershire sauce
1 tablespoon mint sauce or mint jelly
Mashed potato and steamed vegetables, to serve

1. Put the lamb in a slow cooker. Scatter the onion over the lamb. Combine the mushroom soup, French onion soup mix, Worcestershire sauce and mint sauce or jelly in a medium bowl and pour over the lamb. Cover and cook on LOW for 6 hours for chops or up to 8 hours for a large leg of lamb.

2. Serve the lamb with the cooking sauce, creamy mash and steamed vegetables.

Paulene Christie

SLOW-COOKED 'ROAST' LAMB

Simply nothing comes close to this slow-cooked roast lamb. The classic flavours of rosemary and garlic are there, and you can even add the vegies to the slow cooker with the meat and, hey presto, dinner is done.

Serves 6–8 • Preparation 5 mins • Cook 6–8 hours

1–2 kg (2 lb 4 oz–4 lb 8 oz) lamb roast, leg-in or boneless
2–3 garlic cloves, cut in half lengthways
4–6 sprigs rosemary
Vegetables of your choice (optional)
2 teaspoons beef stock powder
125 ml (4 fl oz/½ cup) hot water
1–2 tablespoons mint sauce or 3–4 mint leaves, finely sliced

1. Using a sharp paring knife, make several 1–2 cm (½–¾ inch) deep slits in the lamb and insert half a garlic clove and a rosemary sprig in each hole. Transfer the lamb to a slow cooker. (You can put a layer of vegetables on the base of the slow cooker and put the lamb on top at this point if you like.)

2. Put the stock powder, hot water and mint sauce in a bowl and stir to combine. Pour the mixture into the slow cooker around the lamb. Cook on LOW for 6–8 hours, spooning the juices over the lamb several times during the day if you can.

3. Transfer the lamb to a cutting board and remove the garlic and rosemary sprigs. Carve the meat and serve with vegetables you have roasted in the oven, or those in the slow cooker. Make a gravy with the pan juices to serve with the lamb.

Paulene Christie

LAMB CHOPS WITH ASPARAGUS & MINT SAUCE

I was intending to make my infamous Lamb Obsession recipe but couldn't find the cream of mushroom soup, so I used asparagus soup and found I'd stumbled onto another winner!

Serves 6 • **Preparation** 5 mins • **Cook** 6–8 hours

6 lamb chops
1 onion, diced
420 g (15 oz) tinned condensed cream of asparagus soup
40 g (1½ oz) French onion soup mix, dry
1 tablespoon mint sauce
2 tablespoons Worcestershire sauce

1. Put the chops in a slow cooker. Scatter over the onion.
2. Put the remaining ingredients in a bowl and pour over the chops in the slow cooker.
3. Cover and cook on LOW for 6–8 hours.

Paulene Christie

MINTY LAMB

Based on Paulene's Lamb Obsession, this dish is canola, dairy, egg, gluten, lactose and soy free.

Serves 6 • Preparation 15–20 mins • Cook 3–4 hours

2.5 kg (5.5 lb) lamb, diced
400 g (14 oz) button mushrooms, sliced
1 red onion, diced
4 garlic cloves, diced
6 spring onions (scallions), sliced
1 vegetable stock cube, crushed
2 tablespoons gluten-free cornflour (cornstarch)
2 teaspoons light brown sugar
270 ml (9½ fl oz) tinned coconut cream
2½ tablespoons gluten-free Worcestershire sauce
3 tablespoons gluten-free mint jelly, or to taste
Mashed potato, to serve

1. Put the lamb, mushroom, onion, garlic and spring onion in a slow cooker.

2. Put the stock cube, cornflour, sugar, coconut cream, Worcestershire sauce and mint jelly in a bowl. Mix to combine and pour over the lamb in the slow cooker. Cook on LOW for 3–4 hours.

3. Serve the lamb with mashed potato.

Felicity Barnett

HEARTY LAMB SHANKS

I had lamb shanks out for tea and I was a limited slow-cooker user so I added whatever I had in the pantry, and voila, the outcome was amazing. The flavour, as my partner said, was to die for. So it's been a monthly meal since. I make my own rosemary-infused olive oil, which we dip our bread in to eat with the lamb shanks, by adding a few rosemary sprigs to some olive oil in a bowl and leaving it for about two hours.

Serves 4–6 • Preparation 10 mins • Cook 6 hours

6 potatoes, coarsely chopped
2 onions, cut into wedges
3 carrots, coarsely chopped
2 celery stalks, coarsely chopped
3 garlic cloves, finely diced
2 cups frozen peas, or peas and corn
500 ml (17 fl oz/2 cups) red wine
1 tablespoon soy sauce
4 lamb shanks
800 g (1 lb 1 oz) tinned diced tomatoes
Crusty bread, to serve

1. Spread the potato over the base of a slow cooker. Add the onion, carrot, celery, garlic and peas. Pour over the red wine and soy sauce.

2. Put the lamb shanks on top of the vegetables. Pour the tomatoes over the lamb shanks. Add salt and pepper to taste.

3. Cover and cook on HIGH for 4 hours.

4. Stir, cover again, reduce heat to LOW and cook for 2 hours.

5. When the meat is falling of the bone, serve with a crusty French stick and rosemary-infused oil for dipping.

Kaz Dunemann

FIRST-TIME SHORT-PREP LAMB SHANKS

Designed for first-time slow cookers, this delicious dish takes five minutes to prepare and its warm flavours will delight even the youngest taste buds. The splash of mint lightens an otherwise wintry dish and provides an easy alternative to roast lamb.

Serves 2–4 • Preparation 5 mins • Cook 4–6 hours

4 small potatoes, thickly sliced
2 lamb shanks
3 small onions, cut in half
3 teaspoons minced garlic
Dash of barbecue sauce
2 sprigs rosemary, leaves picked
2 sprigs thyme, leaves picked
Dash of thick mint sauce
800 g (1 lb 12 oz) tinned diced tomatoes
Mashed potato, rice or pasta, to serve

1. Spread the potato slices over the base of a slow cooker. Place lamb shanks on top, followed by the onions.

2. Combine the garlic, barbecue sauce, rosemary and thyme in a small bowl. Spoon the mixture over the lamb shanks and onions.

3. Add the mint sauce to the tomatoes and pour over the top.

4. Cover and cook on HIGH for 4–6 hours, spreading a tea towel (dish towel) under the lid to prevent moisture build-up.

5. Serve the lamb and sauce over mashed potato, rice or pasta.

Jess van Netten

LAMB SHANK CURRY

This is an easy and healthy curry with a great flavour kick. You can add vegetables such as cubed pumpkin, potato or eggplant or stir through some coconut cream at the end if you want a milder, creamier flavour.

Serves 4 • **Preparation** 10 mins • **Cook** 6–8 hours

4 lamb shanks
2 garlic cloves, chopped
1 large onion, chopped
1 tablespoon tomato paste (concentrated purée)
1 teaspoon chopped chilli
1 teaspoon ground ginger
1 teaspoon ground cumin
1 teaspoon ground coriander
1 teaspoon ground cardamom
250 ml (9 fl oz/1 cup) vegetable or chicken stock
Rice, pappadums, fried shallots, coriander (cilantro) and chilli flakes, to serve

1. Put the lamb shanks, garlic, onion, tomato paste, chilli, spices and stock in a slow cooker. Combine gently and season with salt and freshly ground black pepper.

2. Cover and cook on LOW for 6–8 hours.

3. Serve when the meat starts falling off the bone with rice, pappadums, fried shallots, coriander and chilli flakes.

Vicki Rossiter

TWO-IN-ONE LAMB SHANKS & TOMATO

My thinking in creating recipes is to try to use regular pantry and freezer staples and not waste anything. This recipe can give two different meals in one pot. It also hides vegetables in the tomato base. The lamb shanks can be served whole on the plate or the meat shredded with the thick tomato sauce, mashed potatoes and greens. The remaining soup can be stick-blended smooth or left with some chunky bits. The cauliflower thickens the soup, which has an intense lamb flavour. Or you can combine the soup with the shredded meat. The lamb shanks can be substituted for osso buco or any slow cook lamb cuts. So many choices.

Serves 4–6 • Preparation 15 mins • Cook 7–9 hours

Olive oil cooking spray
2 onions, diced
3 carrots, diced
3 stalks celery, diced
500 g (1 lb 2 oz) cauliflower, cut into florets
4 large or 6 medium lamb shanks
800 g (1 lb 12 oz) tinned diced tomatoes
2 tablespoons tomato paste (concentrated purée)
4 tablespoons Worcestershire sauce
4 tablespoons soy sauce
2 teaspoons finely chopped chilli
2 teaspoons minced garlic
2 teaspoons minced fresh ginger
1 tablespoon light brown sugar
1 litre (35 fl oz/4 cups) chicken stock

1. Spray a slow cooker with the olive oil.

2. Put the onion, carrot, celery and cauliflower in a medium bowl and toss to combine. Spread half the vegetable mixture over the base of the slow cooker.

3. Put the lamb shanks on top of the vegetables. Push the remaining vegetables in the gaps around the lamb shanks.

4. Put the tomatoes, tomato paste, Worcestershire and soy sauces, chilli, garlic, ginger, sugar and stock in a medium bowl and stir to combine. Pour over the shanks and vegetables.

5. Cover and cook on HIGH for 1 hour.

6. Reduce the heat to LOW and cook for 6–8 hours.

7. Transfer the lamb shanks to a plate. Blend the vegetable mixture with a stick blender, making it smooth or chunky according to your taste.

8. Serve the lamb and sauce in whatever combination you like. And freeze any leftovers.

Vicky Kemp

LAMB SHANKS IN ONION GRAVY

If you want to, you can add 2 tablespoons of French onion soup mix to this but I prefer it simple.

Serves 2 • Preparation 5–10 mins • Cook 4–8 hours

Cooking oil spray
1 onion, cut in half
2 lamb shanks
½ cup gravy powder
1–2 sprigs rosemary
Garlicky mashed potato, to serve

1. Spray the base of a slow cooker with cooking oil.

2. Slice one half of the onion into rings and spread these over the base of the slow cooker. Put the lamb on top of the onion rings.

3. Finely dice the other onion half. Spray a small saucepan with cooking oil and heat over medium–high heat on the stove. Cook the diced onion until soft and starting to brown. Spoon over the lamb shanks in the slow cooker.

4. Add the gravy powder to the same saucepan and gradually blend in 1½ cups water without heating. Season with salt and freshly ground black pepper, and pour this gravy mixture over the lamb shanks in the slow cooker.

5. Add the rosemary to the slow cooker then cover and cook on HIGH for 4–5 hours or LOW for 6–8 hours.

6. Serve the lamb shanks on a bed of garlicky mashed potato.

Karen Barwick

IRISH STEW

Having an Irish background I wanted to make a stew that was simple but flavoursome to introduce my young daughter to our heritage. This is a family favourite and is always served with fresh bread and butter.

Serves 4 • **Preparation** 5 mins • **Cook** 7 hours

5 potatoes, sliced
3 carrots
2 onions, coarsely chopped
500 ml (17 fl oz/2 cups) chicken stock
1–1.5 kg (2 lb 4 oz–3 lb 5 oz) lamb shoulder
Pinch of pepper, to season
Fresh bread and butter, to serve

1. Put the vegetables in a slow cooker and cover with chicken stock.
2. Place the lamb shoulder on top of vegies, and season with pepper. Cover and cook for 7 hours on LOW.
3. When cooked, shred the lamb with a fork and mix in the vegetables.
4. Serve with fresh bread and butter.

Kris Cosh

⟩━ LAMB NECK CHOP STEW ━●

Picking some herbs from the garden inspired this new way to cook lamb neck chops. Combined with the soy sauce, the rosemary and coriander (cilantro) created a tasty result we couldn't get enough of, and we ate it for the next two nights as well.

Serves 4–6 • Preparation 10 mins • Cook 6–8 hours

2 kg (4 lb 8 oz) lamb neck chops
1 large onion, sliced
3 garlic cloves, thinly sliced
1 sprig rosemary
2–3 sprigs coriander (cilantro)
2–3 basil leaves, including stalk
125 ml (4 fl oz/½ cup) dark soy sauce
Dash of balsamic vinegar
1 tablespoon cornflour (cornstarch)
Mashed potato and steamed vegetables, to serve

1. Put the lamb neck chops in a slow cooker. Season with salt and freshly ground black pepper.

2. Combine the onion, garlic, rosemary, coriander, basil, soy sauce and balsamic vinegar in a large bowl. Spread over the chops in the slow cooker. Add enough water to cover the chops and vegies.

3. Cover and cook on LOW for 6–8 hours.

4. When 30 minutes before cooked, mix the cornflour with a little water and add to the slow cooker.

5. Serve the lamb neck chops with mashed potato and vegetables.

Leigh Baker

➡ 'ROAST' PORK ➡

Now that I have made it in my slow cooker, I will never, ever go back to cooking roast pork in the oven. You need the oven for the crackling, of course, but for moist and tender meat you simply cannot beat the work of the slow cooker.

Serves 6 • **Preparation** 10 mins • **Cook** 5 hours

2 kg (4 lb 8 oz) leg of pork
5 large carrots, cut into quarters
Salt, for rubbing
Gravy, apple sauce and vegetables of choice, to serve

1. Make sure the pork is dry. This can be achieved by leaving it in the fridge, uncovered, for 1–2 days.

2. When dry, score the pork rind down to the flesh at 1 cm (½ inch) intervals, which makes for easy carving and also allows the salt to penetrate.

3. Salt the pork liberally and rub in. Repeat. Salt a final time without rubbing the salt in.

4. Spread the carrots over the base of a slow cooker. Put the pork on top of the carrots.

5. Cook for 5 hours on LOW.

6. When 30 minutes from the pork being cooked, preheat the oven to its highest setting.

7. After the full 5 hours, remove the pork from the slow cooker and put it on a cake rack on a baking tray. Transfer to the oven. Cook until the desired crackling has been achieved.

8. Transfer the carrots to a separate tray and put in the oven to brown, or serve them straight from the slow cooker.

9. Remove the crackling from the pork and break into pieces. Slice the pork and serve with the crackling, gravy, apple sauce, carrots and other vegetables of choice.

Christy Roth

TENDER ROAST PORK

So simple the way the vinaigrette tenderises the meat perfectly and adds a hint of herbs. Smells delish. Tastes good too.

Serves 4–6 • **Preparation** 5 mins • **Cook** 6 hours

Pork roast, netting removed
1 bottle purchased French or any clear herb-based dressing
Roast potatoes and steamed vegetables or salad, to serve

1. Put the pork roast in a slow cooker. Pour over the dressing, cover and cook on LOW for 6 hours.

2. Slice the pork and serve with roast potatoes and steamed vegetables or salad.

Jenny Ford

CREAMY PEPPER PORK CHOPS

The lovely peppery sauce with these pork chops has a bit of bite so you may wish to tone it down by reducing the pepper content for the young or faint-hearted.

Serves 4 • **Preparation** 5 mins • **Cook** 4–6 hours

4 pork chops, rind and excess fat trimmed
2 garlic cloves, minced
1 onion, finely diced
1 teaspoon salt-reduced beef stock powder
1 teaspoon freshly ground black pepper, or to taste
420 g (15 oz) tinned condensed cream of mushroom soup
Baby potatoes or mashed potato, steamed peas and carrots, to serve

1. Put the pork chops in the base of a slow cooker. Scatter the garlic, onion, stock powder and pepper over the pork chops. Pour over the soup. Cook on LOW for 4–6 hours.

2. Serve the pork chops with the creamy sauce and baby potatoes or mash with peas and carrots.

Paulene Christie

SAUCY PULLED PORK

Before I started slow cooking I'd never heard of the pulled meat craze. Then I made this dish and never looked back. I love my saucy sauce and the resulting dish is so versatile. You can serve it with mash and veg, on bread rolls with coleslaw, or even on tortillas with salad. Reduce the salt content by using low-sodium sauce products.

Serves 4–6 • Preparation 5 mins • Cook 6–8 hours

1 kg (2 lb 4 oz) pork shoulder chops or cut of your choice
¼ cup hoisin sauce
¼ cup barbecue sauce
¼ cup soy sauce
¼ cup sweet chilli sauce
¼ cup tomato sauce (ketchup)
¼ cup Worcestershire sauce
4 garlic cloves, minced
Bread rolls and coleslaw or mashed potato and steamed vegetables, to serve

1. Put the pork in a slow cooker.

2. Combine the hoisin, barbecue, soy, sweet chilli, tomato and Worcestershire sauces in a bowl. Add the garlic and ½ cup water, stir and pour the mixture over the pork. Cover and cook on LOW for 6 hours for chops or 8 hours if cooking a large piece of roasting pork.

3. When cooked, use two forks to 'pull' apart the meat and mix through the sauce. Serve on bread rolls with coleslaw or with mashed potato and steamed vegetables.

Paulene Christie

ASIAN-STYLE PORK MEATBALLS

When I am asked my favourite slow-cooker recipe, this is always in my top five. I love the tangy sauce. And here's a tip – don't go stir crazy! The meatballs will come out firm and intact and won't break apart if you leave them to fully seal before going anywhere near them with a spoon. You can buy panko breadcrumbs in the Asian food section at the supermarket.

Serves 4 • Preparation 15 mins • Cook 3–5 hours

500 g (1 lb 2 oz) minced (ground) pork
⅓ cup panko breadcrumbs
1 egg, lightly whisked
1 tablespoon soy sauce
1 tablespoon finely grated fresh ginger
2 garlic cloves, minced
3 spring onions (scallions), sliced
Cooking oil spray
½ cup barbecue sauce
¼ cup plum sauce
2 tablespoons hoisin sauce
Fried rice and steamed Asian greens, to serve

1. Put the mince, breadcrumbs, egg, soy sauce, ginger, garlic and spring onions in a large bowl. Combine gently using your hands and roll into 2.5 cm (1 inch) balls. Spray the inner bowl of a slow cooker with cooking oil. Gently put the meatballs in the slow cooker.

2. Put the barbecue, plum and hoisin sauces in a small bowl and stir to combine. Pour the mixture over the meatballs and stir very gently to coat them. Cover and cook on LOW for 3–5 hours, without stirring or disturbing the meatballs until the end of cooking, when they should be well sealed.

3. Serve with fried rice and steamed Asian greens.

NOTE: If you're using regular breadcrumbs instead of panko, increase the quantity to ½ cup.

Paulene Christie

PORK WITH APPLES & APPLE CIDER

A family favourite that's delicious served with mash for a canola, dairy, egg, gluten, lactose and soy free dinner.

Serves 4–6 • **Preparation** 10–15 mins • **Cook** 4½–7 hours

2 large red onions, sliced
1 kg (2 lb 4 oz) lean pork, diced
600 g (1 lb 5 oz) pork belly, cut into 4–6 pieces
2 garlic cloves, crushed
4–6 apples, peeled and chopped
100 ml (3½ fl oz) apple cider vinegar
500 ml (17 fl oz/2 cups) apple cider or apple juice

1. Spread the onion over the base of a slow cooker. Top with the diced pork and then the pork belly. Spread over the garlic, and season with salt and freshly ground black pepper.

2. Put the apples on top of and around the pork. Pour the cider vinegar and apple cider over the pork.

3. Cover and cook for 4½–5½ hours on HIGH or 6–7 hours on LOW.

Felicity Barnett

SMOKY BARBECUE HONEY BOURBON PULLED PORK

I love how this is not an exact recipe – I have omitted exact portions for the sauce mix because it's all about your taste! Honey and barbecue is a classic mix, but adding bourbon brought a whole other element that marries the toastiness of the barbecue sauce with the sweetness of the honey, giving it a real pop.

Serves 6 • **Preparation** 5 mins • **Cook** 9–10 hours

Large pork shoulder
Barbecue seasoning or seasoning rub of your choice
About 500 g (1 lb 2 oz) smoky barbecue sauce
About 60 ml (2 fl oz/¼ cup) bourbon
About 60 ml (2 fl oz/¼ cup) honey

1. Rub the pork shoulder with the seasoning. Put the pork in a slow cooker.

2. Combine the barbecue sauce, bourbon and honey in a small bowl. Pour the mixture over the pork.

3. Cover and cook on LOW for 8–9 hours.

4. Remove the pork and shred the meat by pulling with two forks. Leaving a little of the sauce in the slow cooker, transfer most of it to a jug or bowl.

5. Return the pork meat to the sauce in the slow cooker and stir through. Cook on HIGH for 30–60 minutes, until the sauce is the perfect thickness.

6. Serve the pulled pork and gravy with baked potatoes and homemade coleslaw or on bread rolls.

Wendy McGinnes

PICKLED PORK

A number of years ago my husband purchased pickled pork and I cooked it up just like I would corned silverside. He was most disappointed and told me the best way to do pickled pork was to roast it. But since doing a lot of cooking in my slow cooker, including roasts, I decided to try roasting the pickled pork in a small amount of pineapple juice to add some sweetness to the meat. It worked really well and the leftover meat is also great on sandwiches or with salad.

Serves 4–6 • Preparation 10 mins • Cook 6 hours

Vegetables of choice, chopped uniformly
Pickled pork
250 ml (9 fl oz/1 cup) pineapple juice

1. Spread the vegetables over the base of the slow cooker. Put the pork on top of the vegetables and pour over the pineapple juice. Cook on LOW for 6 hours.

2. When 30 minutes from being cooked, preheat the oven to the highest setting.

3. When meat and vegetables are cooked, transfer them to baking trays and put in the oven to crisp and brown. Reserve the cooking juices in the slow cooker for gravy.

4. Serve the pork with the vegetables and a gravy made with some of the cooking juices (NB: it will be too salty if you use all the juice).

Chris McInnes

PORK LOIN STACKS

I came up with this recipe as a way of introducing my young child to a new approach to eating meat – instead of serving just plain old pork loins, I made them with stuffing. They worked a treat and the rest of my family enjoyed them as well. We all found them so 'melt in your mouth' tasty. These pork loins are easy and quick to prepare on a busy work day and will go with almost anything as part of a main meal.

Serves 4 • **Preparation** 5 mins • **Cook** 5 hours

4 pork steaks or chops
Homemade or purchased stuffing
1 apple, sliced
1 onion, sliced
4 slices cheddar cheese
4 mushrooms, sliced
1 tomato, sliced
1 tablespoon wholegrain mustard
Roast vegetables and steamed green peas, to serve

1. Put 4 scrunched-up balls of foil in the base of a slow cooker.
2. Place one pork steak or chop on a large sheet of foil. Top with ¼ of stuffing, ¼ of sliced apple, ¼ of sliced onion, 1 sliced mushroom, ¼ of sliced tomato and ¼ tablespoon mustard. Top with another pork steak. Repeat layers of stuffing ingredients and steak until they're all used, then wrap the foil tightly around the parcel to seal.
3. Place the foil parcel on the screwed-up foil in the slow cooker. Add about 2.5 cm (1 inch) water to the base of the slow cooker. Cover and cook on HIGH for 5 hours.
4. Serve with roast vegetables and green peas.

Dawn Robinson

BARBECUED COLA PORK RIBS

My fiancé and I are huge lovers of pork ribs. After receiving our slow cooker for an engagement present, the one thing my fiancé had been nagging me to make was some pork ribs so I decided to have an attempt at my own recipe – and it was to die for! Huge hit with the fiancé. I served this up with a roasted mustard vegie bake, a perfect addition. I hope you all enjoy this as much as we did.

Serves 4 • Preparation 5 mins • Cook 8–10 hours

2 kg (4 lb 8 oz) pork baby back ribs
375 ml (13 fl oz/1½ cups) cola drink
250 ml (9 fl oz/1 cup) barbecue sauce

1. Season the ribs all over with salt and freshly ground black pepper. Put the ribs in the slow cooker, standing them up against the inside of the cooking bowl so they wrap around it.

2. Pour the cola over the ribs, cover and cook on LOW for 8–10 hours.

3. Preheat the grill (broiler) to high. Line a baking tray with foil. Carefully transfer the ribs to the tray, placing them meaty side up. Cover the ribs with the barbecue sauce and put under the grill until the sauce starts to sizzle and caramelise.

4. Remove from the grill and serve.

Brooke Jennings

HAWAIIAN PORK BELLY

The flavours of this Hawaiian dish are perfectly complemented with a side serving of a tropical salad, featuring bacon pieces, pineapple and nuts, and topped with a fresh, zingy salad dressing.

Serves 4 • **Preparation** 20 mins • **Cook** 3 hours

¼ cup vinegar
¼ cup tomato sauce (ketchup)
1 tablespoon soy sauce
110 g (3¾ oz) pineapple pieces in juice, drained and finely chopped
3 teaspoons sugar
½ teaspoon salt
1 tablespoon grated fresh ginger
1 tablespoon chopped garlic
1.2 kg (2 lb 12 oz) pork belly strips, cut into thirds
Salad, to serve

1. To make the marinade, put the vinegar, tomato sauce, soy sauce, pineapple, sugar, salt, ginger and garlic in a medium bowl and mix well.

2. Put the pork belly in the slow cooker, spoon over the marinade and coat the meat well. Cover and cook on LOW for 2 hours.

3. Remove the lid from the slow cooker and cook on HIGH for 1 hour, or until the sauce becomes a thick glaze.

4. Preheat the grill (broiler) on high and line a baking tray with baking paper. Transfer the pork belly from the slow cooker to the tray. Grill the pork belly on both sides until browned.

5. Carve the pork belly and serve with salad.

Tania Whitford

CHILLI PORK & BEANS

I love to serve this on a Sunday family get-together in winter. It adds a fun dimension to the family meal. I serve it in a big bowl on the table with tortillas, diced avocado and sour cream too.

Serves 4 • **Preparation** 10 mins • **Cook** 6 hours

500 g (1 lb 2 oz) minced (ground) pork
400 g (14 oz) tinned diced tomatoes
400 g (14 oz) tinned kidney beans, rinsed
1 onion, finely chopped
2 garlic cloves, crushed
125 ml (4 fl oz/½ cup) vegetable stock
2 tablespoons tomato paste (concentrated purée)
2 teaspoons chilli powder
1 fresh chilli, sliced
Tortillas, diced avocado and sour cream, to serve

1. Put all the ingredients except the tortillas, avocado and sour cream in the slow cooker and stir to combine. Cover and cook on LOW for 6 hours, stirring every now and then.

Melodie Tapp

SPICY PORK RIBS

We use this very tangy pork rib recipe for gatherings, usually serving it with a potato bake and fresh salad. Every time these are made I am asked for the recipe and it never fails to please.

Serves 6–8 • **Preparation** 10 mins • **Cook** 6–8 hours

2 kg (4 lb 8 oz) pork rib racks
¼ cup light brown sugar
¼ cup tomato sauce (ketchup)
¼ cup vinegar
¼ cup Worcestershire sauce
¼ cup honey
2 tablespoons mustard
½ cup sweet chilli sauce

1. Put the ribs in a slow cooker.
2. Put the remaining ingredients in a jug, season with salt and freshly ground black pepper, and pour the mixture over the ribs to coat them evenly.
3. Cover and cook the ribs for 6–8 hours on LOW.

Kris Cosh

SPICY BRAISED PORK

Big on flavour, the slow-cooked pork just melts in your mouth. I love making it for friends and because it has a bit of wow factor, tastes so good and smells so great, but it's deceptively easy!

Serves 6 • **Preparation** 10 mins • **Cook** 3–6 hours

1.5–2 kg (3 lb 5 oz–4 lb 8 oz) pork strips, rind on, cut into 1 cm (½ inch) pieces
1 teaspoon Chinese five spice
25 g (1 oz) minced fresh ginger
10 garlic cloves, crushed
½ teaspoon ground chilli
¼ cup soy sauce
¼ cup oyster sauce
½ cup light brown sugar
2 tablespoons cornflour (cornstarch)
Rice, Asian greens and fresh chilli, to serve

1. Combine all the ingredients (except the cornflour, rice, Asian greens and fresh chilli) and put in a slow cooker. Add 750 ml (26 fl oz/3 cups) water and stir to combine.

2. Cover and cook on HIGH for 3–4 hours or LOW for 6 hours, until the pork is tender and the skin is gelatinous.

3. Transfer the pork to a plate. Keep the heat at, or increase the heat to, HIGH with the lid off the slow cooker until the liquid is bubbling and is reduced by half.

4. Mix the cornflour with some of the liquid and stir into the sauce until it thickens.

5. Serve the pork and sauce on rice with steamed Asian greens and sprinkled with sliced fresh red chillies.

Vicki Rossiter

SLOW-COOKER PORK WITH PEAR, APPLE & CIDER SAUCE

Created for a large family dinner, I wanted a yummy meal that could be eaten and enjoyed by all of us, even those watching their weight, and this was a hit. This meal is great for a social dinner as the cook serves up a delicious meal and still has time to enjoy the company.

Serves 6 • **Preparation** 20 mins • **Cook** 10–12 hours

1 tablespoon vegetable oil
2 onions, cut into quarters
1 skinless pork butt or 1.2 kg (2 lb 12 oz) round shoulder cut
500 g (1 lb 2 oz) new potatoes, cut in half
250 ml (9 fl oz/1 cup) apple cider vinegar
½ cup apple sauce
4 carrots, cut in half lengthways
2 pears, cut into quarters and cored
Sautéed cabbage, to serve

1. Heat the oil in a frying pan over medium heat and sweat the onions. Transfer the onions to a slow cooker.

2. Put the pork in the same frying pan, increase the heat to medium–high and brown on all sides. Transfer to the slow cooker and put on top of the onions.

3. Put the potatoes around the pork in the slow cooker.

4. Mix together the cider vinegar and apple sauce in a bowl and pour over the pork. Cook on HIGH for 4 hours.

5. Put the carrots and pears on top of the pork, cover and cook on LOW for 6–8 hours.

6. Transfer the pork, potatoes and carrots to a baking tray. Blend the sauce with a stick blender, transfer to a medium saucepan over medium–high heat and allow to reduce and thicken.

7. Serve the meat and vegetables with the sauce and sautéed cabbage.

Justine Kamprad

DIJON PORK LOIN CUTLETS

A very simple dish that doesn't require hours of slow cooking, this is still sweet, moist and tender. The meat falls away from the bone and can be served with salads, vegetables, rice or couscous.

Serves 4 • **Preparation** 10 mins • **Cook** 4½ hours

4 pork loin cutlets
1 red onion, sliced
4 tablespoons dijon mustard
2 tablespoons light brown sugar
¼ cup chopped flat-leaf (Italian) parsley leaves
Rice or couscous and salad or steamed vegetables, to serve

1. Put the pork cutlets in a slow cooker. Arrange the onion slices on top.

2. Put the mustard, sugar and parsley in a small bowl and mix to combine. Spoon the mixture generously over the pork cutlets, reserving a small amount for basting.

3. Cover and cook for 2 hours on HIGH.

4. Baste with the cooking liquid and the extra basting mixture if needed. Reduce the temperature to LOW and cook for 2½ hours.

5. Serve with rice or couscous and salad or steamed vegetables.

Will Ford

SCRUMPTIOUS PORK CHOPS WITH YOU-BEAUT CRACKLE

I checked out the pork chop recipes in my slow-cooker recipes file, and thought I'd throw something together with the ingredients I had on hand. Wow! I'm going to keep this one for sure. It got a big thumbs-up from the hubby and I even had enough to make up an extra meal for my elderly father.

Serves 4 • Preparation 5–10 mins • Cook 6 hours

1 onion, cut into quarters
6 pork loin chops, rinds removed and reserved for crackle
½ cup tomato sauce (ketchup)
½ cup barbecue sauce
40 g (1½ oz) salt-reduced French onion soup mix, dry
1 cup light brown sugar
Oil and salt, for crackle
Roast vegetables, steamed broccoli and cauliflower, to serve

1. Spread the onion over the base of a slow cooker. Put the pork chops on top of the onion.

2. Combine the tomato sauce, barbecue sauce and soup mix in a bowl and spoon it over the chops. Toss the chops gently to coat them in the sauce mixture. Sprinkle the brown sugar over the chops.

3. Cover and cook on HIGH for 4 hours.

4. Stir the chops, reduce the temperature to LOW and cook for 2 hours.

5. In the last 30 minutes of cooking, turn a conventional oven to the highest temperature setting.

6. Prepare the pork rinds by soaking them in boiling hot water, to remove any excess oil and maximise the crackle texture. Dry the rinds off with paper towel.

7. Line a baking tray with baking paper. Put the rinds on the tray, drizzle with oil and sprinkle with salt. Cook the rinds in the hot oven for 10–15 minutes, watching closely that they don't burn. Alternatively, you could grill the rinds if you prefer.

8. Serve with roast vegetables and steamed broccoli and cauliflower.

Sandra Schaefer

MEDITERRANEAN MEDLEY WITH PENNE PASTA

This recipe was developed by me for one of the most ambitious, wonderful and amazing women I knew. It was an experience that I will always remember fondly.

Serves 6–8 • Preparation 20 mins • Cook 3 hours 40 mins

1 tablespoon olive oil
2 chorizo sausages, halved lengthways and thinly sliced
200 g (7 oz) rindless middle bacon, diced
1 large red onion, diced
2–3 garlic cloves, crushed
750 ml (26 fl oz/3 cups) tomato pasta sauce (passata)
½ eggplant (aubergine), cut into small cubes
½ cup marinated button mushrooms
250 g (9 oz) cherry tomatoes
400 g (14 oz) penne pasta
1 large green capsicum (pepper), thinly sliced
2 handfuls baby spinach leaves
50 g (1¾ oz) parmesan cheese, shaved, to garnish

1. Heat the olive oil in a large frying pan over medium–high heat. Add the chorizo, bacon, onion and garlic and cook for 3 minutes. Transfer to a slow cooker, spreading the mixture over the base.

2. Add the passata, eggplant, mushrooms and tomatoes to the slow cooker. Mix through the chorizo mixture. Cook for 3 hours on LOW.

3. Bring a large saucepan of salted water to the boil. Add the pasta and cook for just 10 minutes. Drain the pasta and transfer to the slow cooker, stirring through gently so as not to break the tomatoes. Replace the lid and cook for 30 minutes.

4. When 10 minutes away from serving, add the capsicum and spinach to the slow cooker.

5. Serve the pasta in bowls, topped with shaved parmesan.

Kris Cosh

TRUDY'S STICKY CHRISTMAS HAM

I love a sticky Christmas ham. I came up with this recipe because I wanted something sweet and full of flavour but easy to prepare in the Christmas rush. So I looked at what I had left in my cupboard …

Makes 1 ham • **Preparation** 10 mins • **Cook** 5 hours

500 ml (17 fl oz/2 cups) pineapple juice
2 cups light brown sugar
4 teaspoons balsamic vinegar
5 teaspoons dijon mustard
2 teaspoons apple sauce
4 teaspoons honey
1 large ham, leg in or boneless
1 tablespoon cornflour (cornstarch)

1. Put the pineapple juice in a slow cooker.

2. Put the sugar, balsamic vinegar, mustard, apple sauce and honey in a medium bowl and mix to a paste.

3. Spread the sugar paste over the ham. Put it in the slow cooker, cover and cook on low for 5 hours (or less, if required, as it is already cooked), basting every hour or so.

4. Strain any cooking liquid into a small saucepan. Add a little of the liquid to the cornflour in a small bowl and mix to a paste. Add to the saucepan and stir to thicken the sauce. Drizzle the sauce over the ham before serving.

Trudy Lowndes

◗━ GLAZED SLOW-COOKED HAM ━◗

If you can fit your Christmas ham into your slow cooker, then you can glaze it there too. Just keep basting it frequently during cooking for maximum flavour.

Makes 1 ham • **Preparation** 10 mins • **Cook** 5 hours

1 whole or half leg of ham
½ cup maple syrup
½ cup light brown sugar
125 ml (4 fl oz/½ cup) apple juice
2 tablespoons dijon mustard, plus extra to serve
1 tablespoon wholegrain mustard
Whole cloves, to stud the ham

1. Put the ham in a slow cooker. If using a leg ham, prepare it by removing the skin, leaving the fat layer on. Lightly score the top of the ham to form a cross-hatch pattern. (You can use other cuts of ham that don't have a fat layer – just score the surface to allow the flavours to seep in during cooking.)

2. Put a small saucepan over medium heat. Add the maple syrup, sugar, apple juice and mustards and whisk to combine. Stir continuously until sugar has dissolved, and set aside.

3. Stud the ham with cloves, one in each diamond if you like, for presentation purposes.

4. Liberally brush the ham with the glaze and cook on LOW for 5 hours (it's really only heating the ham and infusing the flavours, so this time can be adjusted if need be).

5. Continue to brush with glaze throughout the cooking process – every 30 minutes if possible – for maximum flavour. Remove the cloves before carving, if desired, and serve with extra mustard.

Paulene Christie

KANGAROO SPAGHETTI 'BOLOGNESE'

As a mother always looking for healthier options, I started using kangaroo mince for making spaghetti sauce. Even the fussiest eaters will eat this. This dish is richer than beef but has no fat or oil so it's a much healthier option. I grew up eating kangaroo as we knew the health benefits.

Serves 4–6 • **Preparation** 10 mins • **Cook** 8 hours

1 kg (2 lb 4 oz) kangaroo mince
1 large onion, diced
1 small red capsicum (pepper), diced
1 small orange capsicum (pepper), diced
2 tablespoons minced garlic
2 tablespoons dried mixed herbs
700 g (1 lb 9 oz) pasta sauce with oregano
2 teaspoons Worcestershire sauce
2 teaspoons sugar
2 teaspoons salt
Grated parmesan cheese, to serve
Pasta of choice, to serve

1. Put all the ingredients except the parmesan cheese and pasta in a slow cooker. Cover and cook on HIGH for 1 hour.

2. Stir the sauce vigorously to break up the mince. Turn to the temperature setting to LOW and cook for 7 hours.

3. Top with good-quality parmesan cheese and serve with pasta.

Michelle Quinn

■— VENISON STEW —●

I was brought up eating venison and game meats since I was a young girl so I
made up this slow-cooker recipe to be used as a stew or pie filling and even as
a base for a shepherd's pie. It is a very simple recipe that brings so much flavour
to your plate.

Serves 4 • Preparation 15 mins • Cook 8 hours

1 teaspoon olive oil
1 brown onion, finely chopped
½ teaspoon crushed garlic
500 g (1 lb 2 oz) venison steak, cut into 1 cm (½ inch) strips
1 beef stock cube, crushed
1 litre (35 fl oz/4 cups) boiling water
½ teaspoon salt
½ teaspoon freshly ground black pepper
2 potatoes, peeled and cubed
2 carrots, thickly sliced
1 cup peas
Mashed potato, to serve

1. Heat the olive oil in a large frying pan over medium–high heat. Add the onion and
   garlic and cook for 2–3 minutes, until the onion is translucent. Add the steak and
   cook for 2–3 minutes.

2. Combine the stock cube with the boiling water, and add the salt and pepper.
   Pour the stock mixture into the frying pan and stir well to combine. Transfer the
   meat and the stock mixture to a slow cooker.

3. Put the potato, carrot and peas in the slow cooker and stir to combine.

4. Cover and cook on LOW for 8 hours, stirring the stew once or twice.

5. Serve as a stew on mashed potato, make into a shepherd's pie or even a venison
   puff pastry pie if you thicken the gravy with a little cornflour once cooked.

Erica Simpson

VENISON CASSEROLE

My partner and our boys love to hunt so venison is a part of our regular diet and I'm always looking for new ways to cook it. This was originally a beef recipe that used a packet mix as a base but I tweaked it until I was happy with the taste of the ingredients made from scratch. It's a firm favourite in our household now and great for winter days. Serve with mash and veg or warm crusty bread.

Serves 4 • **Preparation** 10 mins • **Cook** 4 hours

½ cup plain (all-purpose) flour
1 teaspoon salt
½ teaspoon pepper
1 teaspoon paprika
1 teaspoon dried mixed herbs
500 g (1 lb 2 oz) casserole venison, cut into chunks
Vegetable oil, for frying
1 large potato, cut into cubes
1 large sweet potato, cut into cubes
1 large carrot, cut into cubes
2 tablespoons tomato paste (concentrated purée)
250 ml (9 fl oz/1 cup) water, red wine or beef stock
1 cup frozen peas, and/or sliced mushroom, onion, beetroot (beet), corn, celery, broccoli, cauliflower
1 tablespoon cornflour (cornstarch), for thickening (optional)

1. Combine the flour, salt, pepper, paprika and dried herbs in a bowl. Add the venison and toss to coat well.

2. Heat the oil in a large frying pan over medium–high heat. Cook the venison quickly in batches until all browned. Transfer to a slow cooker.

3. Add the potato, sweet potato and carrot and stir to combine. Add the leftover seasoning mixture, tomato paste, water (or wine or stock, if using) and any of the vegetables of choice that aren't frozen.

4. Cover and cook on HIGH for 1 hour.

5. Reduce temperature to LOW and cook for 3 hours.

6. Add the peas and any frozen vegetables approximately 20 minutes before the end of cooking.

7. If the sauce is not thick enough, stir in the cornflour mixed in a little water.

Nikki Willis

SLOW-COOKED GOAT SHANKS

My husband and I have been on a low-fat diet and heard that goat shanks had less fat than the same cut of lamb, so I decided to have a go at my own recipe. The product turned out tasting sweet and falling off the bone, with a lot less fat. Delicious!

Serves 4 • **Preparation** 10–15 mins • **Cook** 7 hours

400 g (14 oz) tinned diced tomatoes
1 teaspoon minced garlic
Good splash of Worcestershire sauce
½ teaspoon dried basil
1 chicken stock cube
200 ml (7 fl oz) hot water
4 goat shanks
2 tablespoons cornflour (cornstarch)
Mashed sweet potato and steamed vegetables, to serve

1. Combine the diced tomatoes, minced garlic, Worcestershire sauce, dried basil and salt and freshly ground black pepper to taste in a slow cooker.

2. Dissolve the chicken stock cube in the hot water and pour into the slow cooker.

3. Put the goat shanks in the slow cooker and spoon over some of the mixture.

4. Cover and cook for 7 hours.

5. Remove the shanks from the slow cooker and set aside on a plate.

6. Combine the cornflour with enough water to make a thin paste and stir into the sauce mixture.

7. Serve the goat shanks with mashed sweet potato and your favourite steamed vegetables, topped with the sauce.

Colleen Doughty

CHICKEN

CHICKEN STOCK

A very simple recipe, and so much better than using a stock cube.

Makes approx 1 litre • **Preparation** 10 mins • **Cook** 8 hours

Roasted free-range chook carcass (and any other parts that haven't been
  nibbled on)
1 large carrot, scrubbed and cut into 4–6 pieces
1 stalk celery (including leaves), washed then cut into 4 pieces
1 brown onion (including papery outer skin, for colour),
  washed then cut into 4 pieces
1 bay leaf
6 peppercorns
1 sprig parsley (optional)
1 stalk thyme (optional)

1. Put all the ingredients in a slow cooker and cover with water. Cook on LOW for
   8 hours.

2. Strain the contents of the slow cooker through a sieve into a large heatproof bowl
   and discard the solids. Cover and refrigerate. If you're not planning to use the
   stock within the next 2 days, pour it into cup-size lidded containers and freeze.

Daisy Yu

SLOW-COOKED HOMEMADE CHICKEN STOCK

I had never made my own stock before, but I will now never buy ready made again. The flavours were so much richer and the smells through the house all day while it was cooking were lovely. And the process couldn't be easier – put all in and away it goes!

Makes 1.9 litres (66½ fl oz) • **Preparation** 5 mins • **Cook** 20 hours

1.5 kg (3 lb 5 oz) whole organic chicken
2 onions, cut in half
2 carrots, coarsely chopped
2 stalks celery, coarsely chopped
1 teaspoon whole black peppercorns
½ bulb garlic, peeled
1 leek, coarsely chopped
3 sprigs thyme
3 sprigs rosemary
4 fresh or dried bay leaves

1. Place all the ingredients in a 6 litre (210 fl oz) slow cooker. Fill with about 3 litres (105 fl oz) water, until the water level is about 2.5 cm (1 inch) from the top of the slow cooker bowl. Cook on LOW for up to 20 hours to develop the full depth of flavour.

2. Use a slotted spoon to remove and discard all the solid pieces from the slow cooker. Pour the liquid contents through a fine sieve to remove any remaining solid pieces of vegetable or herbs. You could also use a leg cut from a new, clean pair of pantyhose – secure the toe end with a knot and stretch it over a bowl to form a fine sieve.

3. Pour the sieved stock into a large bowl. Refrigerate overnight or long enough for any fat in the dish to solidify on top of the stock.

4. Use a slotted spoon again to carefully remove and discard the solidified fat layer from the dish.

5. Refrigerate and use within 3–4 days or freeze and use within 3 months.

Paulene Christie

CHICKEN & ASPARAGUS CARBONARA

This versatile dish is my version of a carbonara due to having no eggs one day. It's also great for those allergic to eggs. Serve in summer with a fresh green salad or turn it into a winter warmer served with garlic bread. It's a handy go-to meal with easy ingredients and low-fuss preparation. Hope you enjoy it as much as I do.

Serves 6–8 • Preparation 15 mins • Cook 4–6 hours

1 kg (2 lb 4 oz) skinless chicken thigh fillets, cut into 2 cm (¾ inch) pieces
200 g (7 oz) ham, shredded
300 g (10½ oz) mushrooms, thinly sliced
1 leek, finely chopped
2 garlic cloves, crushed
250 ml (9 fl oz/1 cup) chicken stock
250 ml (9 fl oz/1 cup) thin (pouring) cream, or cooking cream
½ cup grated parmesan cheese, plus extra, to serve
500 g (1 lb 2 oz) penne pasta
2 bunches asparagus, trimmed and cut into 4 cm (1½ inch) lengths
Garlic bread, to serve

1. Put the chicken, ham, mushroom, leek, garlic, stock, cream and parmesan cheese in a slow cooker. Combine gently and cook on LOW for 4–6 hours.

2. When the chicken is cooked – check it is not still pink inside – cook the pasta in a large saucepan of boiling salted water until al dente. Add the asparagus to the water with the pasta in the last minute of cooking. Drain the pasta and asparagus and add to the slow cooker. Stir gently to combine and serve with garlic bread and extra parmesan cheese to sprinkle.

Melodie Tapp

⚏ CHICKEN SCRACCIATORE ➔

'Cacciatore from scratch' is my version of the classic – which I love – but adapted to my family's taste. I think it's superb. You could add olives and mushrooms if you like. I serve it either with mashed potato and steamed greens, or basmati rice.

Serves 4 • Preparation 15 mins • Cook 4–8 hours

2 skinless chicken breast fillets, cubed
2 garlic cloves, crushed
420 g (15 oz) tinned condensed tomato soup
400 g (14 oz) tinned diced tomatoes with basil and oregano
1 carrot, diced
1 red capsicum (pepper), diced
½ onion, diced
125 ml (4 fl oz/½ cup) dry white wine
1 tablespoon Worcestershire sauce
1 teaspoon dried Italian mixed herbs

1. Put all the ingredients in a slow cooker and stir. Cook on HIGH for 4 hours or LOW for 8 hours.

Krystal Mann

PESTO-STUFFED CHICKEN BREAST

We love our chicken and there are so many things you can do with it. This is one dish I like to cook in the slow cooker. It is something you can make when having guests over but not have to be cooking all day. Very easy but tasty.

Serves 4 • **Preparation** 10 mins • **Cook** 4–5 hours

4 skinless chicken breast fillets
4 tablespoons basil pesto
125 g (4½ oz) camembert cheese, cut into 4 pieces
Garden salad or steamed vegetables, to serve

1. Slice halfway through the chicken to make a pocket. Stuff each breast fillet with a quarter of the pesto and camembert cheese.

2. Place each breast fillet on a large piece of foil and wrap tightly. Put the parcels in a slow cooker and cook on LOW for 4–5 hours.

3. When cooked, unwrap the parcels and serve the chicken with a garden salad or steamed vegetables.

sherrie sutcliffe

CHICKEN PROVENÇALE

Experimenting with a recipe I used to cook in my oven led to this one I now make using the slow cooker. It adapted well and is a lovely winter recipe.

Serves 6 • **Preparation** 20 mins • **Cook** 4–6 hours

1 red capsicum (pepper), quartered and deseeded
1 yellow capsicum (pepper), quartered and deseeded
1 tablespoon olive oil
1.5 kg (3 lb 5 oz) skinless chicken thigh pieces or fillets
2 brown onions, halved and cut into wedges
2 garlic cloves, thinly sliced
125 ml (4 fl oz/½ cup) white wine
600 ml (20 fl oz) tomato pasta sauce
1 teaspoon chicken stock powder
8 sprigs thyme
½ cup pitted black olives
Baby potatoes and green beans, to serve

1. Preheat the grill (broiler) on high and grill the capsicum, skin side up, for 8–10 minutes or until charred and blistered. Transfer to a plastic bag, seal and set aside for 10 minutes.

2. Meanwhile, heat the oil in large frying pan over medium heat. Brown the chicken in two batches for 5 minutes, or until brown. Transfer the chicken to a slow cooker.

3. Remove the skin from the capsicum and cut the flesh into thick strips. Put in the slow cooker with the onion, garlic, wine, pasta sauce, stock powder and thyme. Cook for 4 hours on HIGH or 6 hours on LOW.

4. When 30 minutes from being cooked, add the olives.

5. Serve the chicken and cooking juices with steamed baby potatoes and green beans.

Chris McInnes

CHICKEN LASAGNE CAKE

There was a picture of something similar on the internet so I thought I would try to create a version that suited my taste and could be made in a slow cooker. You can use whatever ingredients your family likes and although the concept is quite simple the results are awesome. And it's a real conversation piece.

Serves 6 • **Preparation** 20 mins • **Cook** 4 hours

Olive oil spray
16 soft pasta sheets or pre-cooked hard pasta sheets
500 g (1 lb 2 oz) minced (ground) chicken
250 g (9 oz) tomato pasta sauce
250 g (9 oz) bottled creamy cheese sauce
12 slices salami
1 large handful baby spinach leaves
3 tablespoons ricotta cheese
½ cup sliced mushrooms
3 tablespoons sliced olives
2 slices ham
3 tablespoons grated cheese of choice
3 tablespoons basil leaves
2 garlic cloves, crushed
Green salad and garlic bread, to serve

1. You will need a 3 litre (105 fl oz/12 cups) bowl or one that fits in your slow cooker. Spray the bowl with oil and line with the pasta sheets, overlapping so the entire bowl is covered.

2. Combine the chicken mince and tomato pasta sauce in a medium bowl.

3. Start layering the ingredients in the pasta-lined bowl, beginning with 1 tablespoon of the cheese sauce and 4 pieces of salami. Top with pasta sheets and repeat three times.

4. Add the spinach and ricotta, then pasta sheets.

5. Add the mushroom and olives, then pasta sheets.

6. Add the ham, grated cheese, basil and garlic, then pasta sheets.

7. Spoon in the chicken mince and pasta sauce mixture. Top with pasta sheets and fold all the sheets down and stick together with cheese sauce, reserving a little to finish.

8. Pressed down on the layers gently but firmly. Prick a small hole in the top of the pasta layer.

9. Place the bowl in the slow cooker and add 5 cm (2 inches) water to the base of the slow cooker. Cook for 4 hours on HIGH.

10. When cooked, take out the bowl and let stand for 15 minutes. Flip onto a plate, pour some of the leftover cheese sauce on top. Serve with salad and garlic bread.

Samantha Steele

BACON LATTICE CHICKEN & PINE NUT MEATLOAF

This chicken and pine nut meatloaf wrapped in crispy bacon is a combination of my two favourite dishes, which are roast chicken and meatloaf. It is a hearty versatile meal that looks fancy and restaurant quality but all kids love to eat it. I would serve it with steamed or roasted vegetables or my favourite wasabi mashed potato in winter or a garden salad in summer.

Serves 4–6 • **Preparation** 30–40 mins • **Cook** 4 hours

1 tablespoon olive oil
1 brown onion, finely chopped
2 garlic cloves, crushed
⅓ cup pine nuts
750 g (1 lb 10 oz) minced (ground) chicken
1½ cups fresh breadcrumbs
¾ cup finely shredded basil leaves
¼ cup finely chopped flat-leaf (Italian) parsley
1 egg, lightly beaten
800 g (1 lb 12 oz) bacon rashers
Mashed potato and steamed green beans, to serve

1. Heat the oil in a large frying pan over medium–high heat. Add the onion, garlic and pine nuts and cook, stirring, for 8 minutes, or until softened. Transfer the mixture to a large bowl and allow to cool.

2. Add the chicken mince, breadcrumbs, basil, parsley and egg to the bowl with the onion mixture and mix well.

3. Transfer the mixture to a 20 x 10 x 7 cm (8 x 4 x 2½ inch) baking dish and press down. Place the bacon rashers over the top to form a lattice.

4. Put a rack or a layer of scrunched-up foil balls in the base of a slow cooker so the meatloaf is above the juice that will be created during cooking. Put the baking dish on top and cook on LOW for 4 hours.

5. Serve with mashed potato and green beans.

Wayne Gatt

PARMIGIANA MEATBALLS

After buying chicken mince and having no idea what to do with it I came up with this recipe to keep a fussy 8-year-old happy. She likes spaghetti and meatballs and chicken parmigiana, so I decided to combine both dishes and it was a huge hit with the whole family. I wasn't sure how the cheese would go, but it browned perfectly. This dish is now a regular meal at our house.

Serves 6 • Preparation 15–20 mins • Cook 5 hours

1 kg (2 lb 4 oz) minced (ground) chicken
1 cup breadcrumbs
1 teaspoon crushed garlic
2 eggs
1 onion, chopped
2 teaspoons dried mixed herbs
400 g (14 oz) tinned diced tomatoes
250 ml (9 fl oz/1 cup) red wine
2 tablespoons tomato paste (concentrated purée)
2 handfuls grated cheddar cheese
Mashed potato, to serve
Mixed salad, to serve

1. Combine the chicken mince, breadcrumbs, garlic and eggs in a bowl. Make meatballs with tablespoonfuls of the mixture and put in the base of a slow cooker.

2. Put the onion, herbs, diced tomato, red wine and tomato paste in a jug and whisk to combine. Pour over the meatballs.

3. Sprinkle the cheese over the chicken meatballs and cook on LOW for 5 hours.

4. Serve the chicken meatballs on top of mashed potato with a mixed salad on the side.

Stacey Goodall

CREAMY CHICKEN & CHORIZO

I adapted the recipe of a fellow slow-cooker fan to include chorizo and capsicum and came up with this! You can also add whatever vegetables you like.

Serves 6 • **Preparation** 15 mins • **Cook** 2 hours

Vegetable oil, for browning
4 skinless chicken thigh fillets, chopped
4 rashers bacon, diced
4 chorizo, sliced
1 onion, diced
1 capsicum (pepper), diced
8 button mushrooms, quartered
2 teaspoons crushed garlic
50 g (1¾ oz/½ cup) finely grated parmesan cheese
250 g (9 oz) cream cheese
Steamed vegetables, to serve

1. Heat the oil in a medium frying pan over medium heat. Add the chicken, cook until browned and transfer to a slow cooker.

2. Add remaining ingredients to the slow cooker. Cook on HIGH for 1½ hours, stir, and cook for a further 30 minutes.

3. Serve with steamed vegetables.

Melissa Negus

CELESTIAL CHICKEN

This is a recipe my mother made up many years ago and has cooked for me on many occasions, so when I eat it I always think of her. It is healthy, delicious and very filling.

Serves 4–6 • Preparation 15 mins • Cook 3 hours 10 mins

Plain (all-purpose) flour, for coating
1½ teaspoons salt
½ teaspoon black pepper
1 teaspoon paprika
700 g (1 lb 7 oz) skinless chicken thigh fillets (or use breast or tenderloins if you prefer), trimmed and diced
Vegetable oil, for shallow frying
450 g (1 lb) tinned pineapple pieces in syrup (or in natural juice if you want it less sweet)
2 x 50 g packets salt-reduced chicken noodle soup mix
6 carrots, thickly sliced
1 big handful cut frozen beans
Mashed potato, to serve

1. Combine the flour, salt, pepper and paprika. Toss through the chicken to coat.

2. Heat the oil in a medium frying pan over medium–high heat. Add the chicken and cook quickly just until browned.

3. Throw the chicken, pineapple, soup mix, carrot and beans into a slow cooker. Mix and cook on HIGH for 3 hours.

4. Serve with mashed potato.

Zara Charles

━● CHICKEN GUMBO ●━

I originally made chicken gumbo purely because I liked the name, but then
I adapted a couple of recipes to come up with the easiest, family-friendliest,
slow-cooker version I could. Since then it has become a family favourite
because it's healthy, colourful and very tasty. It's also easy to adapt by throwing
in whatever vegetables you have on hand. The flavour comes from the chorizo,
the chicken just falls apart, the sauce soaks beautifully into rice, and the kids
are getting some vegetables – plus it's something really different!

Serves 8–10 • Preparation 15 mins • Cook 6–8 hours

2 tablespoons olive oil
1 kg (2 lb 4 oz) skinless chicken thigh fillets (or cut of your choice)
1 tablespoon plain (all-purpose) flour
500 ml (17 fl oz/2 cups) chicken stock
400 g (14 oz) tinned chopped tomatoes
400 g (14 oz) chorizo, diced
1 large red or green capsicum (pepper), diced
3 stalks celery, chopped
1 onion, diced
200–250 g (7–9 oz) okra, sliced diagonally
½ teaspoon cayenne pepper, or to taste
Rice or crusty bread, to serve

1. Heat half the oil in a medium saucepan over medium heat. Brown the chicken
   and transfer to a slow cooker.

2. Put the remaining oil in the saucepan and add the flour. Cook for 1–2 minutes,
   stirring with a wooden spoon. Add the stock and tomato, and bring to boil.
   Transfer to the slow cooker.

3. Add remaining ingredients and cook on LOW for 6–8 hours.

4. Serve with rice or crusty bread.

Alison Tregeagle

SHREDDED CHICKEN ENCHILADAS

My fiancé was always asking me to make chicken tacos but I wasn't a fan of the ones in a hard shell. Then I remembered eating Mexican beef wraps and I thought I would combine both ideas, and use the slow cooker to make the filling. And I'm so glad I did. This is unbelievably delicious – I've really outdone myself! You can add chilli powder or other spices if you like extra heat.

Makes 12 • **Preparation** 5 mins • **Cook** 4–5 hours

6 skinless chicken thigh fillets
1–2 packets taco seasoning (1 for a mild filling, 2 for spicier)
800 g (28 oz) tinned diced tomatoes
2–3 garlic cloves, crushed
1 teaspoon dried oregano
2 teaspoons dried mixed herbs
12 tortilla wraps
1 cup grated cheddar cheese
Shredded lettuce, to serve
Sour cream, to serve

1. Put the chicken in a slow cooker. Sprinkle over the taco seasoning to cover the chicken. Pour over half of the diced tomato, and scatter over the garlic, oregano and half the mixed herbs. Cook on HIGH for 2 hours.

2. Stir the chicken and continue to cook on HIGH for a further 2 hours, or when the chicken is falling apart. If the sauce is quite runny, put a tea towel under the lid and cook on LOW for 1 hour.

3. Preheat the oven to 180°C (350°F) and spray a baking tray with oil.

4. Shred the chicken with two forks. Spoon a portion of the chicken mixture onto a tortilla wrap and roll it up. Place on the baking tray and continue to make 12 enchiladas. Combine the remaining diced tomato and mixed herbs in a bowl and spoon the mixture over the tortilla wraps. Sprinkle grated cheese over the top. Place in the oven until the enchiladas and sauce are heated through and the cheese is melted. Serve on a bed of lettuce with sour cream on top and enjoy!

Jessica Trew

CREAMY MEXICAN CHICKEN MEATBALLS WITH ROASTED CHERRY TOMATOES

When I was given some beautiful homegrown cherry tomatoes I wanted to make something easy and delicious using ingredients I had on hand. The result? A different take on the traditional meatball recipe with pleasing results and clean plates all round! It's a great midweek meal and has become a family favourite. It's now 'Meatball Tuesday' in our household!

Serves 4 • **Preparation** 20 mins • **Cook** 6 hours

500 g (1 lb 2 oz) cherry tomatoes
Olive oil, to drizzle
500 g (1 lb 2 oz) minced (ground) chicken
1 egg
1 tablespoon chopped coriander (cilantro)
½ cup breadcrumbs
2 packets taco seasoning
500ml (17 fl oz/2 cups) chicken stock
250 g (9 oz) light cream cheese
400 g (14 oz) tinned diced tomatoes
1–2 tablespoons cornflour (cornstarch), for thickening
Curly fettuccine, to serve
Grated parmesan cheese, to serve

1. Preheat the oven to 200°C (400°F). Put the cherry tomatoes on a baking tray lined with non-stick baking paper. Drizzle with olive oil and place in the oven for 20 minutes, turning once or twice.

2. Put the mince, egg, coriander, breadcrumbs and half a packet of the taco seasoning in a bowl. Mix together and form tablespoonfuls of the mixture into balls.

3. Put the remaining taco seasoning, stock, cream cheese and diced tomato in a slow cooker and mix gently. Add the cherry tomatoes and drop in the meatballs. Cook on LOW for 6 hours.

4. Add some cornflour mixed with a little water to the slow cooker in the last 30 minutes to thicken up the sauce, if needed. Serve with curly fettuccine or pasta of your choice and sprinkle with parmesan cheese.

Amanda Kenwright

SOMBRERO CHICKEN

I named this recipe for the Mexican flavours brought to it by the taco seasoning. It's such an easy dish to make with just the three ingredients and so versatile, you can change it in several ways. Serve it with vegetables or a salad. Or shred or pull the chicken and use it in tacos or enchiladas. It's also great shredded for school sandwiches.

Serves 4 • **Preparation** 5 mins • **Cook** 4–6 hours

1 kg (2 lb 4 oz) chicken pieces of your choice (eg. fillets, drumsticks, wings)
500 g (1 lb 2 oz) jar apricot jam
1 packet taco seasoning

1. Put the chicken in a slow cooker.
2. Combine the jam and taco seasoning and spoon over the chicken. Cover and cook on LOW for 4–6 hours.

Paulene Christie

HOMESTYLE CHICKEN & VEGIE CASSEROLE

Easily adaptable to whatever vegetables you have on hand, and the addition of grated raw potato towards the end is a great method to thicken up your slow-cooker dish if the dish lends itself to having potato in it. By serving time it's all cooked down and you end up with a lovely thick consistency.

Serves 4–6 • **Preparation** 5 mins • **Cook** 6 hours

0.5–1 kg (1 lb 2 oz–2 lb 4 oz) skinless chicken thigh fillets, cut into chunks
420 g (15 oz) tinned condensed cream of chicken soup
500 g (1 lb 2 oz) frozen diced vegetables or 2–3 cups diced fresh vegetables of your choice
⅓ cup dried peas
1–2 garlic cloves, minced
1 onion, diced
250 ml (9 fl oz/1 cup) chicken stock or broth
1–2 potatoes, grated
Garlic bread or crusty bread rolls, to serve

1. Combine all ingredients except the potato in a slow cooker. Cook on LOW for 6 hours.
2. When 2 hours from being cooked, add the grated potato to the slow cooker.
3. Serve with garlic bread or crusty bread rolls.

Paulene Christie

TOMATOEY CHICKEN

I love this recipe as it is so easy and affordable – I am on a budget so I have converted some of my favourites like this one to help make cooking affordable for us all!

Serves 4 • **Preparation** 5 mins • **Cook** 4–5 hours

1 kg (2 lb 4 oz) chicken pieces
420 g (15 oz) tinned condensed tomato soup
40 g (1½ oz) French onion soup mix, dry
Cream, to serve (optional)

1. Put chicken, tomato soup and French onion soup in a slow cooker and cook on LOW for 4–5 hours.

2. Add a spoonful of cream to each bowl to serve, if you like.

sherrie sutcliffe

CLACKER CHICKEN

Australians often refer to the 'clacker' of the chicken (aka 'the parson's nose', 'the last part over the fence') and that's how this dish got its name. Beautiful flavours infused throughout the chicken make for a tasty meal.

Serves 4–6 • **Preparation** 5 mins • **Cook** 6 hours

1 lemon, plus juice of 1 lemon extra
2 garlic cloves, peeled
1 whole chicken
¼ cup honey
¼ cup soy sauce
1 tablespoon cornflour (cornstarch)

1. Make a cut in the whole lemon and stuff it with the garlic. Push this lemon into the cavity of the chicken via its clacker *wink*. Put the chicken in a slow cooker.

2. Combine the juice of the extra lemon with the honey and soy sauce. Pour this over the chicken. Cook on LOW for 6 hours or until the chicken is cooked through, basting the chicken with the liquid at intervals.

3. When cooked, combine the cornflour with a little water to make a paste and stir through the cooking liquid to thicken it and make an amazing sauce.

Paulene Christie

MANGO CHICKEN

I love chicken and I love mango, so this dish is a sure winner for me. You can choose to add the mango pieces or just nectar, if you prefer. It's lovely served with rice or mashed potato and vegetables.

Serves 4 • **Preparation** 5 mins • **Cook** 4–6 hours

6 chicken thigh cutlets on the bone, or cut of your choice
1 onion, diced
425 g (15 oz) tinned mango pieces in nectar
40 g (1½ oz) French onion soup mix, dry
Rice or mashed potato and steamed vegetables, to serve

1. Put the chicken and onion in a slow cooker.

2. Drain the nectar from the mango. Combine the soup mix with the nectar and pour over the chicken. Scatter the mango pieces over the top.

3. Cover and cook on LOW for 4–6 hours.

4. If using chicken on the bone, when 15 minutes from cooked you can remove the chicken pieces, pull the meat from the bone and return the meat to the slow cooker.

5. Serve the chicken in its sauce with rice or mashed potato and steamed vegetables.

Paulene Christie

CHICKEN & MIXED VEGIES

How did I come up with this recipe? I'd tried a million recipes from websites and cookbooks and got inspired to try different things on my own, so I simply mixed a bunch of stuff together.

Serves 5 • Preparation 15 mins • Cook 7 hours 10 mins

Vegetable oil, for browning
10 chicken drumsticks
2 onions, coarsely chopped
6 potatoes, cut into large chunks
2 carrots, cut into 2.5 cm (1 inch) pieces
800 g (28 oz) tinned diced tomatoes
625 ml (21½ fl oz/2½ cups) chicken stock
2 tablespoons Worcestershire sauce
2 tablespoons cornflour (cornstarch)
4 tablespoons water
2 cups corn kernels
2 cups peas

1. Heat oil in a medium frying pan over medium heat. Brown the drumsticks quickly and transfer to a slow cooker.

2. Add the onion to the frying pan and cook, stirring, until browned. Transfer to the slow cooker.

3. Add the potato, carrot and tomato to the slow cooker. Season with salt and freshly ground black pepper.

4. Heat the stock in a saucepan on the stove or in a microwave until hot. Stir in the Worcestershire sauce and pour into the slow cooker. Cook on LOW for 6½ hours.

5. Combine the cornflour and water in a small bowl. Add to the slow cooker and stir through. Add the corn and peas and stir through. Cook on HIGH for 40 minutes.

Amanda Undy

ORANGE CHICKEN

A great zesty orange dish using ingredients many people have on hand in their pantry. Serve with mashed potato or steamed rice and vegetables, or with fried rice.

Serves 4 • Preparation 5 mins • Cook 6 hours

8 chicken thigh cutlets
Plain (all-purpose) flour, to coat
½ cup orange marmalade
½ cup orange juice
2 tablespoons tomato sauce (ketchup)
¼ cup soy sauce
1 garlic clove, crushed
Mashed potato or rice and steamed vegetables, to serve

1. Coat the chicken in flour, shaking off any excess, and put in a slow cooker.

2. Combine the remaining ingredients in a small bowl and pour over the chicken. Cover and cook on LOW for 6 hours.

3. Serve in bowls with mashed potato or rice and steamed vegetables.

Paulene Christie

BACON-WRAPPED CHICKEN THIGHS

I make them at Christmas but these are great any time of year. They can look quite fancy so they are good for any occasion. Serve with steamed potatoes and garden salad.

Serves 4 • **Preparation** 15 mins • **Cook** 4–5 hours

4 skinless chicken thigh fillets
8 tablespoons (100 g/3½ oz) cream cheese
1 handful dried apricots
1 handful cherries, pitted
4 rashers bacon

1. Flatten out chicken thighs with a mallet. Spread with cream cheese and evenly scatter over apricots and cherries. Roll up the chicken and wrap a rasher of bacon around each roll.

2. Put in a slow cooker and cook on HIGH for 4–5 hours.

Sherrie Sutcliffe

MUSHROOM & BACON CHICKEN

I always use skinless chicken thigh fillets for slow cooking, but if you are using breast meat in this recipe you could add an extra tin of soup to add moisture. You also need to adapt the cooking time depending on the type and size of your slow cooker. I cook this recipe for 8 hours on LOW in my medium slow cooker but for 4 hours in my large one, which cooks much faster.

Serves 4–6 • **Preparation** 5 mins • **Cook** 4–8 hours

1 kg (2 lb 4 oz) skinless chicken fillets of choice
1 onion, diced
6–8 mushrooms, coarsely chopped
1–2 tins (420–840 g/15–30 oz) condensed cream of mushroom soup
3 garlic cloves, minced
40 g (1½ oz) French onion soup mix, dry
200 g (7 oz) bacon, diced
3 tablespoons tomato sauce (ketchup)
Pasta, rice or mashed potato and steamed vegetables, to serve

1. Put the chicken, onion and mushroom in a slow cooker.
2. Combine the remaining ingredients and pour over the chicken.
3. Cover and cook on LOW for 4–8 hours (depending on slow cooker size).
4. Serve the chicken in its sauce with pasta, rice or mashed potato and steamed vegetables.

Paulene Christie

LEMON CHICKEN LOVELY LEGS

Chicken 'lovely legs' are inexpensive compared to other cuts of chicken and I love this simple, healthy dish. It has a refreshing, zingy flavour but it's not too tart for the kids, plus it's easy to prepare and time-efficient for busy families. It's versatile, too – you can serve it with mash, rice or roast vegies, and use the lemon chicken leftovers with a salad the next day.

Serves 6 • **Preparation** 5 mins • **Cook** 4–6 hours

2 kg (4 lb 8 oz) chicken 'lovely legs' (skinless drumsticks with a portion of the bone removed)
Plain (all-purpose) flour, for dusting
1 leek, white part only, chopped
2 heaped teaspoons minced garlic
Zest and juice of 2 lemons
375 ml (13 fl oz/1½ cups) chicken stock
200 g (7 oz) green beans
2 tablespoons chopped flat-leaf (Italian) parsley
Mashed potato, rice or roast vegetables, to serve

1. Dust the chicken pieces in flour to coat.

2. Put the chicken, leek, garlic, lemon zest and juice and stock in a slow cooker and cook for 4 hours on HIGH or 6 hours on LOW, adding the beans when 1 hour from being cooked.

3. Sprinkle with parsley and serve with mashed potato, rice or roast vegetables on the side.

Jenny Ford

BACON-HUGGED CHICKEN

We love chicken, bacon and cheese, so what better way to eat than putting them all together and popping them in the slow cooker?

Serves 4–6 • Preparation 40 mins • **Cook** 6 hours

6 skinless chicken thigh fillets
1 teaspoon wholegrain mustard
1 garlic clove, crushed
125 g (4¼ oz) baby spinach leaves
1 small handful chives
6 bocconcini (fresh baby mozzarella cheese), cut into 3 slices
6 rashers bacon
Steamed seasonal vegetables, to serve

1. Spread out and flatten the chicken thigh fillets as much as possible. Combine the mustard and garlic and spread over the chicken. Lay the spinach leaves and chives along the chicken. Top with 3 bocconcini slices along the middle of each chicken fillet.

2. Roll the fillet as tightly as you can, wrap a bacon rasher around each chicken roll and secure with cooking twine.

3. Place baking paper in the base of a slow cooker. Put the chicken thigh rolls on the baking paper in a single layer. Put a tea towel over the lid and cook on LOW for 6 hours.

4. Remove the twine and serve with steamed seasonal vegetables.

Sharon Paull

MUSTARD MAPLE CHICKEN

A fabulous flavour combination that develops beautifully during slow cooking. The addition of garlic gives a lovely depth to the overall flavour, too.

Serves 4 • **Preparation** 5 mins • **Cook** 4 hours

1 kg (2 lb 4 oz) skinless chicken thigh fillets
125 g (4½ oz/½ cup) dijon mustard
3 tablespoons maple syrup
1 garlic clove, minced
Broccolini, carrots and baby potatoes, to serve

1. Place the chicken in a slow cooker.

2. Combine the remaining ingredients in a small bowl, pour over the chicken and toss to coat the chicken well in the mixture.

3. Cook on LOW for 4 hours.

4. Serve with steamed broccolini, julienne carrots and baby potatoes.

Paulene Christie

CREAMY HERB & GARLIC CHICKEN

A perfect mix of herbs, cream, garlic and chicken! This saucy little number speaks volumes in its title. My only warning is finding some self control to stop eating.

Serves 4 • **Preparation** 5 mins • **Cook** 4–6 hours

1 kg (2 lb 4 oz) skinless chicken thigh fillets
150 g (5½ oz) mushrooms, coarsely chopped
½ red capsicum (pepper), diced
3 spring onions (scallions), finely sliced
250 g (9 oz) light cream cheese
½ teaspoon dried basil
½ teaspoon dried oregano
2 garlic cloves, minced
¼ teaspoon freshly ground black pepper
Brown rice or penne pasta, to serve

1. Brown or seal the chicken if desired, or put it straight into a slow cooker with all the other ingredients to cook on LOW for 4–6 hours.
2. Serve the chicken and sauce over brown rice or penne pasta.

Simon Christie

HONEY MUSTARD CHICKEN
WITH BACON

I love the combination of honey and mustard so I decided to cook it with the other super star pairing – chicken and bacon. The end result was just so tasty! You can choose whatever style of mustard you prefer to personalise this dish.

Serves 4 • **Preparation** 5 mins • **Cook** 6 hours

0.5–1 kg (1 lb 2 oz–2 lb 4 oz) chicken pieces of your choice
1 handful diced bacon
420 g (15 oz) tinned condensed cream of chicken soup
1–2 garlic cloves, minced
2 tablespoons wholegrain mustard, or mustard of your choice
4 tablespoons honey
Mashed potato, snow peas and baby carrots, to serve

1. Put the chicken and bacon in a slow cooker.

2. Combine the remaining ingredients in a medium bowl and pour over the chicken.

3. Cover and cook on LOW for 6 hours.

4. Serve with creamy mashed potato, steamed snow peas and baby carrots.

Paulene Christie

WHOLE CHICKEN IN BARBECUE SAUCE

You could serve this amazingly tasty chicken on its own with a salad, but the best thing to do, I think, is spoon the lovely sauce over the chicken and some rice or mashed potato and vegetables, too. So delicious.

Serves 4–6 • **Preparation** 5 mins • **Cook** 6 hours

1 whole chicken
420 g (15 oz) tinned condensed tomato soup
125 ml (4 fl oz/½ cup) white vinegar
3 tablespoons light brown sugar
1 tablespoon Worcestershire sauce
¼ teaspoon dried basil
¼ teaspoon dried thyme

1. Put the chicken in a slow cooker.

2. Combine the remaining ingredients in a medium bowl and pour over chicken.

3. Cover and cook on LOW for 6 hours or until cooked through.

Paulene Christie

CRANBERRY & ORANGE MARMALADE WHOLE CHICKEN

A very easy way to bring a touch of difference to Christmas or any special occasion, this tasty chicken is full of flavour. You can use the cooking juices at the end to make awesome gravy.

Serves 4 • **Preparation** 10 mins • **Cook** 6–8 hours

4 tablespoons orange marmalade
4 tablespoons cranberry sauce
1 whole chicken
½ orange, cut into quarters
4 sprigs rosemary
½ lemon, sliced

1. Combine the marmalade and cranberry sauce.

2. Cut slits all over the chicken and coat with the marmalade mixture. Push the orange pieces and rosemary inside the chicken (or, as we say in our house, 'up its clacker'). Put the chicken in a slow cooker and place the lemon slices on top. Cover with the lid and cook on LOW for 6–8 hours.

3. When the chicken is cooked, strain the juices into a saucepan and combine with some gravy thickener. Simmer, stirring, until the desired consistency and serve with the chicken.

sherrie sutcliffe

CHICKEN SURPRISE

My family loves chicken and I am always trying new ideas and flavour combinations. This one worked really well and I can just pop everything into the slow cooker and let it do the rest. The house smells great while it's cooking and I serve it with a simple salad.

Serves 4 • **Preparation** 10 mins • **Cook** 3 hours

6 small washed potatoes, thinly sliced
5 rashers bacon
4 skinless chicken breast fillets
4 slices brie cheese
2 tablespoons garlic butter
½ cup grated cheddar cheese
Mixed salad, to serve

1. Layer the potato slices and 1 chopped bacon rasher in the base of a slow cooker. Season with salt and pepper.

2. Cut a slit in the breast fillets and insert a piece of brie and ½ tablespoon of garlic butter in each. Wrap each chicken fillet completely with 1 bacon rasher and secure with toothpicks.

3. Place the wrapped chicken parcels on top of the potato in the slow cooker. Cook on HIGH for 1 hour and then LOW for 2 hours.

4. When cooked, preheat the grill (broiler) to medium–high. Place the chicken under the grill so it crisps up. Scatter the grated cheese over the potato in the slow cooker and cook for 10–15 minutes with the lid off.

5. Remove the toothpicks and serve the chicken with the potato and a simple salad.

Samantha Steele

SOUR CREAM & BACON CHICKEN

Condensed cream soups make a fabulous base for so many slow-cooker dishes. In this case, the bacon, garlic, chicken and sour cream combination makes for an amazing sauce that is perfect served with pasta or rice.

Serves 6 • **Preparation** 5 mins • **Cook** 4–6 hours

1 kg (2 lb 4 oz) skinless chicken thigh fillets
200 g (7 oz) bacon rashers, diced
½ cup plain (all-purpose) flour
420 g (15 oz) tinned condensed cream of mushroom soup (no water added)
1 tablespoon minced garlic
1 cup sour cream
Pasta or rice and vegetables, to serve

1. Put the chicken and bacon in a slow cooker.
2. Combine the flour with the mushroom soup and garlic. Pour this mixture over the chicken.
3. Cover and cook on LOW for 4–6 hours.
4. When 10 minutes until cooked, add the sour cream and stir through.
5. Serve the chicken and its sauce with pasta or rice and vegetables.

Paulene Christie

═— APRICOT CHICKEN ⇒•

A classic dish that is very adaptable to the slow cooker. If you're not a fan of cooked fruit, you can make it with apricot nectar or jam – I give all three options below.

Serves 4 • **Preparation** 5 mins • **Cook** 6 hours

1 kg (2 lb 4 oz) skinless chicken thigh fillets or cut of your choice
1 onion, diced
40 g (1½ oz) French onion soup mix, dry
410 g (14½ oz) tinned apricot halves in juice, OR 425 ml (15 fl oz) tinned apricot nectar, OR 500 g (17½ oz) apricot jam (jelly)
Brown rice and steamed vegetables, to serve

1. Put the chicken and onion in a slow cooker.

2. Combine the soup mix with the apricot juice, nectar or jam and pour over the chicken. Scatter the apricot halves, if using, over the top.

3. Cover and cook on LOW for 6 hours.

4. Serve chicken in its sauce over brown rice with steamed vegetables.

Paulene Christie

DRIED APRICOT CHICKEN

I wanted a thicker sauce and stronger apricot taste than in the various apricot chicken recipes I'd tried, so I used dried apricots. As they broke down, the dried apricots thickened the sauce and gave the dish an intense apricot flavour. The quantity of dried apricots can be adjusted to suit your liking.

Serves 4 • **Preparation** 5 mins • **Cook** 7–9 hours

Olive oil spray
1 litre (35 fl oz/4 cups) apricot nectar
80 g (2¾ oz) French onion soup mix, dry
1 teaspoon minced garlic
250–375 g (9–13oz) dried apricots, cut into quarters
8 skinless chicken thigh fillets, or cut of your choice
Rice, to serve

1. Spray the inside of a slow cooker with olive oil spray. Put the apricot nectar, soup mix, garlic and dried apricots in a jug and stir until combined. Pour a little sauce into the bottom of the slow cooker.

2. Spread the chicken thighs evenly over the base of the slow cooker. Pour over the remaining liquid. Cook on HIGH for 1 hour, then reduce to LOW and cook for 6–8 hours.

3. Lift out the chicken and serve whole or in pieces with the sauce and rice.

Vicky Kemp

WHOLE CHICKEN WITH BACON & HERBS

I came up with this recipe, which is easy and full of flavour, after a bit of experimenting. I like that once it's prepared you can forget about it – there is no basting or turning – and the bacon and butter keep the breast extra moist.

Serves 4 • **Preparation** 15 mins • **Cook** 6–8 hours

1 whole chicken
1 teaspoon chopped garlic, or to taste
3 rashers shortcut bacon, trimmed and chopped
20 g (¾ oz) piece of butter, halved
1 tablespoon dried thyme
1 teaspoon ground sage
Freshly ground pink sea salt, to taste
Freshly ground black pepper, to taste
Chat potatoes and vegetables, to serve

1. Position the chicken with neck facing you. Slide a hand carefully under the skin of the breast, gently separating the skin from the flesh without tearing the skin. Rub half the garlic under the skin and the remaining half all over the breast on each side. Push the bacon under the skin, as evenly as possible. Push half of the butter under the skin on each side.

2. Combine the thyme, sage, salt and pepper in a small bowl. Rub the herb mixture over the skin of the chicken.

3. Put the chicken in a slow cooker. Add enough water to come 2.5 cm (1 inch) up the side of the pot. Cook on LOW for 6–8 hours, depending on the size of the chicken and slow cooker, adding the chat potatoes (pricked with a fork for even cooking) and other vegetables of your choice about halfway through.

4. Slice the chicken, when cooked, and serve with the potatoes and vegetables.

NOTE: For a crispy skin on the chicken, sprinkle a small amount of peanut oil all over and put in a hot oven (200°C/400°F).

TIP: The stock left in the slow cooker can be drained, skimmed of fat and used to make gravy, or frozen for later.

Karen Stuckings

CHICKEN & MUSHROOM PIE

I came up with this recipe by accident. I was making a carbonara sauce and thought it would taste great in a pie, so I tweaked it a bit and now it's a family favourite. You make the pie filling in the slow cooker then cook the pastry in the oven quickly.

Serves 4 • **Preparation** 15 mins • **Cook** 6½ hours

2 skinless chicken breast fillets, chopped into bite-size pieces (or leave whole and shred at the end)
2 cups finely chopped mushroom
1 onion, finely diced
2 garlic cloves, crushed
½ cup cooking cream
1 teaspoon vegetable stock powder
½ cup grated parmesan cheese
Cooking oil spray
1 sheet ready-rolled puff pastry
1 egg, lightly whisked
Mashed potato and steamed vegetables or mixed salad, to serve

1. Put the chicken, mushroom, onion, garlic, cream and stock powder in a slow cooker and mix to combine. Cook on LOW for 6 hours.

2. Add the parmesan cheese and cook with lid off for 15 minutes, or until the sauce is thickened to your liking.

3. Spray a pie dish with non-stick spray, then pour in the chicken filling. Lay the puff pastry over the top, trim the edge and brush the top lightly with the egg. Bake in the oven for 15 minutes or until the pastry is puffed and golden. Serve immediately with mashed potato and steamed vegetables or salad.

Trudy Lowndes

CORONATION CHICKEN

I tried this dish in a restaurant many years ago and loved it. I really wanted to replicate the recipe in the slow cooker – and it worked a treat! The creamy chicken matched with the tomato tang, sweetness of mango and crunch of flaky almonds is surprisingly great and the dish comes together wonderfully. I usually serve it with steamed rice and salad. My family loves this, including Miss 1 and Miss 4.

Serves 4–5 • **Preparation** 20 mins • **Cook** 4 hours

2 skinless chicken breast fillets
1 tablespoon olive or coconut oil
Zest and juice of 1 lemon
1–2 tablespoons butter
1 eschalot or small white or red onion, finely chopped
1 red or green chilli, deseeded and finely chopped
2 teaspoons curry powder
2 tablespoons tomato paste (concentrated purée)
100 ml (3½ fl oz) dry white wine
100 ml (3½ fl oz) chicken stock
1 tablespoon apricot jam (jelly)
150 g (5½ oz) mayonnaise
75 g (2½ oz) crème fraîche
1 teaspoon cornflour (cornstarch)
Dash of Tabasco sauce (optional)
1 large mango, diced
2 tablespoons chopped coriander (cilantro), to garnish
50g (1¾ oz) toasted flaked almonds, to garnish
Rice and green salad, to serve

1. Put the chicken, oil, lemon zest and juice, butter, eschalot, chilli, curry, tomato paste, wine, stock, jam, mayonnaise and crème fraîche in a slow cooker. Mix the cornflour with a little water to make a paste. Add to the slow cooker and stir through the other ingredients. Add the Tabasco sauce, if using. Cook on LOW for 4 hours, stirring once or twice.

2. When 20 minutes from cooked, add the mango.

3. Serve in bowls scattered with coriander and flaked almonds, with rice and a salad on the side.

Jen Hall

HONEY & GARLIC CHICKEN

The flavours in this dish are so yummy and you can use whichever cut of chicken you like. I find drumsticks and thigh fillets are much juicier than breast when cooked this way. Serve it with rice and vegetables.

Serves 4 • **Preparation** 5 mins • **Cook** 4–6 hours

1 kg (2 lb 4 oz) skinless chicken thigh fillets or drumsticks
3 garlic cloves, chopped or grated
⅓ cup soy sauce
125 ml (4 fl oz/½ cup) tomato sauce (ketchup)
125 ml (4 fl oz/½ cup) honey
Brown rice and Asian greens, to serve

1. Put the chicken in a slow cooker.

2. Combine the garlic, soy sauce, tomato sauce and honey in a small bowl and pour over the chicken. Cover and cook on LOW for 4–6 hours.

3. If you have cooked drumsticks, you can debone them at this point and toss the chicken meat pieces back through the sauce before serving with brown rice and Asian greens.

Paulene Christie

FINGER LICKIN' STICKY CHICKEN WINGS

The sweet and savoury sensation associated with this wing dish is perfect with any side, or you can enjoy them on their own while sitting back watching a big game on TV.

Serves 4 • **Preparation** 10 mins • **Cook** 4 hours

1 kg (2 lb 4 oz) chicken wings, tipped and sectioned (discard tips)
½ cup honey
½ cup light brown sugar
⅓ cup balsamic vinegar
⅓ cup soy sauce
3 garlic cloves, minced
1 teaspoon ground ginger
1 tablespoon sweet chilli sauce
1–2 tablespoons cornflour (cornstarch), for thickening
Sesame seeds, to garnish

1. Put the chicken wings, honey, sugar, balsamic, soy sauce, garlic, ginger and sweet chilli sauce in a large saucepan on the stovetop over medium heat or in your searing slow cooker. Bring to a simmer and cook until the sugar is dissolved.

2. Transfer the wings and mixture to the slow cooker and toss to coat. Cook for 4 hours on LOW, stirring gently every now and then.

3. When cooked, remove the chicken wings. Mix the cornflour with a little water to form a paste and stir through the sauce to thicken. Pour the sauce over the wings, sprinkle with sesame seeds and serve.

Simon Christie

CREAMY COCONUT CHICKEN CURRY

We tried many recipes but none got the thumbs up from all five of our family – until we came up with this curry. It is fragrant, mild and tasty, and is now a firm favourite – even with the picky four-year-old. You can tone it down or spice it up, and it's as good served with rice as it is over chips or in jacket potatoes.

Serves 4 • Preparation 20 mins • Cook 4½ hours

Vegetable oil, for browning
500 g (1 lb 2oz) skinless chicken breast fillets, cut into bite-size pieces
1 onion, finely sliced
1 red capsicum (pepper), thinly sliced
1 yellow capsicum (pepper), sliced
3 tablespoons yellow curry paste
200 ml (7 fl oz) chicken stock
¼ teaspoon salt
1 teaspoon sugar
2 heaped teaspoons mild curry powder
2 teaspoons dark soy sauce
2 teaspoons light soy sauce
2 garlic cloves, minced
400 ml (14 fl oz) tinned coconut milk
1–2 teaspoons cornflour (cornstarch)
Rice or potatoes, to serve

1. Heat the oil in a medium frying pan over medium heat. Brown the chicken on all sides and transfer to a slow cooker. Reduce the heat to medium–low, add the onion and capsicum to the pan and cook until soft.

2. Meanwhile, make the curry sauce. Put the curry paste and 3 tablespoons of the stock in a large bowl and mix to form a paste. Add the remaining stock, salt, sugar, curry powder, soy sauces, half the garlic and all of the coconut milk and whisk until smooth.

3. Add the remaining garlic to the frying pan and cook for 1 minute. Add the curry mixture to the pan and bring to the boil.

4. Pour the curry sauce over the chicken in the slow cooker. Cook on LOW for 3–4 hours. When 30 minutes from being cooked, mix the cornflour with a little water to make a thin paste. Add to the slow cooker, stir well, and continue to cook on LOW.

5. Serve with rice or potatoes.

Kerry Miskelly

SIMPLE CHICKEN SATAY

Even though it is so easy to make, this recipe embraces the traditional satay flavours. I like to seal in the chicken flavours with a quick fry before slow cooking, but you don't need to. You can easily whip this up before work for the family to enjoy in the evening.

Serves 4 • Preparation 10 mins • Cook 8 hours

Vegetable oil, for frying
3 tablespoons minced garlic
2 brown onions, finely diced
8 skinless chicken thigh fillets, cut into bite-size pieces
2 carrots, coarsely chopped
1 capsicum (pepper), finely chopped
Juice of 1 lime
½ teaspoon chilli powder (optional)
½ teaspoon ground cumin
1 handful fresh coriander (cilantro)
425 g (15 oz) tinned coconut cream
400 ml (14 fl oz) tinned coconut milk
4 tablespoons Worcestershire sauce
4 tablespoons soy sauce
375 g (13 oz) peanut butter
Rice, pasta or mashed potato, to serve

1. Heat the oil in a medium frying pan over medium heat. Add the garlic and onion until browned. Add the chicken and cook until browned all over.

2. Transfer the chicken to a slow cooker, add the remaining ingredients and stir well. Cook on LOW for 8 hours.

3. Serve the chicken with rice, pasta or mashed potato.

Jess van Netten

SWEET CHILLI CHICKEN

The ingredients in this dish are ones you often have on hand in the pantry. I must confess I tend to double the sauces because we love it that much. Because it uses sweet chilli sauce it's not too hot for the children. Our whole family enjoys this one.

Serves 4 • **Preparation** 5 mins • **Cook** 4–6 hours

6–8 chicken thigh cutlets on the bone, or cut of your choice
Plain (all-purpose) flour, for dusting
4 tablespoons tomato sauce (ketchup)
4 tablespoons soy sauce
4 tablespoons apricot jam (jelly)
4 tablespoons sweet chilli sauce
Mashed potato and vegetables or fried rice, to serve

1. Dust the chicken in flour to coat lightly. Place chicken in a slow cooker.

2. Combine the tomato sauce, soy sauce, jam and sweet chilli sauce in a small bowl and pour over the chicken.

3. Cook on LOW for 4–6 hours.

4. Serve with mashed potato and steamed seasonal vegetables, or with fried rice.

Paulene Christie

ORANGE & GINGER CHICKEN

I wanted to use up some blood oranges, I wanted Asian flavours and I love tender and juicy slow-cooked chicken on the bone for extra nutrients and flavour. I am always looking for ways to use wonderful anti-inflammatory ingredients like turmeric, ginger and garlic. So this dish satisfies all my needs and it's a yummy dinner to come home to after being at work all day. I like to serve it with stir-fried vegetables and hot buttered rice.

Serves 6 • Preparation 10 mins • Cook 4–8 hours

Zest and juice of 2 blood oranges (or any eating variety you like)
1 tablespoon ground turmeric
2 tablespoons ground ginger
3–4 garlic cloves, coarsely chopped
¼ cup soy sauce, tamari or coconut aminos
1 tablespoon honey
1 teaspoon Chinese five spice
12 chicken drumsticks
Rice and stir-fried vegetables, to serve

1. Put the zest and juice in a blender with the turmeric, ginger, garlic, tamari, honey and five spice. Blend to make a paste.

2. Put the drumsticks in a slow cooker and pour over the paste. Cook for 4 hours on HIGH or 7–8 hours on LOW.

3. Strain the liquid and put in a small saucepan over medium heat on the stovetop. (Return the drumsticks to the slow cooker to keep warm.) Simmer the liquid for 10 minutes, or until it is nice and thick.

4. Serve the drumsticks with the sauce, buttered rice and stir-fried vegetables.

TIP: Substitute soy sauce with tamari or coconut aminos for a gluten-free recipe.

Dinielle Farquharson

ORIENTAL-STYLE ORANGE CHICKEN

One of my favourite slow-cooked chicken dishes, I love this recipe and use it regularly. It's child friendly and a hit with the whole family. I usually serve it with brown rice and vegetables.

Serves 4–6 • **Preparation** 5 mins • **Cook** 6–8 hours

1 kg (2 lb 4 oz) skinless chicken thigh fillets
375 ml (13 fl oz/1½ cups) chicken stock
¼ cup teriyaki sauce
3 garlic cloves, crushed
¾ cup orange marmalade
½ cup sliced spring onions (scallions)
1–2 tablespoons cornflour (cornstarch), to thicken
Brown rice and steamed Asian greens or stir-fried vegetables, to serve

1. Place the chicken in a slow cooker.

2. Combine the stock, teriyaki sauce, garlic and marmalade and pour over the chicken. Cover and cook on low for 6–8 hours.

3. When 2 hours from cooked, add the spring onions.

4. When 15 minutes from cooked, combine cornflour with enough water to make a paste and add to the slow cooker; stir to thicken.

5. Serve with brown rice and steamed Asian greens or stir-fried vegetables.

Paulene Christie

SWEET & SOUR CHICKEN

I had planned to use a recipe for sweet and sour chicken I'd found online but lost it. So after searching for ages with no luck, I decided to wing it and make up my own. Success! My accidental slow-cooked sweet and sour chicken went down a treat.

Serves 4 • Preparation 15 mins • Cook 4–8 hours

500 g (1 lb 2 oz) chicken, cut of choice, in bite-size pieces
1 garlic clove, crushed
½ onion, finely chopped
1 handful snow peas, trimmed
1 carrot, coarsely chopped
1 zucchini (courgette), coarsely chopped
1 cup roughly chopped broccoli
½ cup tomato sauce (ketchup)
2 tablespoons soy sauce
2 tablespoons light brown sugar
440 g (15½ oz) tinned pineapple pieces in juice
1 chicken stock cube, dissolved in 250 ml (9 fl oz/1 cup) hot water
Rice, to serve

1. Put the chicken and all the other ingredients in a slow cooker, stir gently and cook away for 4 hours on HIGH or 8 hours on LOW.

2. Serve the chicken in bowls with rice.

Ashlie Bland

TERIYAKI WINGS

This was a simple and easy side to throw together. My children (and I) love any type of flavoured chicken wings. The savoury delight of this version is a perfect compliment to any salad.

Serves 4–6 • **Preparation** 10 mins • **Cook** 4 hours

Olive oil spray
1 kg (2 lb 4 oz) chicken wings, tipped and sectioned (tips discarded)
1 onion, chopped
250 ml (9 fl oz/1 cup) soy sauce
1 cup light brown sugar
1½ teaspoons ground ginger
1 teaspoon minced garlic
Thick-cut potato or sweet potato wedges, to serve
Mixed salad, to serve

1. Heat the oil in a large frying pan over medium heat. Brown the chicken wings then transfer to a slow cooker.

2. Put the onion, soy sauce, sugar, ginger and garlic in a jug and whisk to combine. Pour the sauce over the wings in the slow cooker. Cover and cook for 4 hours on LOW, turning once and spooning over the sauce.

3. Serve the chicken wings with their sauce. Serve with thick cut potato or sweet potato wedges and a garden salad.

Simon Christie

THAI PEANUT CHICKEN

Beautiful Thai flavours cut through with fresh lime juice in this dish. Serve it with brown rice and green vegetables.

Serves 6 • **Preparation** 5 mins • **Cook** 4 hours

1 kg skinless chicken thigh fillets
¾ cup chunky tomato salsa
⅓ cup peanut butter (smooth or crunchy)
2 tablespoons fresh lime juice
1 tablespoon soy sauce
1 teaspoon grated or minced fresh ginger
⅓ cup coarsely chopped peanuts
Brown rice, steamed Asian greens and lime wedges, to serve

1. Put the chicken in a slow cooker.

2. Combine the salsa, peanut butter, lime juice, soy sauce and ginger in a small bowl. Pour the mixture over the chicken. Cook on LOW for 4 hours.

3. Serve in bowls with brown rice and steamed Asian greens. Scatter over the peanuts and pop in a lime wedge for squeezing.

Paulene Christie

ORIENTAL HONEY SOY CHICKEN

When using different cuts of chicken in slow cooking, you may need to adjust the recipes to suit. If I am using a chicken cut that has skin on it, I don't add fats and oils. However, drier cuts, such as skinless breast fillets, may require the added oil.

Serves 4–8 • **Preparation** 5 mins • **Cook** 4–6 hours

Cooking oil spray
8 chicken pieces of your choice (skinless or with skin) or a whole chicken
125 ml (4 fl oz/½ cup) chicken stock
⅓ cup soy sauce
¼ cup honey
1 teaspoon Worcestershire sauce
2 teaspoons balsamic vinegar
2 teaspoons lemon juice
1 teaspoon sesame oil
1 tablespoon minced garlic
1–2 tablespoons cornflour (cornstarch), to thicken
Rice and Asian greens, to serve

1. Lightly spray a slow cooker bowl with cooking oil.

2. Put the chicken in a slow cooker.

3. Combine the stock, soy sauce, honey, Worcestershire sauce, vinegar, lemon juice, sesame oil and garlic in a bowl. Pour this mixture over the chicken.

4. Cover and cook on LOW for 4 hours if using chicken pieces or up to 6 hours if using a whole chicken.

5. When 30 minutes from cooked, skim any excess oil off the surface. Combine cornflour with enough water to form a paste. Add to the slow cooker and stir to thicken the dish.

6. Serve the chicken with rice and steamed Asian greens.

Paulene Christie

JAPANESE STICKY CHICKEN WINGS & SALAD

A simple yet extremely tasty way to marinate your wings, complemented by a light tangy salad. It's mild in spice so is sure to delight even the fussiest eater.

Serves 4 • Preparation 20 mins • Cook 4 hours

2 tablespoons grated fresh ginger
4 dried chillies, sliced
2 star anise
2 teaspoons ground cinnamon
⅓ cup soy sauce
⅓ cup rice vinegar
2 tablespoons sugar
3 tablespoons honey
3 tablespoons oyster sauce
2 spring onions (scallions), thinly sliced
2 tablespoons minced garlic
1.5 kg (3 lb 5 oz) chicken wings, tips removed, cut to make drumettes

SALAD
2 cups thinly sliced cabbage
1 cup julienned carrot
1 cup julienned cucumber
1 sheet nori, toasted and finely sliced
2 cups rocket (arugula)
2 tablespoons rice vinegar
2 tablespoons soy sauce
2 tablespoons caster (superfine) sugar
1 teaspoon grated fresh ginger
2 tablespoons vegetable oil
1 tablespoon tomato sauce (ketchup)

1. In a bowl, combine the ginger, chillies, star anise, cinnamon, soy sauce, rice vinegar, sugar, honey, oyster sauce, spring onions and garlic.

2. Put the chicken in a slow cooker and pour over the seasoning mixture. Cook on LOW for 3 hours.

3. Remove the lid and cook on HIGH for 1 hour to reduce the sauce.

4. To make the salad, put the cabbage, carrot, cucumber, nori and rocket in a bowl and toss to combine.

5. To make the dressing, combine the rice vinegar, soy sauce, sugar, ginger, oil and tomato sauce in a bowl and stir until the sugar has dissolved. Pour over the salad and toss lightly.

6. Serve the chicken wings with the salad.

Tania Whitford

PEKING CHICKEN FRIED RICE

This was inspired by many Chinese Peking duck recipes but it is a simpler version for busy families. It tastes fantastic but does not take that long to prepare and does not have a strong game flavour that sometimes duck can have. I serve mine with fried rice but you can use it in salads or as a main with any sides you like.

Serves 4 • **Preparation** 30 mins + marinate overnight • **Cook** 2 hours

1 teaspoon minced garlic
1 teaspoon finely grated fresh ginger
1 teaspoon Chinese five spice
½ cup light soy sauce
2 tablespoons honey
¼ teaspoon ground chilli
2 teaspoons sesame oil
2 teaspoons red food colouring (optional)
2 skinless chicken breast fillets
Cooking oil spray

FRIED RICE
1½ cups white long-grain rice
Dash of ground tumeric
3 eggs, lightly whisked
2 teaspoons sesame oil
1 carrot, shaved with a potato peeler
3 spring onions (scallions), thinly sliced
2 garlic cloves, crushed
1 long red chilli, finely chopped, plus 1 long red chilli, deseeded, thinly sliced
    lengthways, extra to serve
2 tablespoons salt-reduced soy sauce
1 tablespoon oyster sauce
½ cup frozen peas, thawed

1. To make the marinade, combine the garlic, ginger, five spice, soy sauce, honey, chilli, sesame oil and food colouring, if using, in a medium bowl.

2. Add the chicken to the bowl with the mixture and stir to coat. Cover the bowl and put in the fridge to marinate overnight.

3. To make the fried rice, cook the rice for 10 minutes on HIGH in a microwave, until three-quarters cooked. Spread the rice in a baking tray lined with baking paper to cool. Sprinkle over dash of ground turmeric.

4. When the rice is cool, combine it in a bowl with the egg, sesame oil, carrot, green onion, garlic, chilli, soy sauce, oyster sauce and peas. Put this mixture in a slow cooker.

5. Spray a large frying pan with cooking oil spray and heat over medium–high heat. Cook the chicken until browned. Cut the chicken into thin slices and transfer to the slow cooker. Cook on LOW, with no tea towel (dish towel), for 2 hours.

Wayne Gatt

ISLAND CHICKEN

There is plenty of lovely fresh sauce with this dish, which is great served with rice and stir-fried vegetables.

Serves 6 • **Preparation** 5 mins • **Cook** 4–6 hours

1 kg (2 lb 4 oz) skinless chicken thigh fillets, or cut of your choice
1 garlic clove, finely chopped
1 small onion, sliced
450 g (1 lb) tinned crushed pineapple in natural juice, undrained
¾ cup tomato sauce (ketchup)
3 tablespoons (firmly packed) light brown sugar
3 tablespoons hoisin sauce
1 teaspoon grated fresh ginger
Rice and stir-fried vegetables, to serve

1. Put the chicken in a slow cooker.

2. Combine the remaining ingredients in a medium bowl and pour over the chicken.

3. Cover and cook on LOW for 4–6 hours.

4. Serve the chicken with steamed rice and stir-fried vegetables.

Paulene Christie

CHICKEN TIKKA MASALA

I am happy to be able to share with you my version of chicken tikka masala. I make it to suit all my family so even my toddler will devour it, and even though it's not hot it does have plenty of flavour. It's your choice what you would like to serve it with, but my family enjoy it served on a bed of pilau rice with naan bread and a fresh salad. You can also make it a lighter meal by using low fat yoghurt and cream. Hope you all enjoy making it!

Serves 8 • Preparation 20 mins • Cook 5½ hours

4 tablespoons vegetable oil
25 g (1 oz) butter
8 skinless chicken breast fillets, cut into 2.5 cm (1 inch) cubes
6 tablespoons chicken tikka masala paste
4 onions, coarsely chopped
2 red capsicums (peppers), deseeded and cut into chunks
800 g (1 lb 12 oz) tinned chopped tomatoes
4 tablespoons tomato paste (concentrated purée)
2-3 tablespoons mango chutney
150 g (5½ oz) thick (double) cream
150 g (5½ oz) natural yoghurt
Rice and naan bread, to serve

1. Heat the oil and butter in a large frying pan over medium–high heat. Add the chicken and cook until sealed and slightly browned. Add the tikka masala paste and cook for 5 minutes, stirring, until the chicken is well coated. Transfer to a slow cooker.

2. Add the onion, capsicum, tomato, tomato paste and chutney to the slow cooker. Stir to combine with the chicken. Cook on LOW for 4½ hours.

3. Add the cream and yoghurt and cook for 1 hour.

4. Serve with rice and naan bread.

Adell Cookson

⇒— CHICKEN HEAVEN —●

I called this dish Chicken Heaven because basically it is the tastiest chicken and vegetable dish I have tasted for a long time. I created it when I was attempting to do stuffed and bacon-wrapped chicken but I only had chicken legs. I love that it's so easy to make and jam-packed full of flavour, you don't need to serve it with anything except maybe crusty bread. Surprise your friends and family with this – they're sure to love it and even the kids will ask for more.

Serves 4–6 • Preparation 20 mins • Cook 2½–5½ hours

1 kg (2 lb 4 oz) chicken thighs or breast fillets, cut into bite-size pieces
3 handfuls spinach leaves, coarsely chopped
1–2 cups sliced mushrooms
1–2 tablespoons crushed garlic (I love garlic)
1 teaspoon dried mixed herbs
6 rashers rindless bacon, sliced into 4 pieces
250 g (9 oz) cream cheese
1 tablespoon chicken stock powder
½ cup coarsely chopped onion
420 g (15 oz) tinned condensed cream of chicken soup
Crusty bread, to serve

1. Put all the ingredients in a slow cooker.

2. Cook on HIGH for 2½ hours or on LOW for 5½ hours, stirring occasionally.

3. Serve hot with fresh crusty bread.

Jacqueline Stock

TURKEY MEATBALLS IN TOMATO SAUCE

I usually don't have the patience to cook and turn meatballs, but I needed to make something gluten free and use up a tray of turkey mince in the freezer. So I had a go at making turkey meatballs with the addition of grated parmesan cheese instead of breadcrumbs, and slow-cooking them gently in a tomato-based sauce. It worked a treat and tasted great.

Serves 4 • **Preparation** 10 mins • **Cook** 5½ hours

500 g (1 lb 2 oz) minced (ground) turkey
½ cup breadcrumbs (use gluten-free breadcrumbs if desired) (optional)
½ onion, finely chopped, plus 1½ onions, finely chopped, extra
½ cup finely grated parmesan cheese, plus 1 handful extra
1 egg, beaten
420 g (15 oz) tinned chopped tomatoes
1 tablespoon tomato paste (concentrated purée)
Boiled or steamed rice, to serve

1. Put the turkey mince, breadcrumbs (if using), ½ chopped onion, parmesan cheese and egg in a large bowl. Season with salt and freshly ground black pepper and mix well. Roll into small balls. Put the turkey balls in a slow cooker and cook for 1½ hours on HIGH.

2. Turn the meatballs carefully with tongs so they cook evenly. Add the remaining onion, tomatoes and tomato paste. Mix through, season with salt and freshly ground black pepper if needed. Cook for 3½ hours on HIGH.

3. Sprinkle the extra parmesan cheese over the turkey balls and cook for 30 minutes, until the meatballs are cooked and the cheese is golden.

4. Serve the turkey balls and the sauce with rice.

Sandra Rielly

SEAFOOD

OYSTERS KILPATRICK

Best ever starter for a dinner party, these little beauties are so full of flavour – it's like an explosion in your mouth that really wakes up your taste buds. And using a slow cooker is so much easier than using the oven.

Makes 12 • Preparation 10 mins • Cook 30–45 mins

2 cups rock salt
12 oysters, shucked, in half shells
2 tablespoons Worcestershire sauce
175 g (6 oz) thin rindless bacon rashers, diced and pan-fried until crisp
Lemon wedges, to serve
2 tablespoons chopped flat-leaf (Italian) parsley, to garnish

1. Preheat the slow cooker to HIGH. Put the rock salt in a thick layer on the bottom of the slow cooker. Arrange the oysters on the rock salt.

2. Drizzle Worcestershire sauce over the oysters and top with the pan-fried bacon.

3. Cover, with a tea towel (dish towel) under the lid, and cook for 30–45 minutes.

4. Serve the oysters with wedges of lemon and scattered with parsley.

Cheryl Barrett

CREAMY GARLIC KING PRAWNS

This is an adapted recipe I had been doing for years on my stovetop. I wanted to prove wrong a few of the sceptics who said that prawns couldn't be slow cooked. They sure CAN! The result this recipe provides is restaurant-quality.

Serves 4 • **Preparation** 15 mins • **Cook** 50 mins

115 g (4 oz) butter
2 garlic cloves, crushed
1 tablespoon plain (all-purpose) flour
250 ml (9 fl oz/1 cup) chicken stock
½ cup thin (pouring) cream
½ teaspoon mustard powder
1 kg (2 lb 4 oz) green king prawns, peeled and deveined
Flat-leaf (Italian) parsley leaves, to garnish

1. Preheat the slow cooker to HIGH. Put the butter and garlic in the slow cooker. When the butter is melted, stir in the flour. Cook for 1 minute, stirring, then slowly add the stock and cream, stirring to combine.

2. Cover and cook on HIGH for 30 minutes, or until thickened nicely, stirring every 10 minutes.

3. Add the mustard powder and season with salt and freshly ground black pepper. Add the prawns, cover and cook on HIGH for 15–20 minutes, stirring gently after 10 minutes.

4. Serve scattered with parsley.

Simon Christie

PRAWNS WITH GARLIC & CHIVE-FLAVOURED BUTTER

These prawns taste so good, and the meat pulls away so easily.

Serves 2 • **Preparation** 5 mins • **Cook** 1 hour

4 tablespoons butter, softened
3 garlic cloves, crushed
1 small handful chives, finely chopped
6 jumbo green prawns, sliced down the middle but not right through to butterfly them, washed well under cold running water
Green salad, to serve

1. Combine the butter, garlic and chives. Add prawns and stir so prawns are covered with butter mixture.

2. Put the prawns over the base of a slow cooker. Cook for 1 hour on HIGH.

3. Serve with a leafy green salad.

sherrie sutcliffe

FIJIAN CURRIED PRAWNS

A unique prawn dish, absolutely packed with flavour. Serve yours on a bed of basmati rice for the perfect international dish.

Serves 4 • Preparation 10 mins • Cook 3 hours

400 ml (14 fl oz) tinned coconut milk
50 g (1¾ oz) ghee
1 onion, diced
1 tablespoon minced garlic
1 tablespoon sugar
1 tablespoon grated fresh ginger
5 curry leaves
1 teaspoon ground cinnamon
2 cardamom pods, bruised
½ teaspoon fenugreek
1 teaspoon ground chilli
¼ teaspoon ground turmeric
1 teaspoon ground cumin
2 teaspoons ground coriander
½ teaspoon paprika
1 teaspoon curry powder
2 teaspoons lime juice
500 g (1 lb 2 oz) green prawns
Basmati rice, to serve

1. Put all the ingredients except the prawns and rice in a slow cooker. Cover and cook on LOW for 2½ hours.

2. Add the prawns to the slow cooker and cook for a further 30 minutes, or until the prawns are cooked.

3. Serve the prawns on a bed of basmati rice.

Tania Whitford

TUNA MORNAY

I had made this recipe for years on the stove but when I tried to find one I could do in the slow cooker, they all either used tinned soup or you had to make a sauce before putting it into the slow cooker. I didn't want to do either, so I decided to make the sauce in the slow cooker and it worked. You can also used tinned salmon for a salmon mornay.

Serves 4–6 • **Preparation** 20 mins • **Cook** 2 hours

60 g (2¼ oz) butter
6 tablespoons plain (all-purpose) flour
750 ml (26 fl oz/3 cups) milk
1 chicken stock cube
2 tablespoons coarsely chopped mixed fresh herbs
½ large onion, finely chopped
425 g (15 oz) tinned tuna, drained
½ cup grated cheese
2 tablespoons lemon juice
6 hard-boiled eggs, cut into quarters
Rice or pasta, to serve (optional)

1. Put the butter in a slow cooker on HIGH. Once the butter has melted, add the flour and mix well with a plastic whisk. Allow the butter and flour to cook while you heat the milk in the microwave for 2 minutes. Give the butter and flour another whisk then add the warm milk to the slow cooker. Whisk well until the mixture is smooth. Add the chicken stock cube and mixed herbs, season with salt and freshly ground black pepper and whisk until combined. Add the onion and mix well with a spoon. Cook on HIGH in the slow cooker for 1½ hours, stirring every 20 minutes or so.

2. Add the tuna, grated cheese, lemon juice and eggs, and gently mix to combine. Cook for 30 minutes on HIGH without stirring.

3. Serve with rice or pasta.

Karen Stuckings

EASY TUNA MORNAY

Born from many different tuna mornay recipes I've tried over the years, this has been tweaked and adjusted to become a super easy dish my family loves.

Serves 4 • Preparation 10 mins • Cook 3–5 hours

450 g (1 lb) tinned tuna, drained
420 g (15 oz) tinned cream of asparagus soup
1 cup uncooked rice or pasta
420 g (15 oz) tinned corn kernels, drained
¾ cup thin (pouring) cream
2 teaspoons wholegrain mustard
1 tablespoon lemon juice
2 tablespoons Worcestershire sauce
1 cup grated cheese, plus extra for sprinkling on top
⅔ cup breadcrumbs
Green salad, to serve

1. Put all the ingredients except the cheese and breadcrumbs in a slow cooker and stir to combine. Cover and cook for 2 hours on HIGH or 4 hours on LOW.

2. Add the cheese to the slow cooker and stir through. Scatter the breadcrumbs over the top and sprinkle over the extra grated cheese. Cover and cook for 1 hour or until the rice or pasta has cooked and the cheese has melted or is slightly browned on top.

3. Serve the tuna mornay with a green salad.

Rebecca Burford

CREAMY FISH FILLETS WITH LEMON PEPPER SEASONING

My passion is cooking and sharing ideas. Where we live the summers are very hot so I started looking for cooler meals.

Serves 4 • **Preparation** 5 mins • **Cook** 1–2 hours

4 red emperor fillets
Juice of 1 lemon
Lemon pepper seasoning, to sprinkle
1 tablespoon butter
1 cup thin (pouring) cream
1 teaspoon cornflour (cornstarch)
½ cup grated tasty cheese
Green salad, to serve

1. Line the bowl of a slow cooker with foil to wrap the fish fillets once prepared.

2. Put the fish fillets on the foil. Drizzle the fish with lemon juice and sprinkle over some lemon pepper seasoning. Add the butter and wrap tightly in the foil. Cook for 1–2 hours on HIGH.

3. When the fish is cooked, combine the cream and cornflour. Cook the cream mixture in the microwave until thickened.

4. Unwrap the foil and transfer the fish to a heatproof dish. Spoon the cream mixture over the fish, and sprinkle with the cheese. Put under the hot grill (broiler) until browned.

5. Serve with a green salad.

sherrie sutcliffe

FISH FILLETS WITH COCONUT, LEMON MYRTLE & GARLIC

My husband and son love nothing more than fishing, so I love coming up with different ways to cook the fish they catch. Seafood and fish have such great flavours when done in the slow cooker.

Serves 4 • **Preparation** 10 mins • **Cook** 1–2 hours

4 Spanish mackerel fillets
1 teaspoon lemon myrtle spice
2 tablespoons coconut milk
2 tablespoons shredded coconut, to garnish
Rice and Asian greens, to serve

1. Place the fish fillets in a medium bowl and scatter over the lemon myrtle spice, gently coating well on both sides.
2. Put the fish on individual sheets of foil. Drizzle coconut milk over the fish and wrap tightly.
3. Transfer the fish parcels to a slow cooker, cover and cook for 1–2 hours on HIGH.
4. Unwrap the fish parcels and scatter shredded coconut over the fish.
5. Serve with rice and steamed Asian greens.

Sherrie Sutcliffe

➤ SUGAR 'N' SPICE BARRA FILLETS ➤

I like to try different things every day to make our meals exciting instead of the same thing all the time. The sugar 'n' spice fish has so many flavours and is so easy to cook in the slow cooker. This dish is very popular in my house.

Serves 4 • Preparation 10 mins • Cook 1–2 hours

2 tablespoons light brown sugar
1 teaspoon ground cumin
½ teaspoon crushed garlic
½ teaspoon salt
½ teaspoon freshly ground black pepper
1 tablespoon diced capsicum (pepper)
1 tablespoon finely chopped spring onion (scallion)
4 barramundi fillets
Juice of 1 lemon
1 cup breadcrumbs
1 tablespoon butter, melted
Chunky potato wedges, to serve
Lemon wedges, to serve

1. Combine the sugar, cumin, garlic, salt, pepper, capsicum and spring onion in a medium bowl.

2. Put the fish fillets in the bowl and gently coat each one in the seasoning mixture. Transfer the fish to individual sheets of foil and drizzle lemon juice over them.

3. Combine the breadcrumbs and melted butter in a small bowl. Gently press the breadcrumb mixture on top of the fish and wrap tightly in the foil.

4. Transfer the fish parcels to a slow cooker. Cover and cook on HIGH for 1–2 hours.

5. Serve with potato wedges and lemon wedges.

Sherrie Sutcliffe

⊨— LIME FISH CURRY —●

A 'fast' slow-cooked dish that doesn't take much time or preparation, it is light and healthy with simple, sweet flavours. Colourful and fragrant, you can add other seafood to this dish to your liking.

Serves 4 • **Preparation** 10 mins • **Cook** 2 hours

1 tablespoon honey mustard
1 leek, white part only, rinsed well and sliced
2 teaspoons minced garlic
2 teaspoons minced fresh ginger
2 Roma tomatoes, diced
2 tablespoons lime juice
¼ cup water
¼ cup chopped coriander (cilantro) leaves
600 g (1 lb 5 oz) firm white fish fillets, coarsely chopped
375 ml (13 fl oz) tinned light coconut-flavoured evaporated milk
1–2 tablespoons cornflour (cornstarch)
Basmati rice, to serve

1. Combine the mustard, leek, garlic, ginger, tomato, lime juice, water and coriander In a slow cooker. Add the fish and gently combine.

2. Cover and cook for 2 hours on LOW.

3. When 30 minutes from cooked, add the coconut milk and stir through.

4. When cooked, mix the cornflour with a little water and stir through the curry. Allow to stand in the slow cooker until ready to serve with basmati rice.

Jenny Ford

SWEET & SOUR FISH

The simple things can sometimes be the best, and this is a great simple recipe.

Serves 4 • **Preparation** 5 mins • **Cook** 1–2 hours

4 red emperor fillets
500 g (1 lb) bottled sweet and sour sauce
Rice, to serve

1. Put each fish fillet on a sheet of foil. Pour a generous amount of sweet and sour sauce over each fish fillet. Wrap the fish tightly in the foil and transfer the parcels to a slow cooker.

2. Cover and cook on HIGH for 1–2 hours.

3. Open the parcel and serve the fish with the sauce on a bed of rice.

sherrie sutcliffe

INDIAN SEAFOOD CURRY

This recipe was given to me by one of my sisters, with whom I am always sharing recipes. It's such warming comfort food and that is what our family is all about – caring and sharing.

Serves 4–6 • **Preparation** 10–15 mins • **Cook** 3–4 hours

1 tablespoon vegetable oil
1 brown onion, coarsely chopped
2 tablespoons korma curry paste
270 ml (9½ fl oz) tinned coconut cream
800 g (1 lb 12 oz) seafood marinara mix
2 tablespoons mango chutney
Basmati rice, to serve
Lemon wedges and coriander (cilantro) leaves, to serve

1. Preheat the slow cooker to HIGH and add the oil and onion. Cook until the onion is soft. Add the curry paste and coconut cream and cook, stirring, until combined. Cover and cook for 1 hour.

2. Add the seafood and chutney. Continue to cook on LOW for 1 hour, or until the seafood is cooked through.

3. Serve in bowls with basmati rice, a lemon wedge and scattered with coriander leaves.

Lynne Walters

VEGETABLES

BASIC VEGETABLES SLOW-COOKED STYLE

A large part of the convenience of slow cooking is to have the dish ready to serve straight from the slow cooker at dinnertime. So why not include all your vegetables right alongside your main and have it all ready to go! Tight wrapping is the answer – you can cook your vegies in the same slow cooker as your main dish but keep them firm and intact. As well as cooking whole or large pieces of root vegetables, you can wrap ½–1 cup of softer vegetables – such as zucchini, beans, squash and broccoli – per parcel.

Serves as many as you need • **Preparation** 10 mins
Cook according to vegetable and slow cooker size

Vegetables of your choice, washed and peeled if necessary, cut into uniform size
Salt, freshly ground black pepper, fresh or dried herbs or seasoning of your choice
Butter, 1 teaspoon per parcel

1. Prepare the vegetables. If using washed potatoes with their skin intact, pierce the skin with a skewer a few times to allow the seasoning to penetrate during cooking.

2. Tear up foil into 20 x 20 cm (8 x 8 inch) squares, allowing for two squares per parcel. Lay a piece or pieces of vegetable on a foil square, add seasoning and a teaspoon of butter. Wrap tightly in the foil to form a well-sealed parcel. Wrap the parcel in a second piece of foil, pressing firmly to seal. Put the parcels in the slow cooker with the main meal, occasionally checking whether the vegetables are cooked during cooking time.

NOTES:

Cooking times for vegetables in the slow cooker will vary based on several factors:

- the size of the vegetable pieces and the size of the parcels

- the type of vegetable – a potato may take 4 hours to cook to soft, while a parcel of broccoli may take only 1 hour to steam, and a larger potato will take longer than a baby potato

- the size of your slow cooker – what takes 3 hours on HIGH in my 1.5 litre (52 fl oz/6 cup) cooker, which cooks fairly 'hot', would need longer in my 3 litre (104 fl oz/12 cup) cooker; but the 6.5 litre (220 fl oz) range of cookers run much hotter than the medium ones, so it involves some trial and error until you get to know your cooker

- what else is in the cooker – vegetables will cook faster on their own than if sharing the slow cooker with another dish, and of course it depends on whether the other dish is cooking on HIGH or LOW

The best you can do is test your vegetables at intervals to see if they are cooked until you get to know how long particular vegies take to cook in your slow cooker.

Paulene Christie

⊫— VEGETABLE SLICE —●

If you start with this basic slice, you can then start adding and substituting other vegetables. Just be sure to grate the vegetables finely and if there are a lot more, you'll need to add a few more eggs as well. When a skewer inserted in the centre comes out clean, the egg is cooked and it's ready to eat. This is one of the few 'fast' slow-cooking dishes you can make for a last-minute healthy dinner.

Serves 6–8 • **Preparation** 10 mins • **Cook** 1½–2 hours

6 eggs
80 ml (2½ fl oz/⅓ cup) milk
1 cup grated carrot
1 cup grated zucchini (courgette)
1 cup grated pumpkin (squash)
2 spring onions (scallions), thinly sliced
¼ cup grated cheese
Cooking oil spray

1. Combine the whisked eggs and milk in a medium bowl. Add the carrot, zucchini, pumpkin, spring onion and cheese. Season with salt and freshly ground black pepper and stir well.

2. Line the insert of a slow cooker with baking paper and spray lightly with the cooking oil.

3. Transfer the egg and vegetable mixture to the slow cooker, pouring it carefully onto the baking paper. Cover and cook on HIGH for 1½–2 hours.

Paulene Christie

VEGETARIAN VEGIE SLICE

Trying to use up vegies in the crisper led to the creation of this slice. It's great served with a salad in summer or used in sandwiches, and I'll even pop it into the kids' lunchboxes.

Serves 4–6 • Preparation 15 mins • Cook 3 hours

¼ capsicum (pepper), diced
1 carrot, grated
1 zucchini (courgette), grated
1 cup finely sliced mushrooms
4 slices of Veggie Delights Smoked Slices, or other meat-free deli product, thinly sliced
1 large onion, diced
½ cup corn kernels
1 cup grated cheese
1 cup self-raising flour
¼ cup smoky barbecue sauce
2 vegetable stock cubes dissolved in 2 tablespoons hot water
1 teaspoon crushed garlic
½ teaspoon ground turmeric
½ teaspoon ground paprika
125 ml (4 fl oz/½ cup) olive oil
8 eggs

1. Combine all the ingredients in a bowl and mix together. Season with salt and freshly ground black pepper, to taste.

2. Line the insert of a slow cooker with baking paper (wet the baking paper, scrunch it, squeeze it out and open it up again). Transfer the vegie and egg mixture to the slow cooker. Cover, with a tea towel (dish towel) under the lid (see Hints & Tips, page 9), and cook on HIGH for 3 hours.

Victoria Duncan

VEGETABLE CASSEROLE

Leftover vegetables after cooking ratatouille were what inspired this casserole. I love how jam-packed full of vegies it is, and you can add so many more to it if you like. You can turn it into a soup by adding soup, and you can serve a bowlful to a vegetarian then add chicken or other meat to the remainder for the meat-eaters. You can serve it on its own or as a side to your favourite steak or roast.

Serves 4–6 • **Preparation** 15 mins • **Cook** 4–6 hours

1 pumpkin (squash), peeled and cut into small chunks
2 zucchinis (courgettes), sliced
1 head of broccoli, divided into small florets
½ cauliflower, divided into small florets
1 onion, chopped
½ sweet potato, sliced
2 carrots, sliced
420 g (15 oz) tinned diced tomatoes
420 g (15 oz) tinned pumpkin soup
1–2 teaspoons crushed garlic
2 teaspoons dried mixed Italian herbs
Basil leaves, to garnish

1. Combine all the ingredients in a slow cooker. Cover and cook on HIGH for 4–6 hours.

2. Serve with a garnish of basil leaves.

Jacqueline Stock

EGGY BREKKIE IN RAMEKINS

A great low-fat (if you use low-fat cream and cheese), low-sodium recipe that's full of protein and a variety of vegetables. Great to put on before bed so you wake up to a healthy, nutritious breakfast that can easily be taken to work or school if you run out of time in the morning.

Serves 4 • Preparation 15 mins • Cook 6–8 hours

8 eggs
¼ cup thin (pouring) cream
2 small or 1 large potato, or ¼ sweet potato or pumpkin (squash),
    cut into 1 cm (½ inch) cubes
1 small onion, diced
4 asparagus spears, diced
4 baby or Roma tomatoes, diced
4 small mushrooms, diced
Grated or sliced cheddar cheese

1. Put the eggs and cream in a medium bowl and beat well to combine.

2. Combine the potato, onion, asparagus, tomato and mushroom in a large bowl and toss to combine. Divide the vegetables evenly between four ramekins.

3. Pour the egg and cream mixture over the vegetables in the ramekins and top with the grated cheese or cheese slices.

4. Put 2 cm (¾ inch) water in the slow cooker. Put four egg rings or a silicone stand on the base of the slow cooker and stand the ramekins on top. Cover, with a tea towel (dish towel) under the lid, and cook on LOW for 6–8 hours.

Jo-Anna Wood

BAKED SWEET POTATO

Simple and healthy, these can be served whole or you can scoop out the middle and combine it with other finely diced vegetables, or even diced cooked bacon, for a stuffed sweet potato meal.

Serves 4 as a side • **Preparation** 2 mins • **Cook** 6–7 hours

2 large or 4 small sweet potatoes, scrubbed

1. Put the whole sweet potatoes in a slow cooker. Cover and cook on LOW for 6–7 hours.

2. Slice and serve as a side or scoop out the flesh and stuff with whatever you please.

Paulene Christie

◼— MASHED POTATOES —●

This is the only way my daughter will eat potato. They are canola, dairy, egg, gluten, lactose and soy free, and low FODMAP.

Serves 4 • **Preparation** 5 mins • **Cook** 2–5 hours

4 large potatoes, cut into cubes

1. Put the potato in the slow cooker and just cover with water. Cover and cook for 2–5 hours on HIGH. Cooking time will vary depending on the type of potato used – the softer ones cook quickly, and the firmer ones tend to take longer.

2. When cooked, drain the potatoes and mash as you would normally.

Felicity Barnett

GARLIC BUTTER SPUDS

My family consists of me, my husband and our four kids. We all love food and it's always a favourite topic of conversation: 'What are we having for tea?' When cooking side dishes we always try to serve different things and that's how we came up with Garlic Butter Spuds in the slow cooker! Our family and friends love it and you can serve it with anything you like.

Makes as many as you like • **Preparation** 5 mins • **Cook** 4–12 hours

Gather however many washed potatoes, skin on, as you would like to cook
Homemade or bought garlic butter
Sprigs of fresh flat-leaf (Italian) parsley

1. Slice the potato through the middle without cutting all the way through. Put as much garlic butter as you like on top. Add fresh parsley and grind over some salt and freshly ground back pepper.

2. Wrap the potatoes loosely with foil, making sure there are no gaps. Put the potatoes in the slow cooker. Cover and cook on LOW all day or on HIGH for four hours.

Rebecca Jacobson

BUTTERNUT PUMPKIN WITH GINGERED CREAM SAUCE

I love creamy food and I love this dish.

Serves 6 as a side • **Preparation** 10 mins • **Cook** 3–4 hours

1 butternut pumpkin (squash), cut into 1 cm (½ inch) slices, skin on
125 ml (4 fl oz/½ cup) thin (pouring) cream
125 ml (4 fl oz/½ cup) milk
¼ teaspoon freshly grated or ground ginger
2 tablespoons chopped chives
2 teaspoons cornflour (cornstarch)

1. Put the pumpkin slices in a slow cooker with ½ cup water. Cover and cook on HIGH for 3–4 hours, or until the pumpkin is soft but still keeps its shape.

2. Combine the cream, milk, ginger, chives and cornflour in a medium bowl. Cook in the microwave for 2 minutes, until boiling and thickened, and pour over the cooked pumpkin.

sherrie sutcliffe

GARLIC CREAMED RICE

An unusual dish that tastes delicious and is awesome served with kebabs, chicken or prawns.

Serves 6 as a side • **Preparation** 5 mins • **Cook** 2 hours

500 g (1 lb 2 oz) jasmine rice
3 x 300 ml (10 fl oz) tubs thickened cream
5 garlic cloves, crushed

1. Put the rice, cream and garlic in a slow cooker. Season with freshly ground black pepper and stir to combine. Cover and cook on HIGH for 2 hours, stirring occasionally.

2. Serve warm.

Merinda Haydon

INTENSE ROASTED GARLIC

I purchased a bulk lot of garlic because it was cheaper, and I was then left with the task of working out how to use it before it went bad. I planted one bulb in the garden and decided to try my hand at roasting the rest of the garlic for use at a later time. The smell throughout the house was amazing, and the flavour of the garlic after slow roasting was fabulous – sweet and almost nutty. It has proved a fabulous addition to the freezer (frozen in shot glasses, though you could probably freeze them in an ice cube tray).

Roasted garlic adds a wonderful shot of flavour to stews and other dishes, and is an easy short cut to making richly flavoured garlic bread. The flavour is incredibly intense and far less will be needed than if you were to use standard minced garlic. Roasting the garlic gives it a much sweeter flavour.

Makes approx 250 g (8 oz) • **Preparation** 20 mins • **Cook** 2 hours

6 bulbs garlic
2 tablespooons olive oil

1. Separate the garlic bulbs into cloves. With the side of a large knife, smash the cloves gently. Peel the cloves and put them all in a slow cooker. Splash over the olive oil, tossing the garlic cloves so they are well coated. Cover and cook on HIGH for 1 hour.

2. Stir the cloves, reduce the heat to LOW, cover and cook for 1 hour.

3. Use a potato masher to mash the cloves until smooth. Store in a sealed glass jar in the fridge or freeze in portion sizes in an ice cube tray or small plastic containers.

Christy Roth

⊫— PASTA SAUCE —●

I came up with this dish when I had an excess of cherry tomatoes. It's also a great opportunity to include lots of 'hidden vegies'.

Makes 12 cups • **Preparation** 15 mins • **Cook** 6 hours

2 kg (4 lb 8 oz) tomatoes, coarsely chopped
4 stalks celery, chopped
1 onion, diced
1 zucchini (courgette), grated
2 carrots, grated
150 g (5½ oz) green beans, topped and tailed
250 g (9 oz) mushrooms, sliced
250 ml (9 fl oz/1 cup) vegetable stock
½ cup tomato sauce (ketchup)
1 cup light brown sugar
2 tablespoons minced garlic
2 teaspoons dried mixed herbs
¼ cup Worcestershire sauce

1. Combine all ingredients in a slow cooker. Cover and cook on HIGH for 6 hours.

2. Allow to cool then blend or process to the desired consistency. Use as a sauce for pasta or 2 cups with mince to make savoury mince.

Narelle Youngs

TOMATO RELISH

Over many summers in our house, we would come home to the aroma of Mum's relish cooking on the stove. The smell brings back so many memories and I have now continued on the tradition. There is nothing like this relish served up on a piece of hot toast.

Makes about 12 cups • **Preparation** 45 mins • **Cook** 6 hours

1.8 kg (4 lb) tomatoes, finely chopped
5 large onions, finely chopped
1 tablespoon salt
900 g (2 lb) sugar
1 tablespoon curry paste, or to taste
1 tablespoon mustard powder
1 tablespoon ground turmeric
White vinegar, to cover
4–5 tablespoons plain (all-purpose) flour

1. Put the tomato and onion in a large bowl. Cover with water, add salt and leave overnight.

2. Drain the tomato mixture and put in a slow cooker.

3. In a bowl, combine the sugar, curry paste, mustard powder and turmeric and mix to a paste. Stir it into the tomato mixture in the slow cooker. Pour in enough white vinegar to cover mixture.

4. Cover and cook on LOW for 6 hours.

5. When 15 minutes from cooked, combine the flour with enough water to make a paste and add to the slow cooker; stir to thicken.

6. Allow the relish to cool and pour into clean sterilised jars.

Lynne Walters

SLOW-COOKED MUSHROOMS

A quick and simple side dish.

Serves 4 as a side • **Preparation** 5–10 mins • **Cook** 2–3 hours

12 whole button mushrooms
Olive oil, to drizzle
Dash of balsamic vinegar
Freshly ground black pepper

1. Put the mushrooms in layers in the bowl of a slow cooker. Drizzle a little olive oil, add a dash of balsamic and grind a little pepper on top. Cook on LOW for 2–3 hours.

2. Halfway through cooking, toss the mushrooms through the juices.

Felicity Barnett

CARAMELISED ONIONS

A great base for soups, stews or any meal that asks you to brown onions first. Keeping these on hand can cut down your slow cooker preparation time and bring a stronger flavour to slow-cooker meals.

Makes 2 cups • **Preparation** 5 mins • **Cook** 8–10 hours

5 brown onions, sliced 3 mm (⅛ inch) thick
2–3 tablespoons olive oil

1. Spread the onion over the base of a slow cooker. Drizzle the olive oil over the onion and mix through to coat well.

2. Cover, with a tea towel (dish towel) under the lid, and cook on LOW for 8–10 hours. Check and stir occasionally if you can.

NOTES:

- To make CHEAT'S BARBECUED ONIONS, add ½ teaspoon salt to bring out the flavour if you are making a large batch for a family barbecue or gathering. These can be made ahead, frozen and reheated on the day or served straight from the slow cooker.

- To make CONDIMENT ONIONS, add 2 tablespoons balsamic vinegar. Freeze small portions in ice cube trays to add to sandwiches, etc.

Justine Kamprad

VEGETARIAN CHILLI CON QUORN

As a vegetarian, it isn't always easy to find suitable products to use and certainly not a large variety. The Quorn product range allows for variety and for experimentation so I decided to adapt a meatlovers' recipe and use vegetarian mince. This is suitable for even those who can't imagine a meal without meat.

Serves 4 • **Preparation** 15 mins • **Cook** 8 hours

Chilli con carne flavouring sachet
1 kg (2 lb) bottled tomato pasta sauce
1 large eggplant (aubergine), coarsely chopped
3 brown onions, coarsely chopped
2 capsicums (peppers), coarsely chopped
1 cup water
2 cups corn kernels
2 packets Quorn Meatballs
2 cups cooked pasta of choice
Grated parmesan cheese, to serve

1. Put all the ingredients except the pasta and parmesan in a slow cooker. Cover and cook on LOW for 8 hours.

2. When 30 minutes before cooked, add the pasta and stir through.

3. Serve with freshly grated parmesan cheese on top.

Melissa Walton

THAI YELLOW VEGETABLE CURRY

I adore Thai food and would eat it every day if I could. One day I wanted to make a curry but didn't have meat so I tossed everything I had into the slow cooker and hoped for the best … Needless to say it worked a treat.

Serves 6 • Preparation 15 mins • Cook 4–6 hours

2 x 400 ml (14 fl oz) cans coconut cream
4 heaped tablespoons yellow curry paste
½ butternut pumpkin (squash), peeled and coarsely chopped
2 potatoes, peeled and coarsely chopped
1 cup cauliflower florets
800 g (1 lb 12 oz) tinned chickpeas, drained and rinsed
1 brown onion, coarsely chopped
2 carrots, coarsely chopped
Dash of fish sauce, to taste
150 g (5 oz) baby spinach leaves

1. Put all the ingredients except the baby spinach leaves in a slow cooker. Cover and cook on HIGH for 4 hours or LOW for 6 hours.

2. When 45 minutes from cooked, remove the lid to reduce the sauce.

3. When ready to serve, add the baby spinach leaves and stir through. Serve in bowls.

Kiera Taylor

SWEETS

APPLE CAKE

Perfect for morning tea guests you can also make this cake dessert with ice cream or custard.

Serves 6–8 • **Preparation** 15 mins • **Cook** 1½–2 hours

180 g (6 oz) butter, softened
⅔ cup caster (superfine) sugar
3 eggs, whisked
1 cup self-raising flour
300 g (10½ oz) tinned apple
Cinnamon, to sprinkle

1. Put the butter and sugar in a medium bowl. Using an electric mixer, cream the butter and sugar. Add the eggs and stir until combined. Add the flour and mix well.

2. Line the insert of a slow cooker, or a cake tin that fits into the slow cooker, with baking paper (see page 13 of Hints & Tips on use of cake tins in your slow cooker). Pour half the batter into the slow cooker or cake tin. Spread the tinned apple over the batter and sprinkle with cinnamon. Top with the remaining batter and smooth over.

3. If using a cake tin, put it in the slow cooker. Cover the slow cooker, with a tea towel (dish towel) under the lid, and cook on HIGH for 1½–2 hours.

Melodie Tapp

CARROT CAKE I

I love this cake because it's simple to make with my children. It turns out beautifully moist, yet light and fluffy. Perfect with an afternoon cuppa.

Serves 8–10 • **Preparation** 15 mins • **Cook** 1¼ hour

1 cup self-raising flour
½ cup plain (all-purpose) flour
1 teaspoon bicarbonate of soda (baking soda)
1½ teaspoons cinnamon
Dash of mixed spice
½ cup (firmly packed) light brown sugar
¼ cup vegetable oil
½ cup golden syrup (light treacle)
3 eggs
1 teaspoon vanilla extract or essence
300 g (10½ oz) carrots, grated
Cream cheese icing (optional)

1. Sift the flours, bicarbonate of soda, cinnamon and mixed spice into a large bowl.

2. Put the brown sugar, oil, golden syrup, eggs and vanilla in a medium bowl and whisk until combined.

3. Pour the wet mixture into the dry flour mixture and use a wooden spoon to stir until just combined. Add the carrot and mix through lightly.

4. Line the insert of a slow cooker, or a cake tin that fits into the slow cooker, with baking paper (see page 13 of Hints & Tips on use of cake tins in your slow cooker). Pour the mixture into the slow cooker or tin. If using a cake tin, put it in the slow cooker.

5. Cover the slow cooker, with a tea towel (dish towel) under the lid, and cook on HIGH for 1 hour 15 minutes, or when a skewer inserted in the middle of the cake comes out dry.

6. Transfer the cake to a plate and serve on its own or spread with cream cheese icing.

Ivy Gunn

➤— CARROT CAKE II —➤

My fiancé likes carrot cake the best. I'd never used my slow cooker for baking before when I tried this cake in it, but now I'll never make a carrot cake in the oven ever again.

Serves 12 • **Preparation** 15 mins • **Cook** 1½ hours

2 cups self-raising flour
1 cup coarsely chopped walnuts
1 large carrot, grated
1 cup vegetable oil
3 eggs, lightly beaten
1 cup (firmly packed) light brown sugar
1 teaspoon cinnamon
Cooking oil spray

1. Put all the ingredients in a large bowl and mix well.

2. Spray the insert of a slow cooker, or a cake tin that fits into the slow cooker, with cooking oil (see page 13 of Hints & Tips on use of cake tins in your slow cooker). Pour the batter into the slow cooker insert or cake tin fitted into the slow cooker.

3. Cover the slow cooker, with a tea towel (dish towel) under the lid, and cook on HIGH for 1½ hours, or when a skewer inserted in the middle of the cake comes out dry.

Ashlie Bland

THE NO EGGS, NO BUTTER, NO MILK, NO BOWL, NO PROBLEM CAKE

Perhaps this old recipe came from back when baking supplies were harder to come by and I have converted it to be made in a slow cooker. It is budget friendly and good for those with allergies to dairy or eggs. You don't even need a bowl!

Serves 8–10 • **Preparation** 15 mins • **Cook** 1½ hours

1½ cups plain (all-purpose) flour
3 tablespoons unsweetened cocoa
1 cup sugar
1 teaspoon bicarbonate of soda (baking soda)
½ teaspoon salt
1 teaspoon white vinegar
1 teaspoon vanilla extract
5 tablespoons vegetable oil
30 g (1 oz) flaked chocolate, to scatter
Ice cream, to serve

1. Put the flour, cocoa, sugar, bicarbonate of soda and salt in the insert of a slow cooker or a cake tin that fits within your slow cooker and combine (see page 13 of Hints & Tips on use of cake tins in your slow cooker). Make three holes – two small, one larger – in the dry ingredients. Pour the vinegar in one small hole, the vanilla in the other and the vegetable oil in the larger hole. Pour 250 ml (9 fl oz/1 cup) water over all. Mix well until smooth.

2. Cover, with a tea towel (dish towel) under the lid, and cook on HIGH for 1½ hours.

3. When 10 minutes from cooked, scatter the flaked chocolate over the top for an extra chocolate hit.

4. Serve with ice cream.

Cassandra van Breugel

BANANA, RICE, COCONUT & MANGO CAKE
(NO EGGS, DAIRY OR SUGAR)

A very heavy cake – it will stick to your ribs all day – that would also make a good dessert. I came up with this recipe because there was some leftover rice puddling and a few overripe bananas in my fridge, plus a can of mangoes in the cupboard. The rice pudding was made out of almond milk and the recipe is egg free. Eat the cake on its own or with custard or ice cream.

Serves 8–10 • **Preparation** 15 mins + 2 hours resting • **Cook** 4 hours

3 overripe bananas, mashed
1½ cups coconut rice pudding
1 cup mango pulp, plus ½ cup extra, to top
1 cup rolled (porridge) oats
⅓ cup desiccated coconut
1 cup wholemeal (whole-wheat) self-raising flour
1 cup self-raising flour
185 ml (6 fl oz/¾ cup) almond milk
1 teaspoon cornflour (cornstarch)

1. Put the mashed banana in a large bowl. Add the rice pudding and mix well. Add the remaining ingredients, except the cornflour, one at a time, mixing well between each addition. Cover the bowl and set aside the mixture to rest for 2 hours.

2. Line a slow cooker with baking paper. Pour the cake mixture into the slow cooker. Cover, with a tea towel (dish towel) under the lid, and cook on LOW for 4 hours.

3. Transfer the cooked cake to a plate. Combine the extra ½ cup mango pulp and the cornflour in a small bowl and spread over the top of the cake. This will set nicely.

Veronica Chandler

CHOCOLATE MOLTEN LAVA CAKE

Based on a recipe I found on the internet, I decided to try drinking chocolate instead of cocoa and found that it produced a thick and rich mud cake. Serve it warm with ice cream or cold on its own.

Serves 10 • **Preparation** 10 mins • **Cook** 2 hours

5 eggs
1 cup drinking chocolate, or unsweetened cocoa powder
⅔ cup pure maple syrup
⅔ cup chopped dark chocolate
½ cup frozen raspberries (optional)

1. Put the eggs, drinking chocolate and maple syrup in a large bowl and whisk together.

2. Transfer the mixture to a heatproof bowl that fits into a slow cooker. Put an egg ring or rack on the base of the slow cooker and pour 2.5 cm (1 inch) water into the slow cooker. Sit the bowl with the cake mixture on the egg ring or rack so it sits above the water.

3. Scatter the chopped chocolate and raspberries, if using, over the cake batter in the bowl. Cover, with a tea towel (dish towel) under the lid, and cook on HIGH for 2 hours.

Karen Stuckings

PINEAPPLE UPSIDE-DOWN CAKE

When I couldn't find a slow-cooker recipe for a pineapple upside-down cake on the internet, I decided to try making one with a sponge cake mixture, and put the pineapple in to give some moisture to the cake. We just let it cool and then sliced it for afternoon tea.

Serves 10–12 • Preparation 20 mins • Cook 1½–2 hours

60 g (2¼ oz) butter, softened, plus 50 g (1¾ oz) extra
½ cup (firmly packed) light brown sugar
432 g (15¼ oz) pineapple slices in natural juice (drain and reserve 2 tablespoons juice)
Glazed cherries (one for each pineapple ring)
3 eggs, at room temperature
Pinch of salt
175 g (6 oz) caster (superfine) sugar
125 g (4½ oz) self-raising flour

1. Line a cake tin that fits in your slow cooker with baking paper (see page 13 of Hints & Tips on use of cake tins in your slow cooker).

2. Combine the 60 g (2¼ oz) butter with the brown sugar in a small bowl. Spread this mixture over the bottom and inside of the lined cake tin. Push the pineapple slices, arranged evenly, into the brown sugar mixture on the inside of the tin, and place a glazed cherry in the middle of each pineapple slice.

3. Beat the eggs with the salt in a medium bowl. Add the caster sugar and beat until the mixture is thick and the sugar has dissolved. Fold in the flour gently using a spatula.

4. Heat the reserved pineapple juice in a cup in the microwave. Add the 50 g (1¾ oz) extra butter to the hot juice and stir until melted. Add half of the butter mixture to the cake mixture and stir until just combined, then add the remaining butter mixture and combine gently. Transfer the cake mixture to the cake tin.

5. Put an egg ring or rack on the base of the slow cooker and pour 2.5 cm (1 inch) water into the slow cooker. Sit the cake tin on the egg ring or rack so it sits above the water.

6. Cover, with a tea towel (dish towel) under the lid, and cook on HIGH for 1½–2 hours.

Karen Stuckings

⊫▬— SOFT DRINK CAKE —●

Great for people with allergies to dairy or eggs, this cake has carbonated drink to replace the eggs, milk and butter. There are endless combinations to be made, like red velvet cake made with cola and vanilla cake made with soda water. You use the cake mix dry – do not mix it as per packet instructions.

Serves 10 • **Preparation** 10 mins • **Cook** 1 hour 20 mins

1 packet vanilla cake mix
250 ml (9 fl oz/1 cup) creaming soda
Scoop of strawberry ice cream, to serve (optional)

1. Line a 1.5 litre (52 fl oz/6 cup) slow cooker with baking paper or line a cake tin that fits in your slow cooker with baking paper (see page 13 of Hints & Tips on use of cake tins in your slow cooker).

2. Put the cake mix in a medium bowl and pour over the just-opened creaming soda. Stir until just combined. (Do not over-mix as the bubbles help the cake to rise.)

3. Pour the cake batter into the lined slow cooker or cake tin. If using a cake tin, transfer it to the slow cooker.

4. Cover, with a tea towel (dish towel) under the lid, and cook on HIGH for 1 hour 20 minutes, turning the insert bowl every 20 minutes to avoid hot spots.

5. Serve the cake on its own or with a scoop of strawberry ice cream.

Melodie Tapp

TWO-INGREDIENT CAKE

Could a cake be any easier? By varying the cake mix flavour and fruit you will vary the cake, and there are so many great pairings to be made. Mango and vanilla, and chocolate and cherry are two of my favourites. You use the cake mix dry – do not mix it as per packet instructions.

Serves 8–10 • **Preparation** 5 mins • **Cook** 1½–2 hours

1 packet cake mix, flavour of your choice (I use 320 g mix or larger, up to 440 g)
425 g (15 oz) tinned fruit in juice, type of your choice

1. Line your slow cooker insert with non-stick baking paper.

2. In a bowl, combine the dry cake mix and the tin of fruit, juice included, and stir. Pour the mixture into the prepared slow cooker. You can also place a greased silicone cake tin in the slow cooker bowl and pour the mix into that (see page 13 of Hints & Tips on how to use cake tins in your slow cooker).

3. Cover slow cooker insert with a tea towel under the lid and cook on HIGH for 1½–2 hours, or until a skewer inserted into the middle of the cake comes out clean.

4. Remove cake and allow to cool completely on a wire rack before icing and decorating.

Paulene Christie

HALLOWEEN RED VELVET BROKEN GLASS CAKE

The red velvet broken glass cake is something I make for the kids for special events like Halloween. I make it red velvet because of the colour and texture. The sugar glass looks like broken glass with blood on it but you could make spiderwebs out of spun sugar or decorate with other items.

Serves 8 • Preparation 1½ hours **• Cook** 2½–3 hours

180 g (6 oz) butter, softened, plus extra, to grease
1½ cups caster (superfine) sugar
1 teaspoon vanilla extract
2 eggs
2½ cups self-raising flour
2 tablespoons unsweetened cocoa powder
250 ml (9 fl oz/1 cup) buttermilk
1 tablespoon white vinegar
1 teaspoon bicarbonate of soda (baking soda)
1 tablespoon red liquid food colouring
1 packet royal icing

SUGAR GLASS
1 cup glucose syrup
3½ cups white sugar
¼ teaspoon cream of tartar

EDIBLE BLOOD
½ cup corn syrup
½ cup cornflour (cornstarch)
Red and blue food colouring

1. Grease a square or rectangular silicone cake pan that will fit in the slow cooker you are using (see page 13 of Hints & Tips on use of cake tins in your slow cooker).

2. Use an electric mixer to beat the butter, sugar and vanilla in a large bowl until pale and creamy. Add the eggs, one at a time, beating well after each addition. Add the flour, cocoa powder and buttermilk, in batches, until well combined. Add the vinegar, bicarbonate of soda and food colouring and stir to combine.

3. Spoon the mixture into the prepared pan. Use the back of a spoon to smooth the surface. Cook in the slow cooker with a tea towel (dish towel) under the lid for 2½–3 hours on HIGH, testing with a skewer frequently until done.

4. Set aside to cool completely and then ice using royal icing.

5. To make the sugar glass, put 2 cups water with the glucose syrup, white sugar and cream of tartar in a large saucepan over medium–high heat. Bring to the boil, stirring constantly, then reduce the heat to medium and cook for 1 hour, stirring. The mixture will thicken as the water evaporates. When the mixture has thickened quickly pour it into a metal baking tray.

6. Set aside to cool until completely hardened. Break into 'shards' using a meat mallet.

7. To make the edible blood, combine the corn syrup and cornflour in a large bowl. Slowly stir in ¼ cup water, adding more if necessary, until the corn syrup mixture has thickened to the consistency of blood. Stir in the red and blue food colouring.

8. Stab the iced cake with a few shards of broken sugar glass. Drizzle on drops of edible blood to complete the effect.

Wayne Gatt

CARROT & DATE GINGERBREAD

We were low on ingredients and I wanted something yummy for a get-together with friends, so I put the list of ingredients I had on hand into an online search engine and after reading a variety of carrot cake and date and walnut loaf recipes, I decided to combine the two, plus add a Christmassy edge. After baking it that morning there was none left by evening! It was delicious served piping hot, cut into slices and spread with butter. We also toast it and eat it with honeyed ricotta and berries.

I use a food processor for the whole recipe, however you can also finely grate the carrot and chop the dates and nuts then mix in the other ingredients.

Serves 10 • Preparation 15 mins • Cook 1 hour

2 carrots
200 g (7 oz) dates
1 cup walnuts
1 teaspoon ground ginger
1½ teaspoons ground cinnamon
½ teaspoon freshly grated nutmeg
1 teaspoon vanilla extract
4 tablespoons molasses
2 eggs
¼ cup milk
¼ cup olive oil
1 cup wholemeal (whole-wheat) or spelt flour
1 cup oat flour
2½ teaspoons bicarbonate of soda (baking soda)

1. Using a food processor, process the carrot to a pulp and add the dates until combined. Add the walnuts and pulse quickly until coarsely chopped. Add the ginger, cinnamon, nutmeg, vanilla and molasses and pulse until combined. Add the eggs, milk and oil and pulse until combined. Add the flours and bicarbonate of soda and pulse until just combined.

2. Pour the mixture into a silicone loaf tin. Put the tin in a slow cooker (see page 13 of Hints & Tips on use of cake tins in your slow cooker). Cover, with a tea towel (dish towel) under the lid, and cook on HIGH for 1 hour, or until a skewer inserted into the middle of the cake comes out clean. Cook for an extra 30 minutes if necessary and check again.

Rebecca M Davies

LEMON-LIME CURD
BAKED CHEESECAKE

If you don't like the tartness of this cheesecake, go for plain lemon, or replace the lemon-lime curd with caramel, chopped fruit or whole berries.

Serves 8 • Preparation 15 mins • Cook 3 hours

250 g (9 oz) sweet biscuits
80 g (2¾ oz) butter, melted
500 g (1 lb 2 oz) cream cheese, softened
½ cup caster (superfine) sugar
2 teaspoons vanilla extract
3 eggs
300 ml (10 fl oz) sour cream
375 ml (13 fl oz) lemon-lime curd (homemade or bought)

1. To make the base, pulse the biscuits in a food processor or crush with a rolling pin. Combine the biscuit crumbs and melted butter in a medium bowl. The mixture will be quite crumbly but don't add more butter.

2. Prepare a cake tin that will fit in the slow cooker you are using. Line the base and side with foil and then baking paper. Press the crumbs firmly into the base of the tin. Put the tin in the fridge to chill.

3. To make the filling, put the cream cheese, sugar and vanilla in a large bowl and beat with electric beaters until smooth. Add the eggs and beat until smooth. Fold in the sour cream. Set aside a quarter of the curd and fold the rest into the filling mixture.

4. Pour the filling on top of the chilled base. Smooth the top and swirl the reserved curd through it.

5. Put an egg ring, rack or scrunched up foil balls on the base of the slow cooker and pour 2.5 cm (1 inch) water into the slow cooker. Sit the cake tin on the egg ring, rack or foil balls so it sits above the water. Cover, with a tea towel (dish towel) under the lid, and cook on HIGH for 3 hours, or until the cheesecake is firm when a knife is inserted in the centre.

Karen Stuckings

BOILED PINEAPPLE FRUIT CAKE

My mum used to make dozens of these cakes for family and I thought I would attempt to carry on where she left off. It is such a wonderfully moist and luscious cake, and such a versatile recipe, as you can add or subtract whatever you do or don't want. I add nuts, either slivered almonds or pine nuts, and the rum, which helps it last that little bit longer. And I have adapted it for the slow cooker, and it can also be made as mini Christmas cakes in muffin tins.

Serves 10–12 • **Preparation** 15 mins • **Cook** 5 hours

500 g (1 lb 2 oz) dried mixed fruit
440 g (15½ oz) tinned unsweetened crushed pineapple
1 cup sugar
125 ml (4 fl oz/½ cup) rum
125 g (4½ oz) butter, chopped
1 teaspoon mixed spice
½ teaspoon ground cinnamon
1 teaspoon bicarbonate of soda (baking soda)
2 eggs, beaten
1 cup self-raising flour
1 cup plain (all-purpose) flour
Nuts (optional)

1. Put the dried fruit, crushed pineapple, sugar, rum, butter, mixed spice and cinnamon in a large saucepan over medium–high heat. Boil for 5 minutes. Add the bicarbonate of soda, turn off the heat and allow the mixture to cool.

2. When the mixture is cool, add the eggs and flour and stir to combine.

3. Line the insert of a slow cooker with non-stick baking paper or use a cake tin that fits in the slow cooker (see page 13 of Hints & Tips on use of cake tins in your slow cooker). Pour the cake mixture into the prepared slow cooker insert or cake tin, and top with nuts, if using. Cook on HIGH for 4–5 hours.

4. Transfer to a wire rack to cool. Store in an airtight container.

Lynne Walters

THREE-INGREDIENT CHRISTMAS CAKE

I'd only ever made this recipe that I found on the internet in the oven, and when I gave it a go converting it to a slow-cooker recipe, it turned out perfectly. It's very moist, full of fruit and very tasty, and it really is incredibly easy to make.

Serves 8–10 • **Preparation** 5 mins + 24 hours soaking • **Cook** 8 hours

1 kg (2 lb 4 oz) dried mixed fruit
750 ml (26 fl oz/3 cups) iced coffee flavoured milk
2 cups self-raising flour

1. Put the fruit in a large bowl, add the iced coffee and mix. Cover and put in the fridge to soak for 24 hours.

2. Add the flour to the soaked fruit and mix well.

3. Line the insert of a slow cooker with baking paper. Add the cake mixture and smooth the top. Cover and cook for 4 hours on LOW.

4. Increase temperature setting to HIGH and cook for another 4 hours.

sherrie sutcliffe

ICED FINGER BUNS

It took some experimenting but finally, after making a normal loaf of bread, I added some caster (superfine) sugar and milk, and I got a light and soft bun that was very close to the store-bought variety.

Makes 7 • Preparation 10 mins + 30 mins rising • Cook 1½ hours

3 cups self-raising flour
2 x 7 g sachets dried yeast (½ oz)
½ cup caster (superfine) sugar
1½ cups slightly warm milk
ICING
⅔ cup icing (confectioners') sugar
2 drops red food colouring
Coloured sprinkles or desiccated coconut, for decoration

1. Combine the flour, yeast and sugar in a large bowl. Add the milk and bring together to form a dough. Knead the dough on a lightly floured work surface until it stays together. Cover the bowl with a clean tea towel (dish towel) and set aside in a warm place to rise for 30 minutes.

2. Knead the dough again then separate into 7 evenly sized pieces. Roll each piece into a ball, then into a sausage shape, then flatten down with your hand to make a finger bun.

3. Line the base of a slow cooker with baking paper. Put the buns in the slow cooker. Cover, with a tea towel (dish towel) under the lid, and cook on HIGH for 1½ hours, checking at 1 hour. Allow to cool before icing.

4. To make the icing, combine the icing sugar with 2 drops of red food colouring in a small bowl. Gradually stir in water, one teaspoon at a time, until the icing is smooth but not too runny. Ice the buns using a knife and then dip the iced side into a bowl of sprinkles or desiccated coconut.

Stephanie Wilmen

HOT CROSS BUNS

Next time I cook these I will pop the finished buns in a hot oven or under the grill (broiler) for a few minutes to brown off the top.

Makes 12 • **Preparation** 20 mins + 2 hours rising • **Cook** 1 hour

10 g (¼ oz) dried yeast
1 teaspoon caster (superfine) sugar, plus 2 tablespoons and ⅓ cup extra
185 ml (6 fl oz/¾ cup) warm milk
3½ cups plain (all-purpose) flour, plus ½ cup extra
150 g (5½ oz) sultanas (golden raisins)
50 g (1¾ oz) dried dates, diced
2 teaspoons mixed spice
125 ml (4 fl oz/½ cup) cold milk
50 g (1¾ oz) butter, melted
1 egg, lightly whisked

1. Put the yeast, the 1 teaspoon of sugar and warm milk in a bowl and whisk to combine. Set aside for 10 minutes, or until the mixture becomes frothy and bubbles form on the top.

2. Put the flour, sultanas, dates, the 2 tablespoons of caster sugar, mixed spice and a pinch of salt in a large mixing bowl. Combine and set aside.

3. Put the cold milk, butter and egg in a medium bowl and whisk together lightly. Add to the yeast mixture and stir to combine.

4. Make a well in the dry ingredients and gently pour in the yeast liquid. Fold to combine then work the dough together in the bowl with your hands.

5. Turn the dough out onto a lightly floured work surface and knead for 10–15 minutes. Put the dough in a clean, greased bowl and cover with plastic wrap. Set aside in a warm place for 1½ hours, until doubled in size.

6. Punch down the dough in the centre with your fist. Turn out onto a lightly floured work surface and knead for 2 minutes. Separate the dough into 12 equal parts (divide it into half, then half again to get quarters, then break each quarter into three).

7. Line the insert of a slow cooker with baking paper. Put the buns side by side with a small gap in between in the slow cooker. Cover with a clean tea towel (dish towel) and place in a warm place for 30 minutes, until doubled in size.

8. Mix the extra ½ cup of flour with 170 ml (5½ fl oz/⅔ cup) water to make a paste and transfer to a plastic bag or piping bag. If using a plastic bag, snip a small hole in one corner. Pipe a cross on the top of each bun.

9. Cover, with a tea towel (dish towel) under the lid, and cook on HIGH for 1 hour, or until a skewer inserted in the middle comes out clean and the bottoms are nicely browned. The buns have a lovely soft bread consistency when torn. Use the baking paper to lift the buns out of the slow cooker and place them on a wire rack to cool.

10. Meanwhile, make a glaze. Put the extra ⅓ cup of caster sugar and ⅓ cup water in a saucepan over medium–high heat. Bring to the boil, stirring, and allow to boil for 5 minutes while stirring continuously.

11. Brush the glaze onto the cooling hot cross buns.

Paulene Christie

CHOCOLATE CHOC-CHIP HOT CROSS BUNS

I admit it. I can't go past the chocolate variety of hot cross buns when I see them in the shops. So once I had made my own regular version (see page 287), I had to make the chocolate choc-chip variety too!

Makes 12 buns • **Preparation** 20 mins + 2 hours for rising • **Cook** 1 hour

10 g (¼ oz) dried yeast
1 teaspoon caster (superfine) sugar, plus 2 tablespoons extra
185 ml (6 fl oz/¾ cup) warm milk
4 cups plain (all-purpose) flour
1 tablespoon unsweetened cocoa powder
½ teaspoon ground cinnamon
¼ teaspoon freshly grated or ground nutmeg
1 cup chocolate chips
125 ml (4 fl oz/½ cup) cold milk
50 g (butter), melted
1 egg, lightly whisked
¼ cup chopped dark chocolate (optional, for chocolate crosses)

1. Follow the method for Hot Cross Buns (see page 287), adding the cocoa, cinnamon, nutmeg and chocolate chips to the flour in Step 2 to make up the dry ingredients.

2. If you wish to pipe on chocolate crosses in Step 8, melt the dark chocolate in the microwave. Working fast, transfer the melted chocolate to a plastic bag or piping bag. If using a plastic bag, snip a small hole in one corner. Pipe a cross on the top of each bun.

3. Continue with step 9. Use Steps 10 and 11 if you are opting for a glazed finish instead of chocolate crosses.

Paulene Christie

THREE-INGREDIENT TRADITIONAL SCONES

School lunches sometimes put the pressure on, particularly when the cupboards seem to be bare. These scones were created simply because I needed something for my daughter's lunches for the week. They were so simple to make, and the ingredients are pretty well always on hand. They are easy to jazz up with the addition of some sultanas, dried fruit or other flavours. And the kids love them!

Makes 12 • **Preparation** 15 mins • **Cook** 1½ hours

4 cups self-raising flour
40 g (1½ oz) butter, softened
1¾ cups milk

1. Sift the flour into a bowl.

2. If you forgot to let the butter warm to room temperature first you can cheat, and with a grater, using the fine grate section, grate butter into the bowl.

3. Add the butter and, using your fingers, work the butter and the flour together until there are no more lumps and it has the consistency of fine crumbs. Make a well and add the milk, stirring with a butter knife until combined. Bring the dough together with your hands and turn out onto a lightly floured work surface.

4. Line a slow cooker with baking paper and preheat to HIGH.

5. Work the dough until it is solid (but do not overwork it, or else the scones will be tough) and roll it out to about 3 cm (1¼ inches) thick. Use a cookie cutter or a wine glass, as I did, to cut 12 circles from the dough. You may need to recombine the dough scraps to do this.

6. Put the scones in the slow cooker, with a little space between them. Cover, with a tea towel (dish towel) under the lid, and cook on HIGH for 1½ hours.

7. Serve the scones warm or cold with butter and jam, or pretty well anything you want to put on them.

Christy Roth

⇒— FRUIT & NUT BREAD —●

Friends were coming over and I didn't want to race out to the shops so I rummaged around in the pantry and put together this scrumptious bread with ingredients that needed to be used up. It is delicious served warm with butter and makes a nice afternoon snack.

Serves 4–6 • **Preparation** 15 mins • **Cook** 1½ hours

3 cups plain (all-purpose) flour
300 g (9½ oz) unsalted trail mix
2 teaspoons dried yeast
2 tablespoons ground cinnamon, plus ½ teaspoon extra, to sprinkle
½ cup sugar, plus 1 tablespoon extra, to sprinkle
About 1½ cups almond milk

1. Combine all the ingredients in a large bowl, adding the almond milk gradually until the mixture is well combined and moist. Transfer the mixture to a slow cooker. Mix the extra cinnamon and sugar in a small bowl. Sprinkle the mixture over the cake batter.

2. Cover, with a tea towel (dish towel) under the lid, and cook on HIGH for 1½ hours.

Melissa Walton

➤━ BANANA LOAF ━●

My partner enjoys having bananas, his favourite fruit, sitting in the fruit bowl. I like bananas too but when they turn a little bit brown my partner is the only one who will touch them. He works away from home for a week at a time, so if I find brown bananas they are usually tossed straight in the bin! But one day I decided it was time to stop wasting money and throwing out the brown bananas and instead looked in my cupboard to see how I could use them with what was on hand. I came up with this recipe which exceeded my expectations.

Serves 10 • **Preparation** 15 mins • **Cook** 1½ hours

2 overripe bananas
½ cup (firmly packed) light brown sugar
2 eggs
1½ tablespoons vegetable oil
2 cups self-raising flour
185 ml (6 fl oz/¾ cup) skim milk
Dash of vanilla extract
Golden syrup (light treacle), to drizzle

1. Combine all the ingredients except the golden syrup in a medium bowl. Transfer the mixture to a loaf tin and put inside a slow cooker. (Do not elevate the tin or add water.)

2. Cover, with a tea towel (dish towel) under the lid, and cook on HIGH for 1½ hours, or until a skewer inserted into the centre of the loaf comes out clean.

3. Serve with a drizzle with golden syrup.

Zara Charles

CARAMEL SCROLLS

Combining the ideas behind a three-ingredient dough recipe for savoury scrolls and a condensed milk caramel in the can recipe, I came up with these sweet scrolls. I was pleasantly surprised with the result and my kids gobbled them up for afternoon tea.

Serves 8–10 • Preparation 10 mins • Cook 1½–2 hours

2 cups self-raising flour
1 cup Greek-style yoghurt
Coconut sugar, to sprinkle (substitute with another type of sugar, or omit)
380 g (13½ oz) tinned caramel
3–4 tablespoons icing (confectioners') sugar
2 drops vanilla extract

1. Combine the flour and yoghurt in a medium bowl. Bring together the mixture with your hands and knead, sprinkling over some coconut sugar as you do, if you like, on a lightly floured work surface until smooth.

2. Roll out the mixture to a 20 x 30 cm (8 x 12 inch) rectangle. Spread the caramel over the dough using a knife. Roll the dough into a long sausage shape. Cut into 3 cm (1¼ inch) portions.

3. Arrange the dough scrolls in the base of a slow cooker and allow them to rest for 10 minutes.

4. Cover, with a tea towel (dish towel) under the lid, and cook on HIGH for 1½–2 hours.

5. To get a little crunch on top, I put the slow cooker insert in the oven at 180°C (350°F) for about 5 minutes. But you could omit this step.

6. Transfer the scrolls to a wire rack to cool.

7. To make a glaze for the top, combine the icing sugar, vanilla and a few drops of water in a small bowl. Drizzle the glaze over the scrolls.

Nathalie Goodwin

═══ CHOCOLATE CROISSANT ROLLS ═══

Craving something sweet on a scorching-hot day, I decided to make a sweet without using my oven. Always having a soft spot for chocolate croissants, I adapted an oven recipe and came up with these made in the slow cooker. As I am not really skilled at making proper croissant shapes, I call them Chocolate Croissant Rolls. But my husband thinks this is the best thing yet I've made in the slow cooker.

Makes 8 • Preparation 10 mins • Cook 1¼ hours

2 sheets frozen puff pastry, thawed
225 g (8 oz) chocolate chips

1. Line the base of a slow cooker with baking paper.

2. Cut each sheet of puff pastry into 2 rectangles. Cut each rectangle into 2 triangles.

3. Sprinkle a handful of chocolate chips on the puff pastry triangles and roll up. Squash one end so the baking chips are contained. Do this for every triangle.

4. Arrange the pastries on the base of the slow cooker. Cover, with a tea towel (dish towel) under the lid, and cook on HIGH for 45 minutes.

5. Turn the croissants over and cook for another 30 minutes on HIGH.

6. Serve the croissant rolls warm to enjoy the sensation of the chocolate melting in your mouth.

Roslyn Potter

FRENCH TOAST STICKS WITH CREAM CHEESE & MAPLE SYRUP

The French toast sticks are a classy version of French toast. It can be eaten as a sweet or for breakfast. It is a light dance on the palette because it uses cream cheese instead of cream, and it is not a heavy meal as you can use low fat cream cheese and fresh berries with a drizzle of honey or maple syrup. Perfect for a weekend meal or a snack in a picnic basket.

Serves 4 • **Preparation** 10 mins • **Cook** 1 hour + 5 mins grilling

16 slices white bread, crusts removed
225 g (8 oz) cream cheese
¾ cup icing (confectioners') sugar
¾ cup melted butter
1 cup sugar
2 teaspoons ground cinnamon
Maple syrup, to serve

1. Use a rolling pin to flatten each slice of bread.

2. Use an electric mixer to beat the cream cheese and icing sugar.

3. Put the melted butter in a bowl. Combine the sugar and cinnamon in another bowl.

4. Spread 1–2 tablespoons of the sweetened cream cheese on the flattened bread slices and roll up.

5. Dip the rolled bread firstly in the melted butter and then roll in the cinnamon sugar.

6. Arrange the cinnamon-sugar coated bread rolls in a slow cooker. Cover, with a tea towel (dish towel) under the lid, and cook on HIGH for 1 hour.

7. Preheat a grill (broiler) to medium–high. When the cinnamon-sugar coated rolls are cooked, transfer them to a baking tray and grill (broil) until golden. Drizzle with maple syrup and eat while warm.

Wayne Gatt

MUFFIN JAM DONUTS

Muffin jam donuts aren't fried and so are healthy versions of normal jam donuts. They are perfect with homemade low-GI jam made with seasonal home-grown fruits. The kids love them and parents can control the sugar content. They can be eaten warm or cold with a nice beverage on the side, and depending on their size they can be a dessert or a treat.

Makes 6 • **Preparation** 10 mins • **Cook** 1 hour

300 g (10½ oz/2 cups) self-raising flour
⅔ cup caster (superfine) sugar, plus ½ cup extra, for topping
80 ml (2½ fl oz/⅓ cup) vegetable oil
1 large egg
175 ml (5¾ fl oz) buttermilk
1 teaspoon vanilla extract
3 teaspoons good-quality strawberry jam (jelly)
100 g (3½ oz) unsalted butter
1 teaspoon ground cinnamon

1. Grease a 6-hole silicone muffin pan.

2. Sift the flour into a medium bowl. Add a pinch of salt and the ⅔ cup of caster sugar and combine. In a jug, combine the vegetable oil, egg, buttermilk and vanilla extract. Add the egg and buttermilk mixture to the dry mixture and stir until only just combined.

3. Divide the mixture evenly between the six muffin holes. Make an indent in the centres and fill each with ½ teaspoon strawberry jam.

4. Place a wire rack in the base of a slow cooker. Put the muffin tray on top. Cover, with a tea towel (dish towel) under the lid, and cook on HIGH for 1 hour.

5. Meanwhile, melt the butter. Combine the ½ cup extra sugar and the cinnamon in a medium bowl. When the muffins are cool enough to handle, brush with the melted butter and roll in the cinnamon sugar. Serve while still warm.

Wayne Gatt

CRÈME BRÛLÉE

When I made this dessert for my partner, it looked and tasted just like crème brûlée you might have in a five-star French restaurant – a decadent, silky smooth, melt-in-your-mouth, pure heaven dessert. I was so proud of myself. My partner still cannot stop raving about it and requests this dessert on a weekly basis.

Serves 4 • **Preparation** 15 mins + 4 hours cooling and setting • **Cook** 2 hours

600 ml (20 fl oz) thickened (whipping) cream
1–2 tablespoons vanilla bean paste or 1–2 vanilla beans, split lengthways and
    seeds scraped
6 egg yolks
1–2 tablespoons caster (superfine) sugar, plus extra, for sprinkling

1. Add 2.5 cm (1 inch) boiling water to a slow cooker and turn on to LOW setting.

2. Put the cream and vanilla bean paste or vanilla bean and seeds in a medium saucepan over medium heat. Bring the cream mixture to the boil, removing the saucepan from the heat as soon as it starts to bubble.

3. Put the egg yolks and sugar in a medium bowl and whisk until the sugar dissolves and the mixture is creamy in texture.

4. Slowly and gradually add the hot cream mixture to the egg yolk mixture, whisking continuously as you do.

5. Pour the cream mixture through a sieve into four ramekins.

6. Carefully put the ramekins with the cream mixture into the water bath in the slow cooker. Cover and cook for 2 hours on LOW.

7. When the sides are set but the crème brûlée is still wobbly in the centre, remove the ramekins from the slow cooker. Set aside to cool for 5 minutes then transfer to the fridge to set for 2–4 hours minimum.

8. When ready to serve, sprinkle the extra caster sugar over the top. Use a blow torch to caramelise the sugar. Serve immediately.

Emilia Perito

CHOCOLATE SELF-SAUCING PUDDING

My daughters' favourite recipe to make on a Friday movie night, it is very indulgent. We serve it with vanilla ice cream or homemade custard.

Serves 8 • Preparation 15 mins • Cook 1½–2 hours

1½ cups self-raising flour
6 tablespoons unsweetened cocoa powder
¾ cup white sugar
1 cup milk
1 teaspoon vanilla extract
150 g (5½ oz) butter, melted
1 egg, beaten
1 cup (firmly packed) light brown sugar
2½ cups hot water

1. Sift the flour and 3 tablespoons of the cocoa into a large mixing bowl. Add the white sugar and stir. Add the milk, vanilla, melted butter and egg and stir well to combine.

2. Grease the insert of a small slow cooker. If your slow cooker is large, put 2.5 cm (1 inch) of boiling water in the base and grease a cake tin that will sit in It. Put the pudding batter in the slow cooker or cake tin and smooth the top.

3. Mix the remaining cocoa, brown sugar and hot water, and pour over the back of a tablespoon over the top of the batter.

4. Cover, with a tea towel (dish towel) under the lid, and cook on HIGH for 1½–2 hours. The pudding is ready when the top looks like a cooked cake.

Lilah-Rose Cosh

CHOCOLATE FUDGE SELF-SAUCING PUDDING

My daughter likes chocolate – who doesn't? – but is unable to eat a lot of it. So we tried to make a pudding using carob powder instead of cocoa powder and this was the end result.

Serves 4–6 • **Preparation** 10–15 mins • **Cook** 2–2½ hours

1 cup gluten-free plain (all-purpose) flour
½ cup (firmly packed) light brown or coconut sugar, plus ¾ cup extra
2 tablespoons carob powder, plus ¼ cup extra
2 teaspoons baking powder
½ teaspoon salt
½ cup lactose-free milk
2 tablespoons olive oil
1 teaspoon vanilla extract
1½ cups hot water

1. Put the flour, ½ cup of sugar, 2 tablespoons of carob powder, baking powder and salt in a large bowl and mix well.

2. Add the milk, olive oil and vanilla to the dry ingredients and mix until smooth. Pour the batter evenly into a slow cooker.

3. Mix the extra sugar and extra carob in a small bowl or jug. Add the hot water and stir until smooth. Pour the mixture evenly over the batter in the slow cooker.

4. Cover and cook on HIGH for 2–2½ hours, or until a toothpick inserted in the centre of the pudding comes out clean.

NOTES:

Cocoa powder can be substituted for the carob powder.

Put a tea towel (dish towel) under the lid when cooking for a thicker, fudgier sauce, or go without for a runnier sauce.

Felicity Barnett

CARAMEL SELF-SAUCING PUDDING

I have always enjoyed chocolate self-saucing pudding but was getting bored with it. Everyone loves caramel so I thought I'd give it a go, and I came up with this pudding. I made it in a 3.5 litre (118 fl oz/14 cup) slow cooker and the pudding was about 2.5 cm (1 inch) thick – next time I will try it in the 1.5 litre (52 fl oz/6 cup) slow cooker.

Serves 4 • Preparation 10 mins • Cook 1½ hours

1 cup plain (all-purpose) flour
2 teaspoons baking powder
½ cup white sugar
½ cup milk
½ cup (lightly packed) light brown sugar
1½ cups hot water
2 tablespoons butter, melted

1. Grease the insert of a slow cooker.

2. Put the flour, baking powder, white sugar and milk in a medium bowl and mix well. Transfer this mixture to the slow cooker.

3. Combine the brown sugar, hot water and melted butter in a small bowl or jug and pour gently over the mixture in the slow cooker.

4. Cover, with a tea towel (dish towel) under the lid, and cook on HIGH for 1½ hours.

Sarah Anderson

PEACH COBBLER

The reason I love this peach cobbler is because it's so quick and easy to prepare. And with only three ingredients, you can't complain. You can let it cool and cut it or scoop it straight out of the slow cooker while it's warm and serve it with ice cream or custard.

Serves 6–8 • **Preparation** 5 mins • **Cook** 2 hours

Cooking oil spray
410 g (14½ oz) tinned peaches in juice, drained, 2 tablespoons juice reserved
1 packet vanilla cake mix
1 cup ready-made custard, plus extra, to serve (optional)
Ice cream, to serve (optional)

1. Line the insert of a slow cooker with baking paper and spray with cooking oil. Arrange the drained peaches over the base of the slow cooker insert.

2. Put the dry cake mix, reserved juice from the peaches and custard in a bowl. Combine and pour the mixture over the peaches.

3. Cover, with a tea towel (dish towel) under the lid, and cook on HIGH for 2 hours, rotating the insert every 20 minutes if you can.

4. Allow the peach cobbler to cool in the slow cooker. Lift it out using the baking paper. Peel away the baking paper carefully as the peaches may stick.

5. Serve in bowls with custard or ice cream, if you like.

Tiffany Eagles

COCONUT CREAMED RICE

I added the coconut milk to this recipe I made up because I adore the flavour and I thought it would make the rice perfect with tropical fruit. I love serving it with fresh mango.

Serves 6 • **Preparation** 10 mins • **Cook** 3½–4 hours

400 ml (14 fl oz) tinned coconut milk
600 ml (20 fl oz) skim milk
½ cup white rice
⅓ cup sugar
1 teaspoon vanilla extract
Ice cream, tropical fruit and ground cinnamon, to serve (optional)

1. Put all the ingredients in the insert of a slow cooker. Cover and cook on LOW for 3½–4 hours, stirring every 20–30 minutes, until the rice is cooked and the liquid is absorbed.

2. Serve in bowls with ice cream and tropical fruit and sprinkled with cinnamon, or whatever you please.

Morgan Jane

⊫— SALTED CARAMEL CREAMED RICE —●

Who doesn't like salted caramel? I love creamed rice as well, so I played around with the ingredients and came up with this amazing dish that's yummy but not too sweet.

Serves 6–8 • **Preparation** 5 mins • **Cook** 2 hours

380 g (13½ oz) tinned caramel
1–2 teaspoons salt, mixed into tinned caramel
2 cups arborio rice
1 tablespoon vanilla extract
1.5 litres (52 fl oz/6 cups) milk
Ice cream and extra caramel sauce, to serve

1. Put all the ingredients in the insert of a slow cooker. Cover and cook on HIGH for 2 hours, stirring every 20 minutes if you can. Add more milk if the mixture needs it as it cooks.

2. Serve with ice cream and a drizzle of caramel, if you like.

Angelique Casotti

MAVIS'S BANANA PLUM PUDDING

Christmas was my mother's favourite time of the year, and she'd always go all out when making Christmas lunch. This was her twist on classic Christmas pudding, and the best part of lunch. The bananas make it incredibly moist and I still make it for my family at Christmas as a way of paying homage to her. And using the slow cooker also saves precious stove and oven space on Christmas Day.

Serves 8–10 • Preparation 15 mins • Cook 6–7 hours

5 very ripe bananas
1 egg, beaten
2 cups stale breadcrumbs (use day old-bread and process in a food processor)
1 tablespoon unsweetened cocoa powder
2 cups dried mixed fruit
1 teaspoon bicarbonate of soda (baking soda)
1 tablespoon rum, brandy or orange juice
Cream, ice cream, custard and grated chocolate, to serve (optional)

1. Put the bananas in a large mixing bowl and mash well. Add the egg and combine well. Add the breadcrumbs and cocoa and mix well. Add the dried fruit and combine well.

2. Combine the bicarbonate of soda with the rum and stir into the fruit mixture.

3. Grease a pudding basin (1.5–2 litre/52–70 fl oz/6–8 cup). Transfer the pudding mixture to the basin and secure the lid of the basin. (If there's no lid, cover with a small plate and secure with cooking string.)

4. Put the pudding basin in the slow cooker, making sure the side of the basin is not touching the side of the slow cooker. Add enough water to the slow cooker to reach three-quarters of the way up the side of the pudding basin.

5. Cover the slow cooker and cook on HIGH for 1 hour.

6. Reduce the temperature setting to LOW and cook for 5–6 hours, checking the water level at 2–3 hours and topping up with boiling water if necessary.

7. Carefully remove the pudding basin from the slow cooker. Check the pudding is cooked by inserting a skewer into the centre. Leave the pudding to cool in the basin. When ready to serve, invert onto a serving plate and serve with cream, ice cream or custard (or all three!). Grate some chocolate over the top too, if you like.

Narelle Nightscales

JAM PUDDING IN A MUG

Here's something a bit different I tried. Simple to make and serve for family and guests.

Serves 4 • **Preparation** 5 mins • **Cook** 1–2 hours

2 tablespoons butter, melted
½ cup sugar
2 eggs, beaten
1½ cups self-raising flour
¾ cup milk
4 tablespoons jam (jelly) of choice
Cream, to serve

1. Combine the butter, sugar, eggs, flour and milk in a medium bowl. Divide the mixture between 4 coffee mugs, to just under halfway (too much will cause a mess during cooking). Add a tablespoon of jam to each mug.

2. Put enough boiling water in a slow cooker to just cover the base. Put the coffee mugs in the slow cooker. Cover and cook on HIGH for 1–2 hours.

3. Serve the puddings in the mugs, drizzled with cream.

Sherrie Sutcliffe

APPLE DUMPLINGS

I had some Granny Smith apples and wanted to create a dessert. Not your typical stewed apples, flour dumplings or apple turnovers, this version is a bit of all three.

Serves 4 • **Preparation** 20 mins + resting time • **Cook** 2 hours

4 Granny Smith apples, peeled, cored and cut in half
Cream or ice cream, to serve

PASTRY
1½ cups self-raising flour
½ cup plain (all-purpose) flour
125 g (4½ oz) butter, plus extra for greasing
1 tablespoon sugar
1 teaspoon ground cinnamon
2–3 tablespoons cold water with a squeeze of lemon juice

SYRUP
1 cup (firmly packed) light brown sugar
1 teaspoon butter
Juice of ½ lemon
250 ml (9 fl oz/1 cup) water

1. To make the pastry, combine the ingredients in a food processor or bring together in a bowl and knead by hand. Wrap the dough in cling (plastic) wrap and put in the fridge to rest for 15–20 minutes. Meanwhile, prepare the apples.

2. Remove the dough from the fridge and cut into 8 portions. Roll out each portion into a thin sheet and wrap around a peeled apple half.

3. Grease a slow cooker insert well with butter. Put the dough-wrapped apples, rounded side up, in the slow cooker insert.

4. To make the syrup, put the brown sugar, butter, lemon juice and 250 ml (9 fl oz/1 cup) water in a small saucepan over medium–high heat. Bring to the boil, reduce the heat to medium–low and simmer for 3–4 minutes.

5. Pour the syrup carefully between the apple dumplings in the slow cooker. Cover, with a tea towel (dish towel) under the lid, and cook on HIGH for 2 hours.

6. Check if the apples are cooked using a skewer. The apples should be soft and cooked through but not mushy, and the pastry should be cooked.

7. Serve the apple dumplings with cream or ice cream.

Sandra Rielly

GOLDEN SYRUP PUDDING

What started out as an attempt at doing allergen-friendly golden syrup dumplings for my daughter became a lovely moist pudding when they started merging together in the slow cooker – so I figured 'what the heck?' and poured it all in. This has become a favourite on a cold night.

Serves 4–6 • **Preparation** 25 mins • **Cook** 1½ hours

1¼ cups gluten-free self-raising flour
30 g (1 oz) lactose-free butter
⅓ cup golden syrup (light treacle)
100 ml (3 fl oz) lactose-free milk, warmed

SAUCE
30 g (1 oz) lactose-free butter
¾ cup (firmly packed) light brown sugar
½ cup golden syrup (light treacle)
1⅓ cups water

1. Preheat a slow cooker to HIGH.

2. To make the sauce, combine the butter, sugar, golden syrup and water in a glass jug and heat in a microwave on high until dissolved (approx 1 minute), or over a high heat in a pan on the stovetop. Pour into a slow cooker and set aside for 20 minutes while preparing the pudding mixture.

3. Put the flour and butter in a medium bowl and rub them together. Add the golden syrup and mix with the flour and butter to form a firm ball. Slowly stir in just enough milk so the mixture is smooth enough to pour from the bowl.

4. Gently pour the pudding mixture into the slow cooker with the sauce. Cover and cook on HIGH for 1½ hours.

NOTE: This is a canola, egg, gluten, lactose and soy free dessert – and it could also be made dairy free by using your usual dairy alternative.

Felicity Barnett

INDIVIDUAL SPOTTED DICK PUDDINGS

My amazing mother has an English background and I am constantly introducing her granddaughter to the heritage of strong women before her. In this case, it was with this English recipe.

Serves 4 • **Preparation** 10 mins • **Cook** 3 hours

250 g (9 oz) self-raising flour
Pinch of salt
125 g (4½ oz) shredded suet or butter
180 g (6 oz) currants
80 g (2¾ oz) caster (superfine) sugar
Finely grated zest of 1 lemon
Finely grated zest of 1 small orange
150 ml (5 fl oz) milk
Custard, to serve

1. Combine all the ingredients in a large bowl and bring together to form a ball of dough. Divide the dough between four ramekins, so dough half fills them. Cover with foil.

2. Put the ramekins in a slow cooker. Add enough water to come halfway up the side of the ramekins. Cover the slow cooker and cook for 3 hours on HIGH.

3. Serve the puddings with custard.

Kris Cosh

═━ CHRISTMAS PUDDING ━●

Never having made a Christmas pudding before, I wanted to make a traditional pudding for my grandparents but wasn't too keen on having any peel in the pudding. This recipe is full of flavour but also moist, and processing the fruit made it less chunky. My grandparents loved it.

Serves 10 • **Preparation** 20 mins + 1 week soaking • **Cook** 8 hours

1¼ cup currants
1 cup raisins
1 cup prunes
¾ cup sherry
⅔ cup plain (all-purpose) flour
2⅓ cups breadcrumbs
250 g (9 oz) copha (vegetable shortening/solid cooking oil), grated
¾ cup (firmly packed) dark brown sugar
1 teaspoon ground cinnamon
¼ teaspoon ground cloves
1 teaspoon baking powder
Grated zest of 1 lemon
3 large eggs
1 apple, peeled and grated just before combining
2 tablespoons honey
Custard, to serve

1. Process the currants, raisins and prunes in a food processor until lightly chopped. Transfer to a large heat-proof bowl, pour over the sherry and stir to combine. Cover the bowl with cling (plastic) wrap and put in the fridge for 1 week to soak.

2. When ready to cook, put a saucepan, filled one-third with water, on a stovetop over medium heat. Bring water to a boil, then place the bowl of fruit mixture on top of the uncovered saucepan and heat the contents over simmering water. Remove from the heat, add the remaining ingredients to the warm soaked fruit and combine well.

3. Spray a silicone pudding bowl with a lid lightly with cooking oil. Put the pudding mixture into the bowl and secure the lid.

4. Put ⅔ cup water in a slow cooker. Put the pudding bowl in the slow cooker and cook for 5 hours on LOW.

5. Remove the pudding from the bowl and wrap gently in a tea towel (dish towel). Place wrapped pudding back into slow cooker for 3 more hours.

6. Serve warm or cold with custard.

Stacey Guimaraes

COCONUT CUSTARD

Lovely easy idea for a hot summer's day. Canola, dairy, egg, gluten, lactose and soy free.

Serves 4 • **Preparation** 5 mins • **Cook** 45 mins

2 tablespoons gluten-free cornflour (cornstarch)
2 tablespoons coconut sugar
1 vanilla bean, split lengthways, seeds scraped
540 ml (18 fl oz) coconut milk

1. Put the cornflour, coconut sugar and vanilla bean and seeds in the insert of a slow cooker. Add a little coconut milk and mix to a smooth paste. Turn the slow cooker to HIGH and gradually add the remaining coconut milk, stirring. Continue to cook on HIGH, stirring every 5 minutes or so, for about 45 minutes, until thickened. Remove the vanilla bean.

2. When a thick sauce-like consistency, pour into a bowl, moulds or glasses. Chill in the fridge, uncovered, until the custard is set.

Felicity Barnett

PEAR-STUFFED BAKED APPLES

I am not a regular sweet eater, but I had such a craving one evening with absolutely nothing in the house to satisfy it. So I thought outside the square, grabbed a few apples and anything I could find that might go with them. As the apples cooked, I found myself getting impatient, waiting for them to be ready. And then I devoured them within minutes, served simply as is. Amazing. Such a simple dish but such welcoming, homely flavours and warmth. A definite one to repeat.

Serves 2 • Preparation 15 mins • Cook 1½ hours

1 pear, peeled and chopped into tiny pieces
1 tablespoon light brown sugar
1 teaspoon honey
1 tablespoon sultanas
½ teaspoon ground cinnamon
Pinch of freshly grated or ground nutmeg
2 large apples, cored
Vanilla ice cream, to serve (optional)

1. Put the pear, brown sugar, honey, sultanas, cinnamon and nutmeg in a medium bowl with ½ cup water. Mix well.

2. Stand the apples in a slow cooker. Using a small spoon, fill the centres of the apples with the solids of the mixture, pushing the filling down as you go. Once filled, pour the remaining liquid over the apples.

3. Cover and cook on HIGH for 1½ hours. If you wish to thicken the juices a little, put a tea towel (dish towel) under the lid for the last 15 minutes of cooking.

4. Serve immediately with the juices drizzled over the apples and ice cream on the side, if you like.

Christy Roth

SLOW-COOKED BAKED APPLES

A classic dessert easily converted to slow cooking. You can change it up if you like by adding some sultanas or finely diced dried mixed fruit inside the apples too.

Serves 4 • Preparation 10 mins • Cook 1 hour

4 apples (I like to use Granny Smiths)
¼ cup brown sugar
1 teaspoon cinnamon
2 tablespoons butter
Vanilla ice cream, to serve

1. Core the apples and then peel a small area around the top of each one to stop it from splitting. Place the apples in a slow cooker.

2. In a small bowl, combine the brown sugar and cinnamon. Using a small spoon, fill the apple centres with the sugar mixture, pushing the filling down as you go until it is all used. Once filled, place ½ tablespoon of butter on top of each apple.

3. Cover and cook on HIGH for 1 hour.

4. Serve with creamy vanilla ice cream.

Paulene Christie

CARAMEL APPLE CRUMBLE

This is a super-sweet decadent dessert so even a small serve is a taste-bud treat!

Serves 4–6 • **Preparation** 15 mins • **Cook** 2–4 hours + 1 hour resting

5 large apples, peeled, cored and cut into chunks
¼ teaspoon salt
1 teaspoon ground cinnamon
1 cup (firmly packed) light brown sugar
½ cup white sugar
Vanilla ice cream, to serve

CRUMBLE TOPPING
⅔ cup rolled (porridge) oats
⅔ cup (loosely packed) light brown sugar
¼ cup plain (all-purpose) flour
½ teaspoon ground cinnamon
3–4 tablespoons chilled butter, finely chopped
1 teaspoon vanilla extract

1. Put the apple pieces in a large bowl or plastic bag with the salt and cinnamon and toss to coat well.

2. Combine the brown and white sugars in a separate bowl then spread over the base of a slow cooker. Place the apple pieces in a layer on top of the sugar mixture.

3. Combine all the crumble ingredients in a bowl, using your fingers to completely rub the butter into the dry ingredients.

4. Sprinkle the crumble topping mixture over the layer of apples in the slow cooker. Cook on HIGH for 2 hours or LOW for 4 hours.

5. Turn off the heat and allow the apple crumble to sit, covered, for 1 hour so the sauce will thicken more.

6. Serve the crumble with a scoop of vanilla ice cream.

Paulene Christie

CARAMEL TOFFEE APPLES

I originally found a stovetop recipe that used corn syrup, which I couldn't get, so I used glucose syrup instead. I decided to try it in the slow cooker but was unsure if it would get hot enough. After experimenting with having the lid off, then on, and using a tea towel under the lid, I finally got it to work. I use Granny Smith apples but you can use any type of apple you like. You'll need sturdy sticks for the toffee apples.

Makes 15 • Preparation 15 mins • Cook 4 hours

15 small apples, washed in warm water and dried
2 cups (firmly packed) brown sugar
500 g (1 lb 2 oz) glucose syrup or corn syrup
395 g (14 oz) tinned sweetened condensed milk
250 g (9 oz) butter, cubed
1 teaspoon vanilla extract
125 g (4½ oz) walnuts, crushed, or a topping of choice (optional)

1. Push the sticks into the middle of the apples and put in the fridge. (The colder the apple the better the toffee will set.)

2. Put the brown sugar, glucose syrup, condensed milk and butter in a slow cooker and stir well. Cover, with a tea towel (dish towel) under the lid, and cook on HIGH, stirring every 10–15 minutes, until the mixture becomes caramel and reaches 120°C (250°F) or hard-ball stage (use a candy thermometer, or when a small amount dropped into a glass of cold water forms a ball). Add the vanilla and mix well.

3. Line a tray with baking paper. Take an apple, dry it again, and dip it in caramel. Let any excess caramel drip from the bottom (but not too much) and dip into the nuts or other topping. Put the apple, stick upwards, on the lined tray. Put aside to set at room temperature.

TOFFEE APPLE TIPS
If you forget to stir the toffee a crust may form around the edge, but do not
    panic – just stir the caramel well and it will melt back in.
The butter will sometimes separate, but just stir and as it cooks it will mix in.
Make sure store-bought apples are cleaned so all the wax is removed or the
    caramel won't stick.
Make sure your apples are dry or air bubbles may form.
Put any leftover caramel on a greased and lined tray to set, then cut into
    squares with a sharp knife for a nice fudge.

Karen Stuckings

SOUR CREAM TOFFEE

This has been made in my family for years but I don't know where the original recipe came from. Originally done on the stovetop, I decided to try it in the slow cooker for convenience more than anything else. No more standing there watching it like a hawk. It's great to use up that cream you forgot was in the fridge and sneaking a spoonful as a treat when no-one is watching.

Makes approx 50 small pieces using a 20 x 20 cm (8 x 8 inch) baking tray
Preparation 5 mins • **Cook** 4½ hours

1 litre (35 fl oz/4 cups) sour cream
1.3 kg (3 lb) sugar
115 g (4 oz) butter
2 tablespoons white or malt/brown vinegar
2 tablespoons golden syrup (light treacle)
1 teaspoon salt

1. Put all the ingredients in a slow cooker. With the lid on and the slow cooker on HIGH, bring to the boil, stirring occasionally, for about 1½ hours.

2. Once boiling, remove the slow cooker lid and keep cooking on HIGH, stirring occasionally. (Be aware that when you stir it may cause the mix to bubble up to the top of the cooker.) Keep cooking for about 3 hours on HIGH, until the mixture reaches 120°C (250°F) or hard-ball stage (use a candy thermometer, or when a small amount dropped into a glass of cold water forms a ball).

3. Pour the toffee into a greased dish or container to set.

Nikki Willis

SLOW-COOKER FUDGE

This recipe took the Facebook Group by storm in the lead up to Christmas. Literally every second post for weeks and weeks was someone cooking fudge. And every one was different because a simple swap of the chocolate type or the other ingredients produced a totally different final fudge. Various chocolate flavours can be used for this fudge and you can decorate it with various chocolates or lollies – whatever you like. I've included some of the variations posted to inspire you. A great Christmas gift or a treat for the whole family.

Makes approx 50 small pieces using a 20 x 20 cm (8 x 8 inch) baking tray
Preparation 5 mins • **Cook** 1½–2 hours

500 g (1 lb 2 oz) chocolate
1 tablespoon butter
1 tablespoon vanilla essence
395 g (14 oz) tinned sweetened condensed milk

1. Put all the ingredients in a slow cooker. Cook on LOW with the lid off for 1½–2 hours, stirring every 15 minutes or so.

2. Pour into a baking tin, about 20 cm x 20 cm (8 inch x 8 inch) lined with baking paper and put in the fridge to set. When set firm, cut the fudge into squares and store in the fridge.

Paulene Christie

VARIATIONS

PEANUT BUTTER & HAZELNUT CHOC FUDGE – Paulene Christie
550 g (1 lb 4 oz) hazelnut chocolate, broken into chunks
1 tablespoon butter
1 tablespoon vanilla essence
395 g (14 oz) tinned sweetened condensed milk
3 tablespoons peanut butter, plus 2 tablespoons extra to decorate

Add the chocolate chunks and 3 tablespoons of peanut butter in Step 1. When the fudge is cooked and poured in the tray, heat the extra 2 tablespoons of peanut butter in the microwave until runny. Pour over the fudge in the tray and use a wooden skewer to drag the peanut butter around the surface of the fudge in swirls.

MALTESER FUDGE – Susie Adams

Use the master recipe above, plus a small packet of Maltesers and a little white chocolate for melting and drizzling.

Stir the Maltesers through the fudge mixture at the end of cooking, before pouring into the tray to set. When the fudge has set, melt the white chocolate in the microwave and drizzle over.

JAFFA FUDGE – Melodie Tapp

Use the master recipe above, plus add the zest of ½ orange in Step 1, and press a packet of Jaffa lollies into the fudge when it has been poured into the tray to set.

COOKIES 'N' MINT FUDGE – Demi Cooper

Substitute milk chocolate for white chocolate in the master recipe above, plus 1–2 teaspoons of peppermint essence instead of the vanilla essence, and 3 teaspoons of green food colouring, 1 packet of Oreo biscuits and a squirt of Choc Ice Magic.

Carefully mix the green food colouring into the can of condensed milk, one teaspoon at a time, and add to the fudge mixture in the slow cooker at the start of cooking. After cooking, roughly crush the biscuits and mix ¾ of the packet into the fudge mixture. When fudge has been poured into the tray to set, sprinkle remaining crushed biscuits over the top, and decorate with a swirl of Choc Ice Magic.

CHOC TOP PEANUT BUBBLE BARS

I would like to share this recipe of one of my family's favourites. I originally only put the peanut butter in the chocolate for the topping but then decided to replace the butter in the original recipe with peanut butter as well. This made it taste so much better and I have made it this way ever since.

Makes 24 squares • **Preparation** 10 mins • **Cook** 30 mins

300 g (10½ oz) white marshmallows (include a few pink ones for colour if you
    like)
4 tablespoons peanut butter, plus 1 tablespoon extra
2½ cups rice bubbles
220 g (7¾ oz) milk chocolate
1–2 tablespoons roughly chopped salted peanuts

1. Put the marshmallows and peanut butter in a slow cooker on HIGH and cook until melted.

2. Add the rice bubbles and mix until well combined.

3. Transfer to a baking tray (I use a 26 cm [10½ inch] slice tin) lined with baking paper. Lightly dampen your fingertips with water and use them to press the mixture evenly into the tray.

4. In a medium bowl, melt the chocolate and the extra peanut butter in the microwave at 30-second intervals until melted and smooth.

5. Pour the melted chocolate mixture over the rice bubble mixture in the tray. Spread it out evenly and sprinkle the crushed peanuts over the top.

6. Refrigerate for at least 3 hours to set, then slice into squares.

Tiffany Day

MUESLI BARS

The muesli bars began as an experiment to see if it could be done after a few members on the Facebook group enquired about them. It took three attempts before I got it right but it was worth it. These are great for school and work lunch boxes, or for a healthy breakfast on the run.

Makes 16 • **Preparation** 15 mins • **Cook** 1½ hours

2 cups rolled (porridge) oats
1½ cups plain (all-purpose) flour
1 teaspoon ground cinnamon
½ cup (firmly packed) light brown sugar
1½ cups dried mixed fruit
60 g (2¼ oz) butter
½ cup honey
½ cup golden syrup (light treacle) or maple syrup

1. Combine the oats, flour, cinnamon, sugar and dried fruit in a large bowl.

2. Melt the butter, honey and golden syrup in a medium saucepan over low heat, stirring occasionally.

3. Pour the syrup mixture into the dry mixture and combine until the ingredients clump together.

4. Line the insert of a slow cooker with baking paper. Pour the slice mixture into the slow cooker and press down firmly to the thickness of a muesli bar.

5. Cover, with a tea towel (dish towel) under the lid, and cook on LOW for 1½ hours.

6. Lift the cooked slice out using the baking paper and allow to cool on the bench for 30 minutes. Slice into bars and store in an airtight container. Suitable for freezing.

Simon Christie

CHEWY PEANUT BRITTLE

Inspired by the tasty stovetop treat made grandmothers all over the world, I had to convert one to a slow-cooker version for myself and all the other slow-cooking enthusiasts. Mission accomplished! I purchased the rice bran syrup at a health food store, as they advised against using the traditional corn syrup for health reasons and explained that the rice bran syrup was a healthier alternative. You could also pour the mixture into little patty cake cases to make individual toffees.

Makes 2 baking trays, shattered into size of your choice • **Preparation** 5 mins
Cook 1 hour 50 mins + 1 hour cooling

3 cups white (granulated) sugar
1 cup organic rice bran syrup or corn syrup
4 tablespoons butter
2 tablespoons vanilla extract
2 teaspoons bicarbonate of soda (baking soda)
4 cups roasted unsalted peanuts

1. Line two shallow baking trays with baking paper and set aside.

2. Put the sugar, rice bran syrup, butter and vanilla in a slow cooker. Turn on to HIGH and stir until the ingredients are well combined. Cover and cook on HIGH for 1 hour.

3. Stir the mixture and gradually add the bicarbonate of soda, a pinch at a time, stirring well after each addition. Cover and cook on HIGH for another 30 minutes.

4. Add the nuts and stir to combine. Cover and cook on HIGH for another 20 minutes, or until the mixture is a rich toffee colour. Carefully pour half the mixture into each lined tray (use oven mitts to hold the cooker insert, which will be hot).

5. Spread the mixture out evenly with a spatula and let it cool on the kitchen bench for 1 hour.

6. For easy shattering, put the trays in the freezer for 10 minutes. Cover the tray with a clean tea towel (dish towel) and break apart using a kitchen hammer or a heavy can. Break into rough chunks as large as you like and store in a sealed container at room temperature, or in the fridge in hot climates (the surface of the brittle may go tacky to the touch if refrigerated).

Simon Christie

WHITE CHRISTMAS

When Christmas approaches and everyone is cooking fudge for gifts I like to adapt other traditional treats to the slow cooker. This white chocolate version of White Christmas is actually a delicious and healthier alternative to the traditional stovetop recipe that would feature copha. Ho ho ho.

Makes 40 squares • **Preparation** 5 mins • **Cook** 30 mins

750 g (1 lb 11 oz) white chocolate melts
1 tablespoon vanilla extract
100 g (3½ oz) slivered almonds
1½ cups rice bubbles
100 g (3½ oz) glazed cherries, halved
170 g (5¾ oz) craisins or sultanas
¾ cup desiccated coconut

1. Line a slice tray with baking paper.
2. Put the white chocolate melts and vanilla extract in a slow cooker. Cover and cook on HIGH for 30 minutes with the lid on, until melted.
3. Meanwhile, preheat the oven to 180°C (350°F). Spread the almond slivers out on a baking tray and roast in the oven for 8–9 minutes, until golden, stirring once.
4. Combine the rice bubbles, cherries, craisins, coconut and roasted almond slivers in a bowl.
5. Working fast, add the rice bubble mixture to the melted chocolate mixture in the slow cooker and mix well.
6. Transfer the mixture to the lined slice tray. Spread evenly and press into the tray firmly using your fingers. Refrigerate for 1–2 hours to set. Slice into 40 squares and store in an airtight container in the fridge.

Paulene Christie

LEMON & LIMEADE WITH EXTRA TANG

I love lemonade on a hot day, and I love the addition of lime. This is my own slow-cooker recipe and I can say it is the perfect accompaniment to a slow-cooked dinner that the whole family can enjoy. When I tried it for the first time it was gone before I could even take a photo.

Makes 8 cups • **Preparation** 5 mins • **Cook** 1–1½ hours

8 cups water
1¾ cups white sugar
1 cup freshly squeezed lemon juice
½ cup freshly squeezed lime juice
Ice cubes and lemon or lime slices, to serve

1. Put 1 cup of the water and the sugar in a slow cooker. Cook on HIGH for 1–1½ hours, stirring every now and again, until the sugar has dissolved.

2. Turn off the slow cooker and leave to cool.

3. When completely cool, add the remaining 7 cups of water, and the lemon and lime juices. Taste to see if the mixture needs more sugar, lemon or lime, and add more as necessary. Transfer the mixture to a large glass jug and refrigerate until chilled.

4. Serve with ice cubes and lemon or lime slices.

Cheryl Barrett

STRAWBERRY JAM

I first made this jam after my family and I went strawberry picking and had way too many strawberries to eat fresh. I love this recipe as it is very simple yet tasty and it can be left chunky or blended to make more of a sauce consistency.

Makes 5 x 400 ml (13½ fl oz) jam jars • **Preparation** 20 mins • **Cook** 4–8 hours

Cooking oil spray
900 g (2 lb) strawberries, hulled and sliced
4 cups white sugar
¼ cup lemon juice
Pectin or Jamsetta according to packet instructions, or 1 apple, peeled and
    sliced

1. Spray the insert of a slow cooker with cooking oil.

2. Put the strawberries, sugar, lemon juice and pectin/Jamsetta or apple in the slow cooker and stir until combined.

3. Cover and cook on HIGH for 4 hours or LOW for 8 hours, or until the berries are soft and the jam is starting to thicken. Blend the jam if you like it less chunky. Pour the jam into sterilised jars (it will thicken as it cools). Seal and store in a cool dark place. Refrigerate after opening.

Katrina Renwick

CHRISTMAS MINCEMEAT

I have always made mincemeat at Christmas, and my friends and relatives love to receive jars of it in the hampers I give them. But when an international move meant I was unable to make it my usual way, I did some research and discovered I could put the ingredients in the slow cooker and leave it to its own devices. This recipe makes moister and tastier mincemeat than I'd ever been able to achieve previously.

Makes approx 6 x 350 ml (12 fl oz) jars • **Preparation** 15 mins • **Cook** 2 hours

450 g (1 lb) peeled, cored and chopped cooking apples (about 3 apples with a tart flavour)
115 g (4 oz) candied peel, chopped
115 g (4 oz) glacé cherries, washed and chopped
115 g (4 oz) dried apricots, chopped
115 g (4 oz) blanched almonds, chopped
225 g (8 oz) currants
225 g (8 oz) sultanas (golden raisins)
450 g (1 lb) seedless raisins
225 g (8 oz) dark brown sugar
225 g (8 oz) suet
Grated zest and juice of 2 lemons and 2 oranges
2 teaspoons ground ginger
1 teaspoon ground allspice
1 teaspoon ground ginger
½ teaspoon freshly grated nutmeg (optional)
150 ml (5 fl oz) brandy (optional)

1. Put all the ingredients except half the brandy, if using, in a slow cooker and stir to combine. Cover and cook on HIGH for 1 hour.

2. Reduce the temperature to LOW and cook for 1 hour. Stir and turn off.

3. When the mincemeat is cooked and cooled, stir in the remaining brandy, if using.

4. Spoon the mincemeat into sterilised jars. Store in a cool dark place for up to 1 year. Refrigerate and use within 2 weeks when a jar is opened.

Chris Stanton

FRUIT MINCE SCROLLS

Move over traditional Christmas mince pies, my fruit mince scrolls are a great alternative.

Makes approx 15 • **Preparation** 10 mins • **Cook** 2–3 hours

2 cups self-raising flour
3 tablespoons caster (superfine) sugar
1 teaspoon ground mixed spice
75 g (2½ oz) non-dairy spread (margarine)
½–1 cup milk (I use almond milk for a nuttier taste), plus 2 tablespoons extra for icing
1 x 225 g (8 oz) jar of fruit mince
1 tablespoon raw (demerara) sugar
½ cup icing (confectioners') sugar

1. Combine the flour, caster sugar and mixed spice in a medium bowl. Add the non-dairy spread and rub in with your fingertips until the mixture resembles breadcrumbs. Add the milk gradually and bring together with your hands to form a dough.

2. Roll out the dough on a lightly floured work surface into a 20 x 30 cm (8 x 12 inch) rectangle. Spread the fruit mince evenly over the dough. Roll the dough into a long sausage and cut into 2.5 cm (1 inch) slices.

3. Line the base of a slow cooker with non-stick baking paper. Arrange the scroll slices on the base and sprinkle the raw sugar over them.

4. Cover, with a tea towel (dish towel) under the lid, and cook for 2–3 hours on HIGH.

5. When the scrolls are ready, mix the icing sugar with the extra milk to form a thick but drizzly icing. Drizzle the icing over the scrolls. Eat warm or cold.

Frankie Raines

⚏— LEMON BUTTER —●

Also what you might call lemon curd, you can use this lemon butter on toast, cakes, muffins, or just eat it out of the jar! The recipe can easily be halved if you want.

Makes 3–4 x 225g (7 oz) jars • **Preparation** 10–15 mins • **Cook** 1½–2 hours

8 eggs, whisked
1½ cups white sugar
3–4 teaspoons finely grated lemon zest
1 cup strained lemon juice (from about 7–8 lemons)
250 g (9 oz) butter, chopped

1. Put all the ingredients in a slow cooker. Turn the temperature setting to HIGH and stir continuously until the butter has melted.

2. Turn the temperature setting to LOW. Cover, with a tea towel (dish towel) under the lid, and cook for 1½–2 hours, or until the lemon butter is fairly thick, stirring every 20 minutes or so.

3. Sterilise the jars 10 minutes before you are ready to fill them with the lemon butter. Wash the jars in boiling water, dry them, and put them in the oven at 100°C (210°F) for 10 minutes. Meanwhile, put the lids in a saucepan of boiling water (not in the oven) for 10 minutes.

4. Take the jars out of the oven, pour the lemon butter into them and put on the lids. Allow the lemon butter to cool at room temperature – DO NOT put the jars straight into the fridge or they will crack or explode. Once completely cool, refrigerate the lemon butter and serve for breakfast, lunch or dinner.

Jessica Hooper

INDEX

THANK YOU

I would like to give special thanks to my amazing admin team (past and present) who have helped to keep the massive Facebook group running smoothly: Melodie, Felicity, Nikki, Victoria, Narelle, Karen, Cassandra, Denise, Addatron and Kris. You give up so many of your hours to help the members and in turn help me to achieve my dreams.

To Brigitta Doyle at ABC Books, who came to me with the idea of this book after Belinda at the ABC Shop in Mackay told her all about our group. Because of your combined vision, my children can call me an 'author' and that is truly an amazing gift. Thank you! And to Madeleine James, also at ABC Books, who has guided me through every step of this process.

To Ben, Jackson, Paul and the team at Alyte Creative, who have helped me create a website even bigger and better than I had ever dreamed possible!

To Toni McCulloch who inspired me to turn my far-flung dreams into reality. Without you, Toni, I'd still be saying, 'One day I want to ...'

To my friends and loved ones who've shared in my excitement and my achievements and been right beside me for the ride.

To my husband, Simon, who has been by my side since our school years, and who has always encouraged me to chase my dreams. You had faith in me even when I had none in myself. I couldn't have done this without you, my love. And to our beautiful children who make our life complete and never tire of mummy's slow cooked experiments.

To my dear mum in the heavens who inspires me in every way, every day. I miss you.

And last – but definitely not least – to every single member of our Facebook group, Slow Cooker Recipes 4 Families, and to every visitor to our website, Slow Cooker Central, who have participated in the community family we have there, who share their recipes, share their experience and share their support. Without you this book wouldn't be possible.

Paulene Christie

Slow-cooking internet sensation Paulene Christie is a busy working mum with a passion for sharing new and exciting recipes for the slow cooker. She now has more than 320,000 members in her Facebook group, Slow Cooker Recipes 4 Families, and a hugely successful website, Slow Cooker Central. The Facebook page is so popular Paulene has a team of nine people (including her husband, Simon) to help her administer the thousands of recipes and comments that are posted each day. Paulene lives in Queensland with Simon, their three young children and six slow cookers.

www.slowcookercentral.com
www.facebook.com/groups/SlowCookerRecipes4Families